James E Matthew

A popular history of music, musical instruments, ballet, and opera

James E Matthew

A popular history of music, musical instruments, ballet, and opera

ISBN/EAN: 9783742879103

Manufactured in Europe, USA, Canada, Australia, Japa

Cover: Foto ©Thomas Meinert / pixelio.de

Manufactured and distributed by brebook publishing software
(www.brebook.com)

James E Matthew

A popular history of music, musical instruments, ballet, and opera

A POPULAR

HISTORY OF MUSIC,

Musical Instruments, Ballet, and Opera,

FROM

ST. AMBROSE TO MOZART.

BY

JAMES E. MATTHEW.

WITH ONE HUNDRED AND THIRTY-SEVEN ILLUSTRATIONS,
CONSISTING OF PORTRAITS, MUSICAL INSTRUMENTS, FACSIMILES OF RARE AND EARLY MUSICAL TYPOGRAPHY, ETC.

LONDON:

H. GREVEL AND CO.,

33, KING STREET, COVENT GARDEN, W.C.

1888.

PREFACE.

ALTHOUGH in the present day there is no lack of
Histories of Music, they are either planned on so large
a scale as to be beyond the reach of many who are interested
in the subject, or they are so wanting in detail as to become
little better than dry catalogues of names and dates.

In the following pages I have endeavoured to trace in
a popular manner the History of Music up to the closing years
of the last century. Some space is devoted to the gradual
development of our present system of musical notation, and
this is amply illustrated by examples taken from ancient
manuscripts, without which it would have been difficult to
make the descriptions intelligible. Of the most eminent
musicians portraits are given, and I have also been able to
add facsimiles of the titles of many musical works, mostly
of considerable rarity, which cannot fail to be of interest. In
a work of this nature detailed criticism would be out of place,
for the world has long ago recorded its judgment on the
respective merits of those whose compositions come under
notice.

In treating of our great English musician Henry Purcell, I have followed the guidance of Mr. W. H. Cummings—the acknowledged authority on a subject which he has made his own. I must also express my obligations to **Mr. W. A.** Barrett's excellent little book on *English Church Composers*, which contains in a handy form much information not otherwise readily accessible.

CONTENTS.

CHAPTER I.

EARLY HISTORY OF MUSIC.

PAGE

Music among the Romans—Effects of Christianity on Music—St. Ambrose—St.
Gregory—Introduction of "Neums"—*Antiphonarium* of St. Gregory and its
History—Improvements in Notation—Guido d'Arezzo—Boethius—Infancy of
Harmony—The Troubadours and Minstrels—Minnesingers and Meistersingers
—"Confrérie de St. Julien" in Paris—Adam de la Halle—*Robin et Marion*—
Liturgical Plays 1

CHAPTER II.

THE HISTORY OF MUSICAL INSTRUMENTS.

Difficulties of the Subject—Instruments of Greece and Rome—Classification of
Instruments—Instruments of Percussion: Drums, Cymbals, Bells, Carillons,
Change-ringing—Wind Instruments: Syrinx, Flute, Chorus, Bagpipes, the
Organ, Trumpet, Shophar, Oliphant, Sackbut, Hautboy, Bassoon—Stringed
Instruments: Lyre, Psalterium, Cithara, Nablum, Harp, Dulcimer, Clavichord,
Virginal, Spinet, Harpsichord, Pianoforte, Lute, Theorbo, Guitar—Bowed
Instruments: The Crwth, Rotta, Hurdy-gurdy, Organistrum, Viol, Violin, Mono-
chord 25

CHAPTER III.

THE MUSICAL INFLUENCE OF THE NETHERLANDS.

Dufay—Binchois—John of Dunstable—Hobrecht—Okeghem or Okenheim—Tinctoris—
Obligations to Glareanus for our Knowledge of these Early Musicians—Josquin
de Prés—Willaert—Rabelais on the Musicians of his Time—The Invention of
the Madrigal—Early Music Printers—Orlando di Lassus . . . 61

CHAPTER IV.

MUSIC IN ITALY AND GERMANY.

The Papal Chapel—Palestrina and his Reforms—His Successors—The Music for Holy Week in the Sistine Chapel—Music in Venice—Writers on the Theory of Music—Early German Composers: Isaak and Senfl—The Influence of the Reformation on Music—German Writers on Musical Instruments and Theory . 74

CHAPTER V.

EARLY HISTORY OF MUSIC IN ENGLAND.

Sumer is icumen in—Fairfax, Sheppard, Mulliner, Taverner, Merbecke, Tallis, Redford, Edwards, Tye, and Byrd—Patent for Music-printing granted to Tallis and Byrd—Farrant—The Madrigalian Era—N. Yonge's *Musica Transalpina*—Watson's *Italian Madrigals Englished*—Morley, Bateson, Ward, and O. Gibbons—*Triumphs of Oriana*—Widespread Knowledge of Music—Morley's *Introduction—Parthenia*—Dr. John Bull—Foundation of Gresham College—Ravenscroft—Hilton—Barnard's ' Cathedral Music—Metrical Version of the Psalms 86

CHAPTER VI.

THE ORIGIN OF THE OPERA AND ORATORIO.

Influence of the Renaissance—Study of Greek Music—Vincenzo Galilei—Giulio Caccini and Jacopo Peri—Rinuccini's *Euridice* set to Music by both these Composers—Monteverde—His Instrumentation—The Opera in Venice—Origin of the Oratorio—Carissimi—Alessandro Scarlatti—Durante—Pergolesi—Jomelli—Lotti—Marcello—His Psalms—*Il Teatro alla moda*—Porpora—Corelli and his School—Tartini—Frescobaldi—Domenico Scarlatti 102

CHAPTER VII.

THE RISE OF THE OPERA IN FRANCE.

Chapel Music of the Kings of France—Clément Marot's Psalms—*Ballet Comique de la Royne*—Claude Lejeune—E. de Caurroy—Italian Singers brought into France by Mazarin—Skill of Louis XIV. in Music—Introduction of French Opera by Perrin and Cambert—Jean Baptiste Lully—His Career and Influence—Colasse—Desmarets—Campra—Destouches—Cultivation of Instrumental Music —Descartes—Père Mersenne 120

CHAPTER VIII.

MUSIC IN GERMANY.

The "Stadt-pfeiffer"—The Bach Family—J. S. Bach—His Sons and Pupils—Founda-
tion of the Gewandhaus Concerts—The Opera in Germany—Reinhard Keiser—
Early Career of Handel—Johann Mattheson—Hasse—Graun—Musical Journalism
—Marpurg—Music in Vienna—J. J. Fux—Gluck—His Musical Reforms   .   . 151

CHAPTER IX.

MUSIC IN ENGLAND AT THE TIME OF THE RESTORATION.

Discouragement of Music during the Commonwealth—The Resumption of the
Cathedral Service—"Captain" Cooke—Matthew Lock—The "Salmon and
Lock" Controversy—Pelham Humfrey, Blow, and Wise—The "Verse" Anthem
—Jeremiah Clark and Croft—Henry Purcell—Boyce's "Cathedral Music"—
The Progress of Organ-building in England—"Father Smith" and Renatus
Harris—The Temple Organ—John Playford, the Music-publisher—Christopher
Simpson—Mace's *Musick's Monument*—Tom d'Urfey   194

CHAPTER X.

THE RISE OF OPERA AND ORATORIO IN ENGLAND.

Early Attempts at English Opera—Celebrated Singers of that Time—Addison's
Criticisms—Arrival of Handel in England—His Success in Opera—Story of
his "Water Music"—Enters the Service of the Duke of Chandos—His First
Oratorio, *Esther—Acis and Galatœa*—The "Royal Academy of Music"—
Buononcini and Ariosti—The Singers Francesca Cuzzoni and Faustina Bordoni
—Collapse of the Royal Academy of Music—The Beggar's Opera—Handel's
Partnership with Heidegger and Resumption of Italian Opera—First Public
Performances of Oratorio—Buononcini's Rival Opera—His Disgrace—Heidegger's
Perfidy—Handel joins Rich—His Illness—Further Failure of Opera—Handel's
Oratorios—*Saul—Israel in Egypt—The Messiah*—Its Success in Dublin—
Samson—Dettingen *Te Deum—Belshazzar*—His Bankruptcy—*Judas Maccabæus*
—*Joshua—Solomon*—His Blindness and Death   221

PAGE

CHAPTER XI.

FURTHER HISTORY OF MUSIC IN ENGLAND.

Dr. Arne—Lampe's *Dragon of Wantley*—Henry Carey—Thomas Britton, "the
Musical Small-coal Man"—Ballad Operas—Charles Dibdin—Early Concerts—
Foundation of the "Concert of Antient Musick"—Cultivation of Part-singing
—Catches—Samuel Webbe and the Glee-writers—The Catch Club and its
Secretary, E. T. Warren Hall—The Histories of Burney and Hawkins—Visit
of Mozart to England   249

CHAPTER XII.

MUSIC IN FRANCE DURING THE EIGHTEENTH CENTURY.

Rameau as a Theorist and Composer—The "Théâtre de la Foire"—*La Serva
Padrona* of Pergolesi in Paris and the "Guerre des Bouffons"—J. J. Rousseau
—His Dictionary—Gossec—Monsigny—Gluck in Paris—Piccinni—Grétry—The
Philidors—Foundation of the "Concerts Spirituels"—Instrumental Composers
—Leclair—Couperin—The Ballet 263

THE HISTORY OF MUSIC.

CHAPTER I.

EARLY HISTORY OF MUSIC.

Music among the Romans—Effects of Christianity on Music—St. Ambrose—St. Gregory —Introduction of "Neums"—*Antiphonarium* of St. Gregory and its History— Improvements in Notation—Guido d'Arezzo—Boethius—Infancy of Harmony—The Troubadours and Minstrels—Minnesingers and Meistersingers—"Confrérie de St. Julien" in Paris—Adam de la Halle—*Robin et Marion*—Liturgical Plays.

HOWEVER widely the appreciation of art may have been diffused among the inhabitants of ancient Rome, it is certain that the Romans themselves showed but little originality in its practice. For their sculpture, which was probably the manifestation of art in the greatest favour, they were almost entirely dependent on Greeks, who were attracted to Rome in large numbers by the liberal patronage which they received. In music they relied equally on foreign talent, its professors being also almost invariably drawn from the shores of Greece. All the treatises on music which have come down to us from ancient time are written in the Greek language. No original work on the subject in Latin is known earlier in date than the treatise of Boethius.

A new direction was given to the practice of music by

I

the spread of the Christian religion. The persecution which they suffered in their own land drove many of the early Jewish converts into Rome, where they performed their religious rites in secrecy. It is reasonable to suppose that they brought with them many regretful memories of the sacred melodies of their beloved land. But music was in those days an unwritten language, which had a natural tendency to become deteriorated, especially as the ranks of the early Christians were soon recruited by converts from among the people whose hospitality they had sought, who added the melodies of their pagan hymns to the common stock. The practice of music was carried on with difficulty, for, owing to a constant succession of persecutions, their meetings for public worship were held by stealth—most frequently in the secrecy of the catacombs.

It is no wonder, then, that the ancient melodies, thus handed down by tradition alone, should become corrupted. Under Constantine a happier time was in store for the Christians, and they were enabled to celebrate their worship in public. It soon became evident that great variety of practice existed in the performance of the vocal portions of the services. St. Ambrose, who had become Bishop of Milan, was about the year 384 engaged in building his cathedral there. He determined that the music performed within its walls should be the purest obtainable. As a first step he collected all the melodies at that time in use, and then proceeded to lay down fixed rules for the future guidance of his choristers. He allowed the four following tonalities only, in which all the melodies receiving his sanction were written. We have attached to them the equivalent terms according to the Greek nomenclature, and have marked the position of the semitone with a circumflex. ·

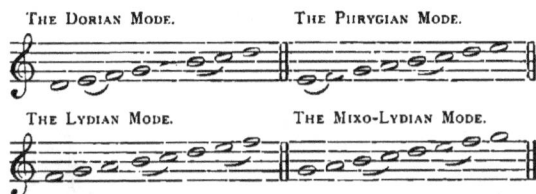

THE DORIAN MODE.   THE PHRYGIAN MODE.

THE LYDIAN MODE.   THE MIXO-LYDIAN MODE.

It is said that Pope Damasus was the first to introduce, at Rome in 371, the practice of chanting the Psalms, which up to that time had been recited in a loud voice by the congregation ; and no doubt the introduction of music in public worship spread rapidly. Gregory of Tours records that the baptism of Clovis in the church of Rheims was accompanied by beautiful music, which impressed the royal catechumen so deeply that when he signed a treaty of peace with Theodoric, King of the Ostrogoths, he made a condition that the prince should send him from Italy a party of singers and a skilful performer on the cithara.

Two centuries after the time of Ambrose, St. Gregory the Great, who was elected pope in 590, supplemented the work of his predecessor by making a further collection of the melodies in Church use. He increased the number of modes to eight, but in addition to this he drew up an *Antiphonarium*, consisting of hymns, with suitable melodies, adapted to all the principal seasons of the Church's year. These have ever since remained in use in the Roman Catholic Church, and are now familiar to all under the name of " Gregorian," which they owe to their collector, although the proper name for them is Plain-Chant or Plain-Song.

Fig. 1.—Flute-player accompanying priests during a sacrifice (from a Roman bas-relief).

For the notation of his melodies Gregory is said to have made use of the letters of the Latin alphabet, the capitals A, B, C, D, E, F, G standing for the seven lowest notes of his scale, while the small letters, from *a* to *g*, continued the octave above. The enthusiasm of Gregory for the worthy performance of the musical services of the Church does not admit of question. He established in Rome schools for the education of choristers, and insisted on a knowledge of music among the bishops, refusing to ordain to that dignity a priest who was wanting in a sufficient knowledge of plain-song.

For Gregory also has been claimed—on doubtful grounds —the system of musical notation which came into general use soon after his time,—that of "neums," a word supposed to be derived from the Greek word πνεῦμα, breath. As an example, we refer to the facsimile of part of the so-called *Antiphonarium* of St. Gregory (fig. 2), supposed to be the oldest musical manuscript in existence, the historical value of which cannot be exaggerated. It has been for many centuries the property of the monastery of St. Gall, in Switzerland. Towards the end of the eighth century, Charlemagne was desirous of introducing uniformity of practice in ritual throughout the whole of his vast empire. With that view he begged Pope Adrian I. to send him two choristers well instructed in the practice of plain-song. To so laudable a request the Pope readily acceded. Two choristers named Peter and Romanus were selected, and they both started for Metz, at which place the reform was to commence, each in charge of a copy accurately made from the precious manuscript actually drawn up under the supervision of Gregory the Great. On the road, Peter fell ill, and was glad to claim the hospitality of the monks of St. Gall. By the express command of Charlemagne, he was received as a permanent resident in the monastery,—

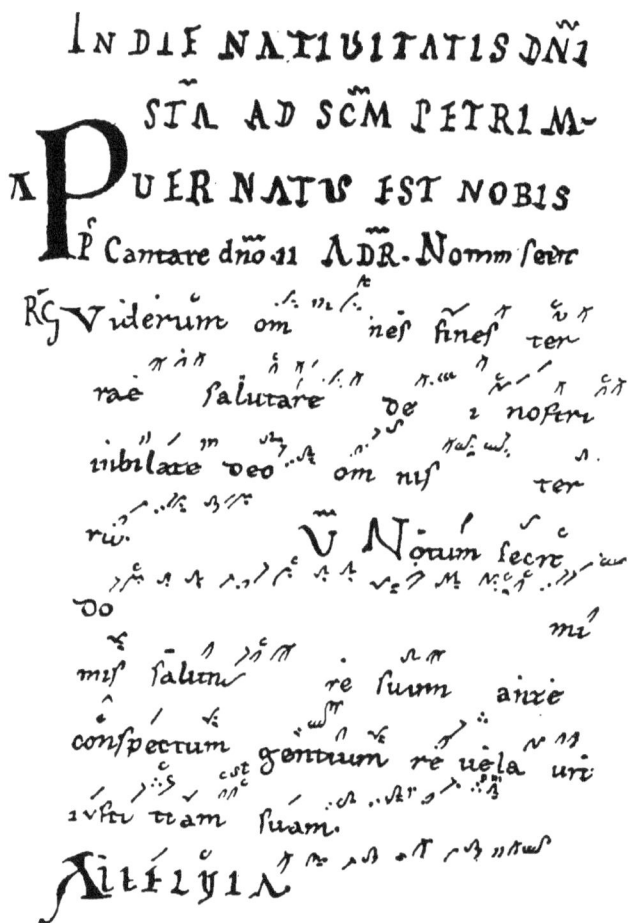

Fig. 2.—Facsimile of a portion of the *Antiphonarium* of St. Gregory belonging to the monastery of St. Gall (A.D. 790).

possibly with a view of making another centre for the diffusion of the true principles of plain-song ; and thus the *Antiphonarium* has become the most cherished possession of the monastery. By a fortunate accident, Père Lambillotte, one of a small body of men who have been instrumental of late years in restoring the ancient practice of the Roman Church, was enabled to make a facsimile of it in the year 1848, which was subsequently published ; and in 1885 the manuscript itself was actually shown in the exhibition of musical manuscripts, etc., which was given in the Albert Hall at South Kensington.

The origin of neums is lost. Several theories have been started to explain them, but none quite satisfactory. According to some authorities, including the learned historian of music, Kiesewetter, they are of Roman origin, having some analogy with a species of shorthand invented by Tiro, the freedman and secretary of Cicero. Fétis claimed for them an Oriental origin, while Coussemaker thought they were simply the acute, grave, and circumflex accents. The question will probably never be settled. Their interpretation into modern notation presents equal difficulty, especially as the practice of writing them varied considerably. It may be taken for granted that no absolute pitch was intended. The rising and falling of the voice were indicated by the distance at which the neums were placed above the words, although the interval could not be clearly defined by this method. It must be borne in mind, however, that the melodies were familiar to the singers, so that but little assistance was required for that purpose. When

the signs became a little more definite in shape, they probably
represented certain well-known and frequently recurring sequences
of notes so constantly met with in plain-song. Of these Gerbert
gives a "memoria technica" from an eleventh-century manuscript, in which the names of the figures are arranged in
hexameter verses, with the signs representing them (fig. 3).

The use of neums was not confined to ecclesiastical music

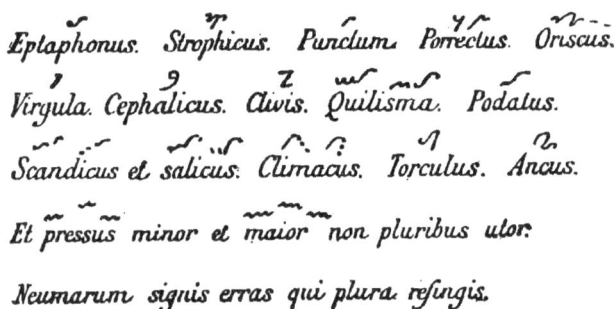

Eptaphonus. Strophicus. Punctum. Porrectus. Oriscus.

Virgula. Cephalicus. Clivis. Quilisma. Podatus.

Scandicus et salicus. Climacus. Torculus. Ancus.

Et pressus minor et maior non pluribus utor:

Neumarum signis erras qui plura refingis.

Fig. 3.— Nomenclature of the Neums, given in the Breviarium de Musica,
a MS. of the eleventh century (from Gerbert).

alone. Many manuscripts exist in which they are added to
secular poems. Of some of these facsimiles are given by Coussemaker. We give that of a song composed by a Frank named
Angilbert in 841 (fig. 4) to celebrate the battle of Fontanet
or Fontenailles in Auxerrois, between the sons of Louis le
Debonnaire, with the translation of the same into modern
notation. Fig. 5 is a dirge on the death of Charlemagne, by
a contemporary monk named Colomban.

In confirmation of the opinion that neums were of assistance
to those only who already were familiar with the melodies

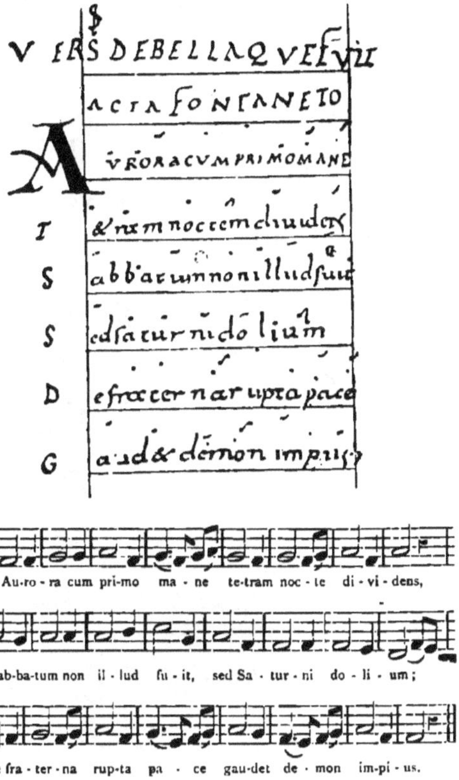

Fig. 4.—First strophe of a song in commemoration of the battle of Fontanet,
eleventh century (from the National Library, Paris).

they were designed to represent, the contemporary testimony
of St. Isidore, Bishop of Seville, a friend of Gregory, may

be brought forward. He says expressly : " Unless sounds are retained in the memory they perish, for they cannot be written

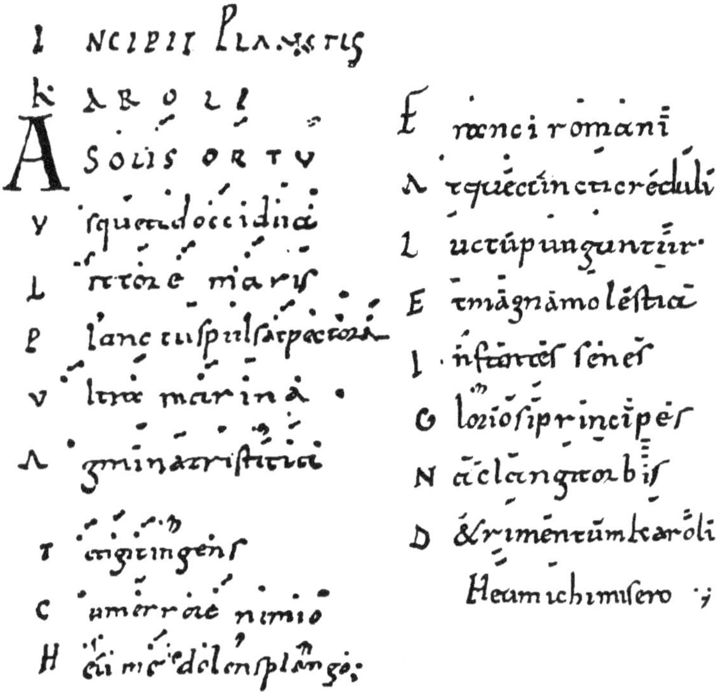

Fig. 5.—Dirge on the death of Charlemagne, probably written about 814 or 815, attributed to Colombanus, Abbot of St. Tron (MS. from the National Library, Paris).

down." A very simple invention paved the way to a reversal of this opinion. It occurred to some scribe, whose name has, unfortunately, not come down to us,—for without doubt he deserves to be remembered with gratitude,—to draw with his bodkin a line across the parchment above the words to which the music was to be given. At the beginning of this line was written the letter F, signifying that all the neums placed upon the line represented the note of that name (fig. 6). At once we have a definite pitch to start from, and the germ

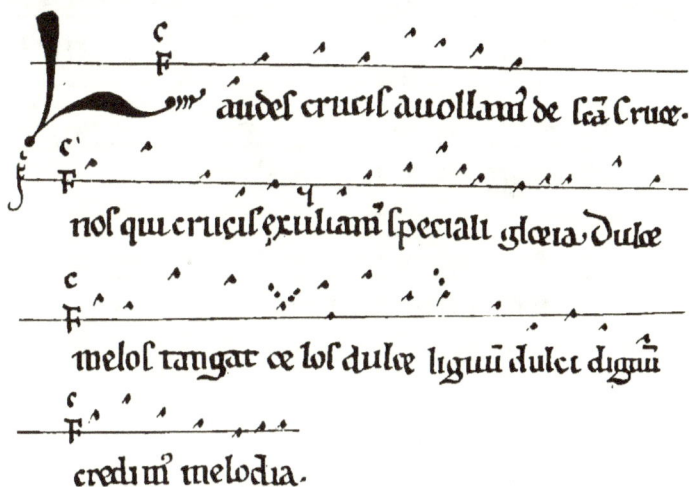

Fig. 6.—Commencement of the "Prose," or Hymn for the Festival of the Holy Cross (MS. twelfth century).

of the musical staff, which soon suggested itself. The first step was the addition of another line above the F, representing the note C; and it became the practice to use a red line for the F, while the upper line was drawn in yellow or green ink. It was a natural advance to draw a line, either with a

bodkin or in black ink, between the coloured lines, and another
line below the red soon followed. The four-line stave was now
complete (fig. 7), and embraced a sufficient portion of the
scale for most purposes of plain-song ; but, if necessary,

Fig. 7.—Notation on four lines (from a Lombardic gradual of the fourteenth century).

another line was added either above or below the four-line
staff, as convenience dictated. The introduction of the single
line appears to have been made at the end of the tenth
century, although it was some time before its use became
general. On the introduction of the complete staff, neums
were gradually abandoned in favour of notes bearing more
resemblance to those with which we are now familiar.

The invention of the use of coloured lines has been
attributed to Guido d'Arezzo (*circa* 990—1070), apparently
without foundation, and it is only fair to say that he does

not claim it. M. Fétis remarks that "Guido's fame has rested far more on what has been attributed to him than on what he really did." There can be no doubt that he was a very successful teacher of youth, in which capacity he invented the method of reading music now known as "*Solfeggio*." He observed that the melody sung to the hymn to St. John the Baptist—

> *Ut* queant laxis
> *Re*sonare fibris
> *Mi*ra gestorum
> *Fa*muli tuorum,
> *Sol*ve polluti
> *La*bii reatum,
> Sancte Johannes—

rose a degree of the scale with the commencement of each line. It occurred to him to use these syllables—Ut, Re, Mi, Fa, Sol, La—to designate those notes of the scale, and he taught his pupils to sing these intervals by carrying back their thoughts to a melody so familiar to them all, instead of referring to the interval on an instrument.

The important part which music filled in the service of religion made some acquaintance with it a necessary part of the education of every ecclesiastic. The mild wisdom of the writings of Boethius, which caused him to be looked on as a Christian, led to their extraordinary popularity. Among them was unfortunately a treatise on music, and this was selected as the text-book. It has been abundantly proved that he entirely misunderstood the subject which he attempted to

explain ; and the blind confidence which for so long a
time was placed in his knowledge proved a great hindrance
to the true study of the science. But in truth it was a subject on which the divorce between theory and practice was
almost complete. The priest and the chorister were content
to acquire sufficient knowledge to go through their duties
with credit, while the student indulged in the useless inquiries
then in vogue.

We are fortunately not called on here to decide whether
the ancient Greeks and Romans were acquainted with har
mony, a question which has been discussed with great warmth
by many learned musicians ; there can be no doubt, however,
that rude attempts at harmony were made at a very early
period of the middle ages. It must be admitted that they
were of such a nature that the performance of them in the
present day would strike the musician with horror ; but it is
equally certain that at the time in which they were in
use they were received with enthusiasm. A monk who wrote
soon after the time of Charlemagne mentions that the Roman
singers taught the French singers the art of "organizing,"
which was the term by which the earliest attempts at harmony
were described. On this statement Coussemaker makes the
very sound reflection that if the monk was mistaken in the
fact which he reports, it proves at least that the practice
existed at the time when he wrote, which was in the early
part of the ninth century.

The first attempt to describe the principles of harmony

as then understood is given by the monk Hucbald, who
lived at the end of the ninth and the beginning of the tenth
centuries, in his treatise entitled *Musica Enchiriadis.* In the
earliest specimens the melody was accompanied by notes of
equal length, preserving the same interval throughout the
whole of the composition. The intervals allowed were the
octave, the fifth, and the fourth, which were admissible when
the work was in two parts only, but these parts might be
doubled in the octave above when a larger number of parts
were employed. This style of writing was called diaphony or
organum. The meaning of the former term offers no difficulty;
Hucbald explains it to be so called "because it consists, not
of a melody produced by a single voice, but of a harmonious
composition of sounds of a different nature heard at the same
time." But the term "*organum*" is not so easy of explanation. The word had been in use before the time of Hucbald,
who makes no attempt to unravel the difficulty. The first to
do so was the monk John Cotton, who fancied that it was
so called from the resemblance it had to the sounds of the
organ. We will now give from Hucbald a specimen of this
method of harmonising (fig. 8), and this was considered by
the critics of the time to be a "*suavem concentum*"!

Soon after the adoption of "organum," "discant" was
introduced, which made its way almost simultaneously. It was
originally in two parts only, the principal melody called the
"tenor," while the accompanying part was called the "discant;"
but at a later time other parts were added. The main

difference between diaphony or organum and discant consists in the fact that while in the former the accompanying parts were note against note, in the latter these parts might consist of notes of different value from those of the "tenor" which they accompanied. In its earliest days the discant was often improvised by the singer, for whose guidance certain rules were current; but it is difficult to suppose that the practice was possible except with the smallest number of singers. This was called in France "chant sur le livre," and in Italy "contra-

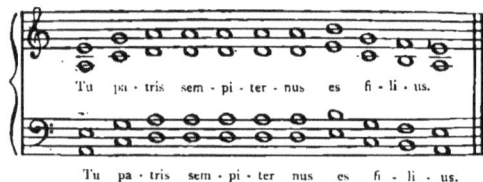

Fig. 8.—Diaphony in fifths, for four voices (from the *Enchiridion Musica* of Hucbald, ninth century).

punto a mente." It is not surprising that the practice led to abuses; a desire for display would naturally lead the singer into a style of singing quite foreign to the spirit of plainsong; and thus we find that several of the popes attempted to suppress it.

From such humble beginnings the modern science of harmony was developed.

Secular music was kept alive by the troubadours, who were both poets and musicians. Their art is supposed to have had its origin in the East, and to have passed into Provence from the neighbouring country of Spain. The troubadours were the aristocrats of the world of art, many of the body being of noble and even royal origin, among whom may be numbered Thibaut, King of Navarre, the Châtelain de Coucy, the Count of Anjou, the Count of Soissons, and the Duke of Brabant. But a more humble birth, if accompanied by commanding ability, was no obstacle to admission to the honoured ranks, and among such we find Adam de la Halle, Blondeau de Nesle, the devoted friend of Richard Cœur de Lion, Richard de Fournival, and others. Their efforts enlivened the tedium of

In modern
notation.

Fig. 9.—Diaphony, passing from the unison to the fifth and back to the unison (from a MS. of Francon from the Ambrosian Library, Milan ; eleventh century).

the courts to which they generally attached themselves ; their rules compelled them to choose some lady whose charms formed the prevailing subject of their songs.

Unlike the troubadours, the jongleurs and minstrels wandered about from place to place, certain of being well received in the houses of the rich, where their lays ensured them a welcome ; they were always well lodged and fed, and dismissed with an ample reward. This roving life was far from exercising a beneficial effect on them, and they were too apt to deserve the character of being rogues and drunkards.

In Germany the troubadours and minstrels existed under

the names of minnesingers and meistersingers. The minnesingers were selected from the members of the noble classes,
while the meistersingers answered to the professional
musicians or minstrels. Election into the body was a
proceeding of great solemnity. The candidate performed
before four judges, who were hidden from sight by a silken
curtain. One of these had to watch carefully for any
grammatical error ; the others paid attention to the rhyme
and metre, and the melody of the postulant. If the judges

Fig. 10.   Fig. 11.   Fig. 12.

Crowned minstrels playing on various instruments (from a MS. in the National Library, Paris).

agreed in thinking him worthy, he was admitted with all due
ceremony, being decorated with a silver chain and badge, on
which was represented David playing on the harp. To be a
meistersinger was not incompatible with a much more prosaic
calling ; Hans Sachs, of Nuremburg, one of the most celebrated,
was, it will be remembered, a shoemaker.

An attempt was made in France by some of the worthier
members of the body of minstrels to recover the position
which they had forfeited by the somewhat disreputable character

of many who followed the calling. Two of them, Jacques Grue
and Hugues or Huet le Lorrain, bought a piece of ground

Fig. 13. Church of St. Julien des Menestriers, founded in the fourteenth century by two
jongleurs, Jacques Grue and Huet le Lorrain.

in Paris, in the Rue Saint Martin, on which they built, with
money which they contrived to collect among the inhabitants

of Paris, a church (fig. 13), dedicated to St. Julien and St.
Genesius,—the latter a saint who followed the profession of
comedian in the fourth century, and suffered martyrdom for
embracing the Christian religion,—who were chosen as the
patron saints of the order.   In addition to the church there
was also a house of refuge for minstrels in want of a few days'
lodging.   Under such respectable auspices the minstrels united
into a duly organised society, and made rules for their own
guidance and protection, to which the Provost of Paris, William
de Germont, was induced to give his official sanction.   The
laws of the guild provided imprisonment for any member who
should be guilty of singing scandalous or offensive verses, but
were still more directed against any outsider who should presume
to exercise his art in Paris, the penalty for which was banish-
ment for a year and a day.   It is only fair, however, to state
that hospitality was extended to the unauthorised performer
who required it, on the sole condition that he made no attempt to
exercise his talents.   In 1401 the guild received letters patent
from Charles VI. which empowered them to elect a head of
the "Confrérie de St. Julien" (for that was the title they
adopted), under the name of "King of the Minstrels," which
was subsequently changed into that of "King of the Violins."
Under such patronage the Confrérie acquired great power,
which as time went on tended to retard rather than to advance
the cause it was designed to protect.   It gradually became a
machinery for extracting large sums of money from performers
who were not members of the body, which had long ceased to

take the lead in the art of music. In 1658 Louis XIV. confirmed their privilege ; but the extravagant pretensions which they soon afterwards advanced led to the extinction of the society.

A - dieu commant a - moure - tes, Car je men vois Dolans pour les dou-
chetes Fors dou dous pa - is d'Artois Qui est si mus et destrois,
Pour che que li bourgois Ont es - té si four - menés Qu'il n'i queurt
drois ne lo's Gros tournois Ont a - nu - lés contes et rois, Jus-ti-ches et
prelas tant de fois Que mainte be - le compaigne Dont Ar - ras me-
hain gne Laissant a - mis et maisons et harnois, Et fui - ent chà deus,
chà trois, Sou-spirant en terre es-train-gne.

Fig. 14.—Original notation of a motet by Adam de la Halle (from a MS. of the fourteenth century from the National Library, Paris).

Among the troubadours whose names we have mentioned was Adam de la Halle, who was born early in the thirteenth century.   Thanks to the researches of M. Coussemaker, the

most learned authority on the music of this period, we possess
a very large collection of his works, which comprise numerous
songs, rondeaux, motets (fig. 14) (a word which had not at that
time acquired the meaning of a *sacred* composition) ; in all
of these both words and music were of his composition ; but
what is still more interesting, a regular drama set to music,
entitled *Li Gieus de Robin et de Marion*, which one is
almost justified in calling an opera.   The story is of the

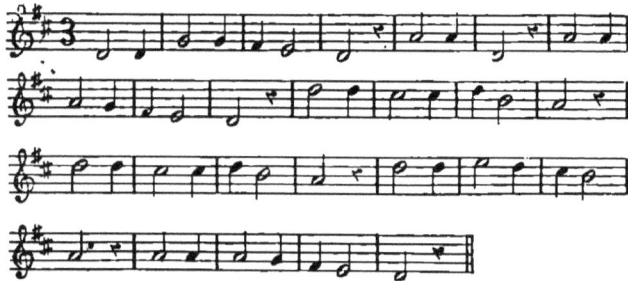

Fig. 15.—The air *L'Homme Armé* (thirteenth century) in modern notation.

simplest.   Marion is betrothed to the shepherd Robin,
when a knight appears on the scene who tries to steal away
her affections ; however, she proves faithful, and everything
ends happily.   In the course of this piece Adam de la Halle
introduces the famous air *L'Homme Armé* (fig. 15), which was
so often in after-times used as a subject for musical treatment.   Tradition has it that this was the air which the
triumphant Crusaders sang on their entry into Jerusalem.

Allied to this little musical play are the liturgical dramas of the middle ages, which were performed in churches as a means of instructing the people in the main facts of the Christian religion. Several of these have also been published by the indefatigable M. Coussemaker, and among them we find such subjects as the Resurrection, the Adoration of the Magi, the Massacre of the Innocents, the Holy Women at the Sepulchre, and other subjects of a like nature. The characters were personated by the priests and choir of the church; they were

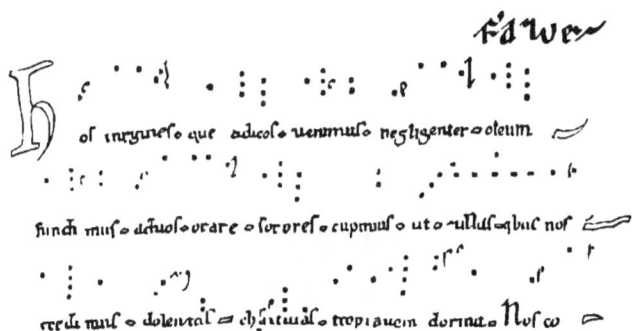

Fig. 16. —Song of the Foolish Virgins (from the liturgical drama of *The Wise and Foolish Virgins*). Notation in neums (from a MS. of the eleventh century in the National Library, Paris).

performed at the appropriate seasons of the Church's year, and no feeling of irreverence had any place whatever in thus representing the principal facts of religious belief. It is interesting to notice that the melodies in *Robin and Marion* are decidedly light in character compared with the music of these dramas, which are of the nature of plain-song. M. Coussemaker prints twenty-two of these compositions, ranging from the eleventh to the fourteenth centuries. The

earliest of these is the Parable of the Wise and the Foolish
Virgins; the music to this is inserted in neums. We are
enabled to give a facsimile of a portion of this interesting
work (fig. 16).

The knowledge and cultivation of music spread rapidly over
Europe, but it was in the Low Countries that the greatest
advance was made, as will be seen in our third chapter.

CHAPTER II.

THE HISTORY OF MUSICAL INSTRUMENTS.

Difficulties of the Subject—Instruments of Greece and Rome—Classification of Instruments —Instruments of Percussion: Drums, Cymbals, Bells, Carillons, Change-ringing— Wind Instruments: Syrinx, Flute, Chorus, Bagpipes, The Organ, Trumpet, Shophar, Oliphant, Sackbut, Hautboy, Bassoon—Stringed Instruments: Lyre, Psalterium, Cithara, Nablum, Harp, Dulcimer, Clavichord, Virginal, Spinet, Harpsichord, Piano- forte, Lute, Theorbo, Guitar—Bowed Instruments: The Crwth, Rotta, Hurdy-gurdy, Organistrum, Viol, Violin, Monochord.

THE investigation into the nature and construction of the musical instruments of early times is surrounded with many difficulties. The earliest are known to us only by the representations which have been preserved on sculptured monuments, with such scanty elucidations as contemporary writers have given. Nor can these representations always be accepted in perfect faith. Even in our own day many of the attempts at the representation by otherwise skilled artists of instruments perfectly well known to musicians frequently result in abject failure. In such trivial details it is thought perfectly allowable to draw on the imagina- tion. There is no reason to suppose that any greater con- scientiousness actuated the artist of a former age ; it is therefore unsafe to rely too implicitly on representations of this character for such details, for instance, as the number of strings with

which a particular instrument was furnished.   In addition to these
difficulties, the nomenclature is much involved, the same instrument receiving during the course of years a succession of different
names, while, on the other hand, the same name, from a
fancied but false analogy, has, in many cases, done duty for

Fig. 17.—Theatrical scene, with a woman playing the pipes (from a bas-relief in the
Museum at Naples).

an instrument of an entirely different nature.   Many attempts
have been made by men of learning to investigate the nature
of the instruments of Biblical and classic times,—it must be
added, with a very inadequate result.   A similar attempt, embracing instruments of a more modern day, was made by Father
Bonanni, an industrious writer, in his *Gabinetto Armonico* (Rome

1722), but with no greater success.   He had no special knowledge
of the subject ; his aim was to produce a book of handsome
plates of instruments, into the design of many of which an
exuberant fancy entered, for it is certain that nothing of the
sort ever existed.   No scientific investigation was made till the
question was taken up in our own day by the late Mr. C. Engel,
whose excellent catalogue of the musical instruments at the

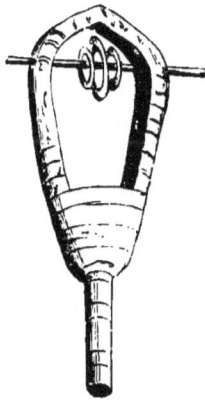

Fig. 18.—Egyptian sistrum.

South Kensington Museum contains nearly all the solid facts
on the subject which are available.

The favourite instruments of Greece and Rome belonged
mostly to the families of the lyre and the flute (fig. 17), but
the latter nation seems to have adopted many of the instruments
in use among the peoples which they conquered ; thus drums
and trumpets are supposed to have been borrowed from the
warlike nations of the North, while the sistrum (fig. 18), a frame

of bronze, through holes in the side of which metal rods were
loosely inserted, producing a jingling noise when shaken, was
introduced from Egypt with the worship of Isis. The Romans
seem also to have possessed the hydraulic organ, which is
represented on a coin of the time of Nero, now in the British
Museum. The organ is mentioned by St. Jerome in a letter
in which he speaks of the different kinds of musical instruments
of his day (A.D. 331—420). His account of it is a very good
example of the difficulties which have to be contended with
in trying to understand these ancient descriptions. He says it
was composed of fifteen brazen tubes, and two reservoirs of air
of elephant skin, and of twelve forge bellows to imitate the
sound of thunder. He goes on to describe, under the generic
name of *tuba*, several sorts of trumpets: that which gathered
together the people, that which directed the marching of troops,
that which proclaimed a victory, that which sounded the charge
against the enemy, that which announced the closing of the
city gates, etc. He further mentions the cithara of the Hebrews,
an instrument triangular in shape, with twenty-four strings ;
the sambuca, a wind instrument of wooden tubes sliding one
in the other, something like the modern trombone ; the psalterium, a small harp of ten strings ; and the tympanum, which
resembled the tambourine.

The obvious division of musical instruments is into three
classes—instruments of percussion, wind instruments, and stringed
instruments. Indeed, a modern writer on the subject, Mr. J. F.
Rowbotham, maintains that in uncivilized nations musical instru-

ments have always been invented in the order of "the drum, the pipe, and the lyre;" and he maintains his theory with much learning and research.

INSTRUMENTS OF PERCUSSION.

There can be no doubt that some form of the drum is known to almost every nation, however low in the scale of civilization. It is so familiar that description is needless. At a very early date the kettledrum was in use in France, as it is referred to by Joinville under the title of "Nacaire" (fig 19), and was an Oriental importation. The modern tambourine, so associated with Spanish life, under different names was popular in most countries. A curious sculpture is to be seen on the

Fig. 19.—Oriental Nacaire.

House of the Musicians at Rheims (fig. 20), in which a musician is represented as playing on a pipe, while he strikes the tambourine, which is fastened to his elbow, with his head. The tabour was long popular in England, associated with the pipe, both instruments being played by the same person. It was a small hand drum, and has its counterpart down to the present time in Provence, under the name of Tambourin, where, in conjunction with the flageolet, it serves for village dances.

It should be mentioned that most of the instruments of the drum order give no definite musical pitch. Their use is simply to accentuate the rhythm. This, however, is not the case with the modern orchestral kettledrums, which are susceptible

Fig. 20. —Musician playing the tambourine and pipe (from the House of the Musicians at Rheims).

of tuning by tightening or relaxing the heads. These instruments are generally used in pairs.

We have already mentioned the Egyptian sistrum. Allied to these are cymbals, also of Oriental origin, and even now those in general use are nearly all made in Constantinople. The crotala were small cymbals, used in dancing much in the same way as castagnettes were employed in Spain. The triangle is also of great antiquity (fig. 21).

The use of the bell was soon appropriated to the purposes of religion, for calling together the congregation. At first it

Fig. 21.—Triangle of the ninth century (from a MS.).

was no larger than a hand-bell (fig. 22), which was rung in front of the church door, or from a raised platform ; but with increased skill the size was developed, and the bells were hung

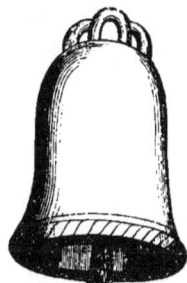

Fig. 22.—Hand-bell, ninth century (from a MS. at Boulogne).

in the towers and campaniles,—the word signifies bell-towers,— and required mechanical assistance to ring them. In early times these large bells were made of hammered plates of metal, riveted together, as in the large bell of St. Cecilia at Cologne, re-

presented in fig. 23. But the practice of casting them soon
became general. One of the most ancient now existing is that

Fig. 23.—Bell of St. Cecilia at Cologne, made of riveted plates.

of the cathedral at Siena (fig. 24), which bears the date 1159.
It is barrel-shaped, and gives a very acute sound. The variety

Fig. 24.—Bell in the tower of the cathedral at Siena, twelfth century.

of pitch in different bells soon suggested the chime or carillon,
which first consisted of a series of bells struck by the performer

with a small hammer (fig. 25). But with the increase in the size and number of the bells it became necessary to replace the hammer of the performer by mechanism. Carillons were a source of great delight to the inhabitants of the Low Countries, where they are still to be heard in their greatest perfection.

Fig. 25.—Carillon played with a hammer (from a MS. of the ninth century at St. Blaise, in the Black Forest).

They are generally set in motion by a system of pins on a barrel, so disposed as to produce the melody, as in the familiar musical box; but they can also be played upon by trained performers, some of whom have been musicians of eminence, as, for instance, Matthias van den Gheyn, of Louvain, who was an excellent composer and a fine organist.

3

The Russian bells are among the largest in the world. The great bell at Moscow is a familiar example; but this has never been rung, as it was cracked, immediately after it was cast, by an unfortunate influx of water before the bell was cold. The habit in Russia appears to be to ring all the bells at once, the din from which is terrific. The practice of what is called change-ringing is peculiar to England. By change-ringing is meant a continual variation of the order in which the bells are sounded, according to certain rules laid down.

WIND INSTRUMENTS.

The reed gave to our progenitors a musical instrument almost ready to their hands. It was a natural step to the

Fig. 26.—Syrinx (MS. in the Library at Angers).

Fig. 27.— Oblique flute and syrinx (from an Etruscan bas-relief).

combination of reeds of different lengths into the syrinx or Pan's pipes (figs. 26, 27), now only associated in our minds

with the ancient and popular drama of *Punch and Judy*.
The tibia or flute was originally made out of a
shin bone of an animal, and its shape was retained when it came to be constructed of other
materials. It was blown at the end, and was
frequently used double, either with a common
mouthpiece (fig. 28) or separately ; and in
Greece and Rome it was usual to employ a
capistrum or bandage round the cheeks, which
embraced the mouth. The flutes were of
different lengths, to produce a more extended
range of
sounds.
The hori-

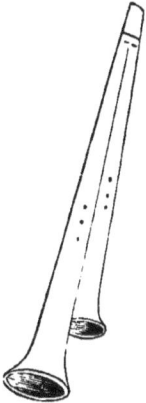

Fig. 28.—Double
flute.

zontal flute, blown through
a hole in the side, was in
use in early times (fig. 27),
but was for a long time
abandoned. The modern
flute was in its earliest days
known as the "German"
flute (fig. 29), to distinguish
it from the flute à-bec,
which was blown into by
means of a mouthpiece
containing some modification

Fig. 29.—Musicians playing the flute and other instruments (from Jost Amman, sixteenth century).

of the reed, having greater resemblance to the flageolet.

The "chorus" (fig. 30) was an instrument of one or two
speaking tubes attached to a bladder, or sometimes the skin of
an animal, as a pig, into which a mouthpiece was inserted to
blow it by. To show the confusion in which the subject of
these ancient instruments is involved, the name of chorus was
also applied to a stringed instrument. That which we have

Fig. 30.—Chorus (from a MS. of the ninth century at St. Blaise).

been describing evidently paved the way to the *cornemuse*, or
bagpipe (fig. 31), a contrivance to which some have refused the
name of a musical instrument, while, on the other hand, it is
held in exaggerated reverence in the northern parts of these
realms. The bagpipes consist of a wind-bag, which is usually
supplied from the mouth of the player; a reservoir to contain
the wind, a certain number of the tubes forming the drones,

which are not under the control of the player ; and the chaunter,
a pierced tube on which the melody is performed.   It is an
instrument of great antiquity, and is found, even in our own
day, over a wide extent of the globe.   It exists in Italy in the
rude "*zampogna*" of the Calabrian peasant, the bag formed of

Fig. 31. —Cornemuse, or bagpipe (from the House of the Musicians at Rheims).

the skin of a pig ; and in Scotland in the finished instrument of
torture of Her Majesty's pipers.

Sometimes the wind was supplied to the wind-bag by
means of a pair of bellows, worked by the pressure of the
elbow.   This is the case with the Irish and also with the
Lowland Scotch bagpipe.   Under the name of " Musette " a

similar instrument, of smaller dimensions, became very fashionable
in France during the reign of Louis XIV. It was constructed
in very ornamental fashion, and was a favourite instrument in
the hands of ladies.

It is evident that the bagpipes contain all the elements of

Fig. 32.—Primitive organ (sculpture in the museum at Arles).

the organ. A sculpture now in the museum at Arles (fig. 32)
shows that in its most primitive form the organ was actually
blown by the breath of two attendants, who of course had to
blow alternately to keep up the pressure of wind. The difficulty
of doing this successfully seems to have suggested the hydraulic
organ. Of that instrument there is an elaborate description in

Vitruvius, which has greatly exercised the ingenuity of those interested in the question. There can be no doubt, however, that it was "hydraulic" only so far that the weight of a column of water was used to produce the necessary pressure of wind. The pneumatic organ soon came into use, for on an obelisk erected by Theodosius, who died in 393, is a representation of an organ (fig. 33), in which the pressure of air is produced by a couple of attendants who are standing on the upper board of the bellows. There were probably two pairs, side by side, or the pressure could not have been uniform. Here we have the

Fig. 33.—Sculpture on an obelisk erected by Theodosius at Constantinople in the fourth century, representing organs in which the pressure of air is produced by the weight of the blowers.

method which has been retained in Germany even to the present day.

The suitability of the organ for use in religious service appears to have soon suggested itself. It is stated to have been common in the churches of Spain as early as A.D. 450. In France its introduction was later. In 757 the Byzantine emperor Constantine Copronymus sent one for a present to Pépin, and seventy years later Haroun Alraschid made a similar gift to Charlemagne. In the next century organs had become common. The earliest representation of an organ in which the

bellows are worked by means of levers is given in a MS. Psalter
of Edwin, in the library of Trinity College, Cambridge (fig. 34).
It is played upon by two performers, both of whom appear to
be chiding the unfortunate blowers, a custom which even now
has not gone out of use. That two performers were required
for so small an instrument may be accounted for by the fact
that keys had not come into use. Each particular pipe was

Fig. 34.—Organ with bellows worked by levers (from a MS. of the twelfth century in the library
of Trinity College, Cambridge).

allowed to speak by the withdrawal of a broad piece of wood
which slid under the foot of the pipe. In 951 an organ of
considerable dimensions was erected in Winchester Cathedral,
which was described with great enthusiasm in a poem by a
monk named Wolstan, although it must be admitted that the
description is by no means easy of comprehension. On their
introduction the keys were vastly broader than we are accustomed

to in the present day, for they required to be struck by the whole fist, and thus performers on this instrument came to be called organ-beaters.

While the dimensions of organs continued to increase, those of small size still remained in use, under the names of Portative, Positive, or Regal (figs. 36, 37), in the accompaniment of the plain-song, and also for domestic enjoyment. The

Fig. 35.—Organ (from a MS. Psalter of the fourteenth century, National Library, Paris).

addition of pedals, which have so largely added to the resources of the organ, is attributed to Bernhard, a German living in Venice about the year 1470. With the invention of the swell, a box containing the pipes which opened with Venetian or sliding shutters, thus allowing of a crescendo, the organ may be considered complete. This improvement was first applied to an organ by Jordan in the Church of St.

Magnus, by London Bridge. It is almost confined to England, as the use of it on the Continent has been very rarely adopted.

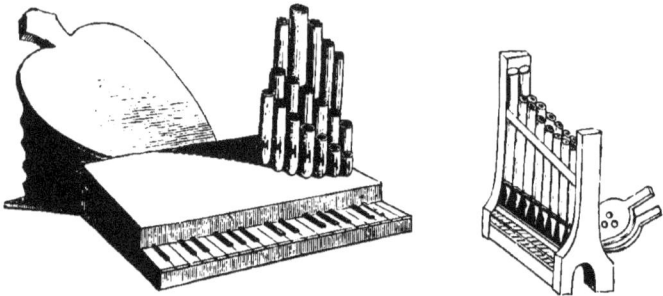

Figs. 36 and 37.—Small organs, called "Portative," "Positive," or "Regal."

The instruments of the trumpet order were numerous. The earliest were made from the horns of animals, and this type is still preserved in the Jewish "*shophar*," made of

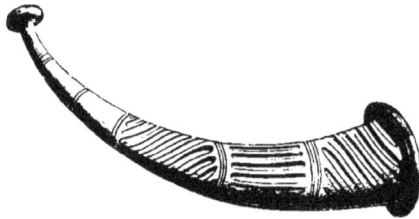

Fig. 38.—Oliphant (fourteenth century).

ram's horn, which is still used in the synagogues at the Festival of the New Year. Another was the "oliphant" (fig. 38), so called because it was constructed from the tusk of an elephant, and was used in the middle ages as a hunting-horn, and also for announcing the arrival of distinguished guests. Many of these still remain, and are frequently so exquisitely carved that they are admirable works of art. In mountainous districts enormous trumpets were used as a means of communication between the shepherds on neighbouring hills (fig. 39). These were generally constructed of wood, bound

Fig. 39.—Shepherds' trumpets (eighth century, from a MS. in the British Museum).

together by metal bands, or thongs of hide. In this form they are familiar to Swiss travellers at every spot where there exists an echo.

But it was for military purposes that the trumpet was chiefly brought into requisition. The use of metal soon became almost universal in its construction. In the earliest times it was made perfectly straight, or only slightly curved; and when the length was excessive, some sort of prop or support became

necessary (figs. 40, 41). It was soon found, however, that the
tube could be doubled on itself with no harm to the quality
of tone, but with the advantage of much greater convenience
of handling (fig. 42). With the addition of the slide, by
which the pitch of the instrument could be varied, the trumpet
became available as an orchestral instrument, and as such

Fig. 40. —Bent trumpet (eleventh century,   Fig. 41. —Trumpet with support (eleventh
Cottonian MS. British Museum).   century, Cottonian MS. British Museum).

was a great favourite of Handel, who has written *obligato*
parts for it to several of his songs. The sackbut (fig. 43)
was also made of metal, furnished with a sliding piece, and
was the equivalent of the modern trombone.

The "shawm" (*i.e.* "chalumeau"), which was a reed
instrument, developed into the modern hautboy, to which the

bassoon serves as a bass.   These were the only reed instruments
in general use in the orchestra till the adoption of the clarionet
in the latter part of the last century.   The "recorder," which

Fig. 42.—Military trumpet (from Jost Amman, sixteenth century).

is often mentioned in seventeenth-century works, was also a
reed instrument, but on the side, near the mouthpiece, there
was a hole covered with a piece of bladder, which modified the
quality of sound.

STRINGED INSTRUMENTS.

The fabled invention of the lyre does not concern us
here, but the instrument remained in use for a long period,

and continued to be represented in the illuminations of manuscripts (figs. 44, 45). The psalterium, which succeeded it,
differed in name rather than character, being simply a frame
on which the strings were stretched (figs. 46, 47). The
resonant chamber indeed was smaller, or even absent, so that
the tone must have been less powerful. The only advantage
would seem to have been the increased number of the strings.

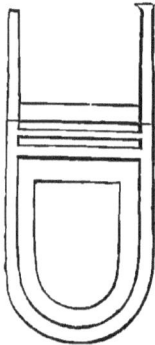

Fig. 43.—Sackbut (from   Fig. 44.—Ancient lyre (from a MS. at   Fig. 45.—Lyre used in the
a MS. of the ninth   Angers).   north (ninth century).
century at Boulogne).

The frame assumed several different shapes. In fig. 48, for
example, the upper part of it was prolonged to enable it to
rest against the shoulder. Differing only in having the strings
arranged diagonally is the instrument figured by the Abbot
Gerbert (fig. 49) from a manuscript in the library of his
monastery at St. Blaise in the Black Forest under the title
of "cithara." The "nablum" had a semicircular frame (fig. 50),
and it will be noticed in this that the resonant chamber be-

came larger. The strings of these instruments were plucked
with the finger, but in many cases with a plectrum, in the way
the zither is played in the present day.

Some form of the harp was almost universal (figs. 51—

Fig. 46.—Psalterium (ninth century, from a MS. in the National Library, Paris).

58), and its shape was the natural result of the different lengths
of string required to produce the musical scale. In its
earliest construction it was simply a wooden framework for
carrying the strings, but the want of a " sound-board " to

reinforce the tone was soon felt. This was supplied by
making the portion of the frame nearest the body of the

Fig. 47.—Round psalterium
(twelfth century).

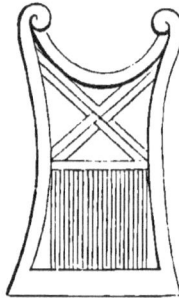

Fig. 48.—Psalterium (ninth
century, MS. Boulogne).

Fig. 49.—Cithara (from
Gerbert).

performer to consist of a hollow box. That this plan soon
suggested itself is proved by the "Harp of O'Brien" (fig. 55)
in the Museum of the Royal Irish Academy, Dublin, for

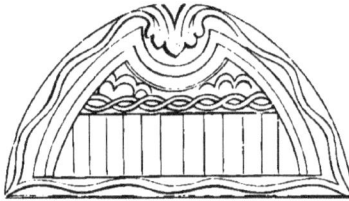

Fig. 50.—Nablum (ninth century, from MS. at
Angers).

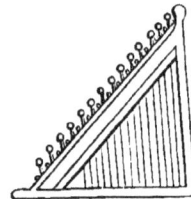

Fig. 51.—Triangular Saxon harp
(ninth century, from the Bible of
Charles the Bald).

which the date of the tenth century is claimed. The Welsh
"triple" harp, on the merits of which the inhabitants of the

Principality are eloquent, is so named from the fact that the

Fig. 52.—Harp (tenth century, Saxon Psalter, British Museum).

Fig. 53.—Harp (tenth century, University Library, Cambridge).

strings are arranged in three parallel rows. The outer rows

Fig. 54.—Harp (twelfth century, MS. National Library, Paris).

Fig. 55.—Harp of O'Brien, King of Ireland (tenth century, in the Dublin Museum).

on each side are tuned in unison, and thus by plucking the

4

string on each side successively it is possible with great skill
to produce almost the effect of a sustained note. The inner
row contains the chromatic intervals. In this position they
must be very difficult of access.

The harp is an instrument around which numerous poetical

Fig. 56.—Players on the harp (twelfth century, from a Bible, National Library, Paris).

Fig. 57.—Harpist (fifteenth century, from an enamel found near Soissons).

associations have gathered, from the days when David played
before Saul, and Alfred entered the Danish camp ; but its
resources were very restricted until the invention of the
" pedal " harp in the year 1720, by a Bavarian named Hoch-
brucher. By means of a pedal working a little plate armed

with projecting pins, it was in the power of the performer to raise the pitch of each string a semitone (fig. 59). The mechanism passed up the front pillar, and each note was affected in all its octaves. Up to this time the only way of altering the pitch of the string was by pressing it with the finger. This mechanism was subsequently much improved by Erard.

Fig. 58.—Minstrel's harp (fifteenth century).

A favourite instrument was the dulcimer (fig. 60), which even now may occasionally be met with. It consisted of a flat box, acting as a resonating chamber over which the strings of wire were stretched. They were struck by little hammers. This instrument was also known as the psaltery.

An attempt was made, as early as the first half of the sixteenth century, to apply keys to stringed instruments ; in the first attempt, under the name of "clavicytherium," the strings were of gut, but these were soon replaced with wire, and the instrument was then called the clavichord (fig. 61). The use of these instruments was mainly confined to Germany.

Fig. 59.—Harp with pedals, made by Naderman in 1780 for Queen Marie Antoinette (now in the South Kensington Museum).

The peculiarity of them was that one string only served for
each tone and the semitone above, the vibrating length of
each string being shortened by the action of the same key
which set it in vibration. This latter was produced by the
plucking of a slip of quill on a " jack," which was raised by

Fig. 60.—Dulcimer (fourteenth century, MS. National Library, Paris).

the key. This action, with slight modifications, served for
the " virginal " or " spinet," which were small and portable
instruments. It is supposed by some that the name of virginal
was given it in honour of Queen Elizabeth, with whom it was
a favourite. This in its turn was superseded by the harpsichord,

a much larger instrument, resembling in shape our modern grand pianofortes. The action was still that of the "jack" and quill, but more than one wire was used to each note, sometimes even as many as four ; and there were elaborate

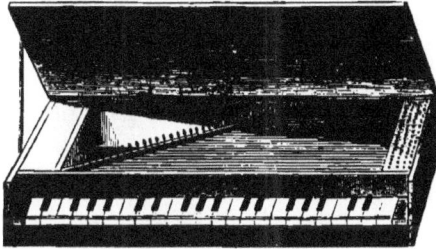

Fig. 61.—Clavichord (beginning of the fifteenth century, from Martin Agricola).

contrivances to enable a part of these only to be set in vibration, so as to produce variety of power. Kirkman, whose house still exists under the same name, and Tschudi, the founder of the well-known firm of Broadwood, were both eminent makers of harpsichords. The dulcimer no doubt

Fig. 62.—Lute (thirteenth century).

suggested the application of hammers instead of quills. This invention has been claimed for both Germany, France, and Italy, but there can be little doubt that the latter country was a few years the earliest, in the person of Bartolomeo

Cristofali. The new "pianoforte" was destined in a very short time to drive the harpsichord quite out of the field.

Among the most popular instruments during a long period commencing with the sixteenth century was the lute (fig. 62),

Fig. 63.—Crwth of the ninth century.

and that throughout the greater part of Europe. The strings were arranged in pairs tuned in unison, with a single string called the *chanterelle*, on which the melody was performed. The neck had frets at the required distances for producing the semitones. These frets were generally made of catgut, tightly fastened round the neck. Lutes were made of various sizes, and in the seventeenth century such instruments, of very large dimensions, with extra strings at the side of the finger-board,

Fig. 64.— King David playing the rotta (from a window of the thirteenth century in the cathedral of Troyes).

became very popular, under the names of theorbo, archlute, and chittarrone. The use of the guitar, which requires no description, was more popular in Spain, but it also had its period of fashion both in France and England.

Fig. 65.

Fig. 66.

Figs. 65 and 66.-- Concert (portions of a bas-relief of the capital of a column at the
Church of St. George's, Boscherville).

It will be noticed that all the stringed instruments of which we have spoken as yet were incapable of sustaining the sound. This was rendered possible by the use of the bow, which came into use in very early times. The most ancient was the Welsh crwth (fig. 63), pronounced "crowd," although some such instrument was no doubt known even earlier in the East. On the Continent a similar instrument was known under the name of "*rotta*" (fig. 64), which has been by some supposed to be an attempt to represent the same word. The term has been productive of some confusion, on account of its similarity

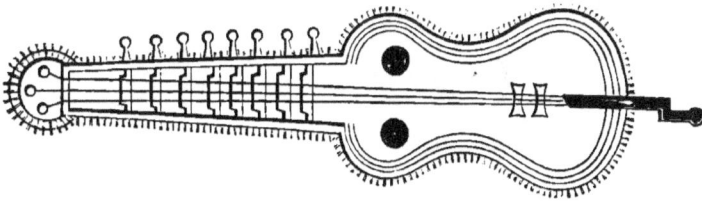

Fig. 67.—Organistrum (ninth century, from Gerbert).

with "*rota*," *a wheel*, by which was understood the hurdy-gurdy, an instrument of great antiquity. It may be found represented on a bas-relief from the Church of St. George's, Boscherville (figs. 65 and 66), in Normandy, dating from the eleventh century, and still earlier in a manuscript of the ninth century, described by Gerbert, under the title of "*organistrum*" (fig. 67). It will be seen from the figure that instead of frets the string was stopped by turning the handles at the side of the neck, which brought the projecting "feather" on the axis sufficiently above the level of the neck to effect that purpose.

It appears that two performers were necessary. The size of the instrument was soon reduced so as to adapt it to the powers of a single performer, and at a later period it became very fashionable in France, under the name of the "*vielle*," and in the eighteenth century shared with the musette the attention of the ladies.

For many years the viol (figs. 68—72), under various shapes, put in vibration with the bow, remained in vogue. The

Fig. 68.—Devil playing the viol (thirteenth century, Amiens Cathedral).

Fig. 69.—Minstrel playing the viol (fifteenth century, Book of Hours of King René, MS. Library of the Arsenal).

position of the tones and semitones was fixed by frets attached to the finger-board. For completeness it became necessary to have a "chest of viols," which contained two treble viols, a tenor and a bass-viol. The latter was also known as the Viola da Gamba, as it was held between the knees.

But the violin and its family were soon to oust the viol. Its invention is claimed for Gaspar Duiffoprugcar, of Bologna. It is probable that, although living in Bologna, he was in reality a Tyrolese, and his real name Tieffenbrücker. It was certain, however, that at almost the same time, in the second half of the sixteenth century, both Gaspar di Salo in Brescia and Andreas Amati in Cremona began to make violins, agreeing in all important particulars with those now in use. From that time the town of Cremona acquired a reputation for these instruments which is universal. Several members of the Amati

Fig. 70.—Viol-player (thirteenth century enamel found at Soissons).

Fig. 71.—Angel playing the viol (Amiens Cathedral).

family sustained its reputation, and they were succeeded by Antonius Straduarius and Joseph Guarnerius, who carried their skill to a pitch of excellence which more modern times have not succeeded in equalling.

The monochord was more used for purposes of scientific investigation into the division of the scale than as a musical instrument, but an old manuscript of Froissart's *Chronicles*

serves to show that it was occasionally brought into requisition
(fig. 73). Allied to this was the "trumpet-marine," the

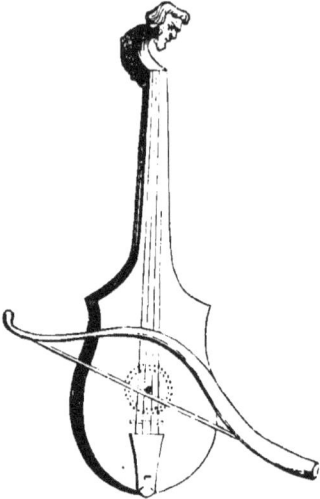

Fig. 72.– Rebec (sixteenth century).

Fig. 73.–Monochord (fifteenth century, from a MS. Froissart, National Library, Paris).

favourite instrument of M. Jourdain in the *Bourgeois Gentilhomme* of Molière, which, in spite of its name, was a stringed
instrument.

CHAPTER III.

THE MUSICAL INFLUENCE OF THE NETHERLANDS.

Dufay—Binchois—John of Dunstable—Hobrecht—Okeghem or Okenheim—Tinctoris' Obligations to Glareanus for our Knowledge of these Early Musicians—Josquin de Prés—Willaert—Rabelais on the Musicians of his Time—The Invention of the Madrigal—Early Music Printers—Orlando di Lassus.

As we have seen in Chapter I., the plain-song of the Church had now assumed a definite form, which the improvements in musical notation placed beyond the reach of those corruptions which are inseparable from oral tradition, while examples that have come down to us show that secular music had also adopted the same improvements.

The progress of music was about to receive a great impetus from the genius of a school of composers which arose in Flanders, the influence of which in a short time made itself paramount over the whole of Europe, both by the originality of the works which it produced and by the personal influence of its members, whose assistance was in request at all the centres of musical life. The founders of this school were Guillaume Dufay (1350—1432), Egidius Binchois (1400—1465), and John of Dunstable, the latter of whom was of English birth. Their reputation is based on the testimony of con-

temporaries rather than on any specimens of their powers
which have been handed down to us, although Dufay became
attached as tenor singer to the Pontifical Chapel in Rome in
the year 1380, retaining this position until his death ; and
while thus employed he wrote several masses, which are still
preserved in its archives.

In the second half of the fifteenth century three other
distinguished musicians came to the front : Hobrecht, Okeghem
or Okenheim, and Tinctoris. Hobrecht was master of the
music at the cathedral of Utrecht, and it is interesting to
note that in that capacity he had as pupil the eminent Erasmus,
who sang there as a choir-boy about the year 1471. For our
acquaintance with the works of Hobrecht and several other of
the distinguished musicians of those early times we are indebted to a distinguished philosopher and mathematician, named
Glareanus, from the fact that he was a native of the canton
of Glarus. He enjoyed the intimacy of Erasmus, and among
the many fields of learning which he cultivated, took great
delight in music, on which subject he wrote two works, in
addition to editing Boethius, whose treatise on music was then
looked on as containing the highest knowledge on the subject.
The most important of the works of Glareanus on the
subject of music was called *Dodecachordon*. The theory
which it was designed to support does not concern us here ;
its interest for our present purpose lies in the fact that a
large number of specimens of· the compositions of contemporary
and earlier musicians, which it would be exceedingly difficult to

find elsewhere, are preserved in this work, as well as many interesting particulars of their composers.   The work, which is an excellent example of typography and music printing, was published at Basle in 1547.   Speaking of Hobrecht, he tells us that he was a man who composed with remarkable facility,

Fig. 74.—Viol-players (after Jost Amman, sixteenth century).

one night sufficing for the composition of a mass which was the admiration of musicians.   In 1492 he was elected musical director of the cathedral at Antwerp, from a number of competitors who, during a whole year, took charge of the services in turn ; and this appointment he held till his death, about the year 1507.   He exercised important influence on the development of music, and was looked on as a great authority, receiving visits from all the principal musicians of his time. A collection of five of his masses was published during his lifetime by Petrucci, as well as many of his motets.

It is supposed that Okenheim, who was born about 1430, began his career as a choir-boy in Antwerp Cathedral, and there are strong grounds for believing that he continued his studies, after the breaking of his voice, under Binchois. It is certain, however, that in 1461 he was chaplain to Charles VII. of France, and afterwards to his successors Louis XI. and Charles VIII.; he subsequently became treasurer of St. Martin at Tours without resigning his other appointment. The testimony of contemporary writers unites in showing the respect in which he was held, and his death formed the subject of a poem, *La Déploration de Crétin sur le Trepas de feu Okeghem,*—which has been reprinted in Paris within the last few years by M. Thoinan,—as well as of dirges to his memory by more than one of his pupils. Glareanus claims for him the invention of the form of musical composition called " canon." Many of his works remain in manuscript, and of those which were published the original editions are of the greatest rarity. As a teacher, Okenheim's reputation was equally great, many of the leading musicians at the end of the fourteenth and beginning of the fifteenth centuries having been his pupils ; among these the most famous was Josquin de Prés, of whom we shall have to speak presently.

Tinctoris is better known as a theorist than as a composer. He was born at Nivelles, seemingly about 1434 or 1435, and at an early age went to Italy, where he became *maître de chapelle* to Ferdinand, King of Naples, by whom he was held in great estimation. He there founded a school of music. To Tinctoris belongs the merit of writing the first dictionary of music, under the title of *Terminorum Musicæ Definitorium*, a book of the very greatest rarity, being the first work printed on the subject of music. It is distinguished by great clearness of statement, and has been reprinted several times during the present century.

But a still greater light appeared in the person of Josquin de Prés (1450?—1521), a man who had been taught all that could be taught by his master Okenheim, but who possessed that true genius which enabled him to use his vast learning as a means to an end—the production of works of true beauty. Till that time no one had appealed so directly to the heart. Early in life he was master of the music at the cathedral of Cambrai, but he was soon called to become one of the singers in the Pontifical Chapel at Rome, under Pope Sixtus IV. At the death of the latter he entered the service of Ercole d'Este, Duke of Ferrara, and subsequently that of Lorenzo de Medici, of Louis XII. of France, and of the Emperor Maximilian I. Josquin appears to have been a man of much address, as the following anecdotes will show. Louis XII. wished him to write a piece of music for several voices, in which he could himself take part. The King was

5

an indifferent musician, with a weak voice, and sang much out
of tune. The composer wrote a part which he called *vox regis*,
consisting of the repetition of a single note throughout—an
example which many years later was followed by Mendelssohn
in his *Son and Stranger*. At another time the King promised
him some preferment, but delayed to perform his promise, on
which the composer wrote and executed a motet to the words

Fig. 75.—Musical instruments (from a thirteenth century MS.).

Memor esto verbi tui. The hint was not taken, whereupon he
tried the effect of a second motet, *Portio mea non est in terra
viventium.* At last he received the long-wished-for benefice,
and expressed his gratitude in a third motet, *Bonitatem fecisti
cum servo tuo, Domine.* A number of his masses were printed
by Petrucci and others, as well as a large collection of motets
and other sacred music, in addition to many chansons, etc.

We have spoken only of the leaders of the Flemish school, but it was very numerous, and comprised many men whose works were only inferior to those of the great masters whose scholars they were. Among these we must name Pierre de la Rue, Brumel, Jannequin, Mouton, Arcadelt, Verdelot, Gombert, Clemens non Papa, Goudimel (who settled in Rome and founded a school, but was subsequently killed in Lyons during the massacre of St. Bartholomew), Philippe de Monte, Waelrent, and Claude le Jeune.

Another distinguished man, Adrian Willaert, founded a school in Venice, from which issued, among others, Costanzo Porta, Cypriano di Rore, and the great theorist Zarlino.

Rabelais, in a very interesting passage of his *Pantagruel*, has collected, in two distinct groups, the names of fifty-eight musicians, French, Belgian, and Italian, who were in great esteem as composers and performers at two different epochs of the reign of Francis I., the first about 1515, the other about 1551. Rabelais was himself a dialectician and theorist in music, for he was master of all the sciences which could be acquired in the schools of the university of Paris. He calls to mind, therefore, with delight having heard, doubtless at the house of the brothers Du Bellay, his college companions, a fine vocal and instrumental concert, given in May, *en ung beau parterre*—on a beautiful lawn—by the following artists : Josquin de Prés, Ockeghem, Hobrecht, Agricola, Brumel, Camelin, Vigoris, De la Fage, Bruyer, Prioris, Seguin, Delarue, Midy, Moulu, Mouton, Gascogne, Loysel, Compère, Pevet, Fevin,

Rouzée, Richafford, Rousseau, Consilion, Constancio Festi, and
Jacques Bercan. The larger part of these musicians were
pupils of the venerable Flemish master Jean Ockeghem, who
died at Tours about 1510 at a very advanced age, and of his
learned scholar Josquin de Prés.

Thirty-five years later Rabelais again found himself with
the Cardinal du Bellay, but at Rome, "in a secluded garden,
under a beautiful leafy shade," and there he listened to another
concert, no less exquisite, performed by thirty-three musicians
belonging to the Flemish-Italian school. The chief performer
was Adrian Willaert, pupil of Josquin de Prés, and chapel-
master of St. Mark's at Venice, and by the side of this great
Flemish contrapuntist stood Claude Goudimel.

We have seen how widely extended was the influence of
the Flemish school. One of its greatest achievements is the
invention of the madrigal—a form of composition which at once
met with the greatest favour both in the Netherlands and in
Italy. Circumstances greatly favoured this result. The art of
printing music with movable type had just been invented by
Ottaviano dei Petrucci, of Fossombrone, in the duchy of
Urbino, about the year 1503, who set up a press in Venice.
Others quickly followed. Gardano, Vincenti, and Scotto in
Venice, Phalèse in Antwerp, as well as others, printed edition
after edition of sets of madrigals, for which the demand seems
to have been inexhaustible. Everything published in Italy was
at once reprinted at Antwerp, frequently at Nuremburg also,
and *vice versá*. They were invariably printed in separate parts

Fig. 76.— Jesse-tree, fifteenth century, with musical instruments.

for convenience of performance,—a score was unknown. It
naturally follows that complete sets of parts of early madrigals

are among the rarities of musical literature, for singers were doubtless no more careful in those days of the music they took home to practise than they are at present. This remarkable multiplication of copies proves that the knowledge of music and the power of singing must have been very widespread.

We have still to speak of one more of the glories of the Flemish school—with whom it seems to have died out—Roland de Lathe, better known as Orlando di Lasso or di Lassus, for even he adopted both forms of his name. He was born at Mons, most probably in the year 1520, according to some authorities in 1530. At an early age he became a choir-boy at the Church of St. Nicolas, and so beautiful was his voice that three separate attempts were made to kidnap him. On the first two occasions his parents were fortunate enough to recover their child, but on the third they allowed him to remain with Ferdinand Gonzaga, Viceroy of Sicily, who was at that time in command of an army of the Emperor Charles V. at St. Dizier. By him the young Orlando was taken to Milan, and subsequently to Sicily. He appears to have remained three years at Naples with the Marquis of Terza, and then to have gone to Rome, where for six months he was the guest of the Archbishop of Florence, until he received the appointment of director of the choir at St. John Lateran, a post which at that time was always entrusted to musicians of eminence. After two years he returned to his native land, and entering the service of Julius Cæsar Brancanio, visited in his train the court of our Henry VIII., by whom he was well received.   He had decided on settling in this country, when he was called to Antwerp to assume the post of director of the music.   There he made himself so much esteemed that he proposed to make that city his permanent abode.   But his reputation had become so great that Duke Albert V. of Bavaria, a true lover of music, made him the most flattering offers, with the result that in 1557 he removed to Munich, which from that time became his home.

The intercourse between the Duke and the musician was of the most intimate nature, and did honour to them both. The Duke took a deep and personal interest in all the works of the musician ; the latter was a man of charming and courtly manners, whose knowledge was not confined to the art which he practised.   He married a young maid-of-honour attached to the court, and was subsequently ennobled by the Emperor Maximilian II.   He died in Munich in 1594, having passed his life in the most congenial surroundings which could fall to the lot of a musician.

The number of works which he left behind him was enormous, in all departments of musical composition.   They comprise 51 masses, 180 magnificats, 780 motets, and many other works of sacred music, while among the secular are contained 233 madrigals and 371 chansons, altogether 1,572 sacred and 765 secular works.   A magnificent collection of his works is still to be seen in the Royal Library at Munich, superbly written on vellum, with illuminations, and in the

Fig. 77.—Orlando di Lassus.

richest binding. These volumes alone are a splendid testimony
to the consideration in which he was held. Many of his works

are included in the *Patrocinium Musices*, printed by Adam Berg in Munich, a splendid work, of which seven volumes only were issued, of the largest folio, and printed in notes which could be read by a whole choir.   After the death of Orlando di Lassus his sons Ferdinand and Rudolph brought out a complete collection of his motets in separate parts, in six volumes, under the title of *Magnum Opus Musicum.*   It is most clearly printed, and if the bars were inserted, could be read from by any choir in the present day.

With Orlando di Lassus ceases the predominance of musical activity in the Netherlands.   As we have seen, its influence had extended over the whole of the continent of Europe. From this time Italy became for a while the chosen home of music.

CHAPTER IV.

MUSIC IN ITALY AND GERMANY.

The Papal Chapel—Palestrina and his Reforms—His Successors—The Music for Holy
Week in the Sistine Chapel—Music in Venice—Writers on the Theory of Music—
Early German Composers : Isaak and Senfl—The Influence of the Reformation on
Music—German Writers on Musical Instruments and Theory.

It will scarcely appear surprising that Rome, the centre of all
that was most magnificent in the pomp of religious ceremonial,
should attract within its walls the most eminent artists of the
day, and we have seen how many of the Flemish musicians
were drawn to it ; indeed, the majority of the Papal
Chapel were of that nation. Under the influence of Josquin
de Prés, and still more of Orlando di Lassus, the school
of the Low Countries had in a great measure broken away
from the mere exhibition of technical contrivance—although
that was not wanting—in favour of greater beauty of expression.
The practice, however, was still maintained of employing
secular melodies as the subjects of religious compositions ; for
instance, every writer of the day felt it due to his reputation
to write a mass on the air *L'Homme Armé;* and many of
the subjects in vogue were even more mundane in their
associations.

In addition to this practice, which to the musicians of those days suggested no lack of reverence, corruptions had also crept into the authorised text of the mass, the singers even venturing at times to sing the very words of the secular melodies on which the masses were written ; in fact, great laxity had become common, and had been the occasion of grave scandal.

The Council of Trent was now (1564) sitting, and this abuse was one of the subjects which it was called on to consider. It is needless to say that it was condemned absolutely, a proposition being very seriously entertained to forbid any other music than the plain-song.   Pope Pius IV., however, decided on referring the whole question to a commission of eight cardinals, with the saintly Carlo Borromeo at its head.   The commission appears to have taken great pains to act rightly, and sought the advice of many of the papal singers.   Cardinal Borromeo was personally strongly opposed to the proposition of confining ecclesiastical music to the ancient plain-song, and persuaded his fellow-members to suspend their judgment, having in the meantime requested Palestrina, who had already attained some eminence, to compose a mass which should reconcile the claims of religion and of art.

The composer was not content with writing a single mass ; he submitted three, which were sung in succession by the papal singers before the commission. It was at once seen that the great composer had solved the problem.   Both the first and the second mass were heard with delight, but the third with absolute enthusiasm. Nothing so solemn had been heard up to that time. This was the famous *Missa Papæ Marcelli*, so named in memory of Pope Marcellus, who filled the office for a few days only. It remains a model of all that religious music should be—the highest type of unaccompanied vocal music, and at the same time most devotional and expressive. It was at once sung before the Pope in the Sistine Chapel, when it impressed all hearers with its beauty.

Giovanni Pierluigi du Palestrina was so named from the place of his birth, the date of which was 1524. At an early age he went to Rome, singing in the choir of Santa Maria Maggiore. He became a pupil of Claude Gondimel, and, after holding different offices, was in 1555 appointed by Julius III. a singer in the Sistine Chapel. Shortly afterwards Paul IV., who had succeeded to the papacy, deprived him of his office on the ground that he was not in orders, and that he was also married. In the same year, however, he was made director of the music at St. John Lateran, and in 1561 at Santa Maria Maggiore. As a result of the success of his *Missa Papæ Marcelli*, the office of composer to the Sistine Chapel was created for him. He was a man of great saintliness of character, living in the greatest intimacy with St. Philip Neri, in whose arms he expired in the year 1594. His works, which are very numerous, including no less than ninety-three masses, are masterpieces of the art of writing for unaccompanied voices; they are full of learned contrivance, but the learning is kept in the background by the devotional feeling which is their prominent characteristic ; no vocal music is capable of giving greater delight to the true musician ; no music is more admirably suited to the requirements of religious worship. Such fitness had never been attained before his time, and the term "alla Palestrina" has ever since been applied to the highest development of sacred music. Many of his compositions are still unpublished, but this reproach is being removed by Messrs. Breitkopf and Härtel, of Leipzig, who are bringing out a complete and critical edition of his works.

It will be supposed that the traditions of such a master would be perpetuated. Among those who followed in his footsteps were Giovanni Maria and Bernardino Nanini, Felice and Francesco Anerio, Giovanni Animuccia, Luca Marenzio, and Gregorio Allegri. The Papal Chapel had always numbered among its members several Spanish musicians. Among the most eminent of these were Cristoforo Morales—a motet by whom, *Lamentabatur Jacob*, is a masterpiece of expressive music—Bartolomeo Escobedo, Francesco Guerrero, and, perhaps greatest of all, Loreto Vittoria.

The choir of the Sistine Chapel carried the practice of unaccompanied vocal music to the highest pitch of excellence, and was the admiration of all musicians. The performance of the music during Holy Week was especially admirable. This was the composition of Palestrina, Allegri, and Bai. The *Miserere* of Allegri was so jealously guarded that no member of the choir was allowed to take one of the parts out of the

chapel, under pain of excommunication. Our own Dr. Burney,
however, succeeded in obtaining a copy, which he published
in 1771, and it will be remembered how the youthful Mozart,
at that time fourteen years of age, wrote it down from
memory after hearing it once, taking his manuscript in his hat
for correction on a second occasion. When it is remembered
that the composition is written for two choruses of four and
five parts, and that the two choruses finally unite, the
wonderful nature of the feat becomes the more remarkable.

We have already mentioned that a school of music was
founded at Venice under the auspices of the Flemish musician
Adrian Willaert. It produced many good musicians, among
whom were Cipriano di Rore, who, in spite of his name, was
of Flemish origin, Giovanni della Croce, renowned for his
madrigals, Andrea Gabrieli, and his nephew Giovanni Gabrieli.
Its influence made itself felt in its turn in Germany, Hans
Leo Hassler (fig. 78), who was among the earliest musicians
in Nuremburg, having learned his art in Venice at the feet of
the elder Gabrieli. Among other musicians of Northern Italy,
we must name Orazio Vecchi and Giangiacomo Gastoldi, who
both carried on their art in Milan, and Costanzo Porta, another
pupil of Willaert, who was successively director of the music
at Padua, Ravenna, and Loretto.

In addition to the numerous composers of whom we have
spoken, there was no lack of writers on the theory of music.
Among the earliest of these was Franchinus Gaforius, who
published his first work in the year 1480, and it is a proof of

the interest taken in the subject, so soon after the invention
of printing, that several editions of his treatises were called
for.   So great indeed was the interest excited, that controversies
soon arose between rival theorists, which were carried on with

Fig. 78.—Hans Leo Hassler.

a bitterness proceeding from thorough conviction.   A Spanish
musician, Ramis de Pareja, having attacked the doctrines of
Guido d'Arezzo, was answered in 1487 by Nicolas Burci or
Burtius in a treatise " *adversus quemdam Hyspanum veritatis
prevaricatorem*"! and the style of the book is in keeping with

the title. Spartaro, a pupil of Ramis, flew to the rescue of his master, and Gaforius was soon drawn into the controversy, with an *Apologia adversus Johannem Spartarium et complices musicos Bononienses.* Among other eminent theorists must be mentioned Peter Aron, and somewhat later Zarlino, who was director of the music of St. Mark's at Venice. It was the fashion of those early days to bring out handbooks to the seven liberal arts, of which, of course, music formed one ; these were generally dry treatises epitomized from Boethius— our frontispiece is taken from such a work—and as a knowledge of plain-song was part of the education of every priest, it naturally follows that the works on this subject were almost countless.

In Germany, among the earliest musicians of eminence we find Heinrich Isaak. The place and time of his birth are doubtful, but he was a contemporary—some say a pupil—of Josquin de Prés. He became director of the choir of St. Giovanni in Florence, from which place he was called back to Germany by Maximilian I. Many of his works remain in manuscript, but some were published, and several handed down to us in the works of Glareanus and other writers. His pupil Ludwig Senfl (fig. 79), of Swiss birth, wrote masses, as well as many motets, and among his miscellaneous writings set to music some of the odes of Horace. The names of Jakob Händl and Gregoir Aichinger must also be recorded.

About this time the Reformation took place. It is well known that Luther was a profound lover of music, several well-known chorales being attributed to him. There can be no doubt

Fig. 79. - Ludwig Senfl.

that one of the effects of the Reformation was to alter the direction of musical activity. The laity were encouraged to join

6

in the musical portions of the service. It is obvious that works
of any elaboration were unsuited for such a purpose, and to
this feeling must be attributed the multiplication of chorales, many
of which form the cherished inheritance of the Protestant portions
of the German nation, to whom they are universally familiar.
Among the best-known of these, and one identified with the
great Reformer's career, is *Ein' feste Burg ist unser Gott*, and
this is additionally familiar from its introduction and magnificent
treatment by Meyerbeer in his *Huguenots*. *Nun danket alle Gott*
is another which in Germany occupies much the same position
that the Old Hundredth Psalm does with Englishmen. The
beauty and appropriateness of the German chorale are incontest-
able, but there can be little doubt that its exclusive use has
tended to cramp the development of religious music.

Germany produced a large number of didactic and theoretical
works, among the earliest and most curious of which is the
Flores Musicæ, by Hugo von Reuthingen, printed by Pryss at
Strasburg in 1488, although probably written more than a century
earlier. As its title indicates, it is in Latin, and while printed
as prose, in reality consists of hexameter verses, with a running
commentary by a later hand. Among our greatest obligations
to the Germans is the information they have given us on the
form and construction of the musical instruments of that time.
The *Musica Getutscht* of Sebastian Virdung (Basle, 1511) gives
descriptions, with figures, of most of these. It is a work of
very great rarity, five copies only being known, three of which
are in public libraries abroad, the others both in this country

in private hands. Fortunately an excellent facsimile has been published. It is written in the German language, but in 1536 Ottomar Luscinius (*i.e.*, Nachtigall) brought out a similar book in Latin, illustrated with the identical blocks used for Virdung's work, of which it was in great part a translation. Lastly, we

Fig. 80.—Michael Prætorius.

must mention another and a later work, also of the greatest rarity, the *Syntagma Musicum* of Michael Prætorius (fig. 80) (Wittemburg and Wolfenbüttel, 1615—1620), designed by the author to be a complete encyclopædia of the art and practice

Fig. 81.—Title-page of the volume of plates of the *Syntagma* of Michael Prætorius (1620).

of music, which also contains descriptions and woodcuts of the instruments then in use (fig. 81). Of these plates an excellent facsimile has been issued, but the letterpress has not been reprinted. As the date of the work is nearly a century after that of Virdung, its historical value is important.

We have already spoken of the debt we owe to Glareanus for preserving to us in his great work *Dodecachordon* many compositions by distinguished musicians of an earlier date which would have been otherwise lost. For the same reason must be mentioned Sebaldus Heyden's *Ars Canendi*. The number of books on the science of music published in Germany during this period is very large, and the Germans soon became, as they have since remained, the most prolific writers on the art.

CHAPTER V.

EARLY HISTORY OF MUSIC IN ENGLAND.

Sumer is icumen in—Fairfax, Sheppard, Mulliner, Taverner, Merbecke, Tallis, Redford, Edwards, Tye, and Byrd—Patent for Music-printing granted to Tallis and Byrd— Farrant—The Madrigalian Era—N. Yonge's *Musica Transalpina*—Watson's *Italian Madrigals Englished*— Morley, Bateson, Ward, and O. Gibbons — *Triumphs oj Oriana*—Widespread Knowledge of Music—Morley's *Introduction—Parthenia—* Dr. John Bull—Foundation of Gresham College—Ravenscroft—Hilton—Barnard's Cathedral Music—Metrical Version of the Psalms.

IF, in consequence of its geographical position, England was in a great measure cut off from the musical influences which were at work in the continent of Europe, there is one fact to which it may point with pride—the possession of the earliest secular composition in parts existing in any country. This is the famous *rota*, or *round*, *Sumer is icumen in*. It is contained in one of the Harleian manuscripts, and was exhibited in the King's Library at the British Museum as part of the interesting musical collection which was shown there in the summer of 1885, when no doubt many of our readers saw it. An excellent facsimile forms the frontispiece of Mr. W. Chappell's *Popular Music of the Olden Time*, and another is to be found in Sir George Grove's *Dictionary of Music* (vol. iii.). We do not therefore reproduce it here. In the judgment of those best qualified to form an opinion, the manuscript belongs to the first half of the thirteenth century. This was the opinion of the late Sir F. Madden among others, and lest it should be supposed that national feeling may have influenced this decision, it may be well to mention that M. Coussemaker concurred in it. The composition is a canon for four voices, with two others forming the *pes*, or burden. The style of the composition, both in melody and harmony, is far in advance of anything known at that time, which was a hundred and fifty years before the rise of the Flemish school.

With so long a step in advance, it is humiliating to be unable to continue the record, and we are forced to suppose that much music was lost at the suppression of the monasteries in the time of Henry VIII. We have already spoken of John of Dunstable. Of musicians before the Reformation very little beyond the names has come down to us. Robert Fairfax, Doctor of Music (and England is the only country in which degrees in music have been conferred), was organist, or perhaps precentor, of St. Albans in the reign of Henry VII. About the same time flourished John Sheppard, organist of Magdalen College, Oxford, who received his education from Thomas Mulliner, master of the boys of St. Paul's, London. Taverner was organist of Boston, and subsequently of Cardinal College (now Christchurch), Oxford. Having joined the Reformed religion, his life was in some peril, but fortunately his skill in music helped to secure his acquittal.

We now come to one whose name is more widely known

in our own time—John Merbecke, to whom was entrusted
the duty of arranging the musical portions of the first
Reformed Prayer-book of Edward VI., which was published
in 1550, under the title of *The Booke of Common Praier
Noted.* This was an adaptation of the plain-song to the new
form of liturgy. The author was a man of some learning in
other departments of knowledge, having compiled a concord-
ance to the Bible. He was a very staunch adherent to the
new doctrines, and nearly fell a martyr to his opinions, having
been condemned to death with two of his friends, who were
actually executed, his own life being saved by Bishop Gardiner's
intervention. The choral portions of the services of the
Reformed Church were also set to music by the celebrated Tallis.
He made use of the resources of harmony, and his noble
setting has held its place to the present day wherever the
choral service of the English Church is performed.

John Redford succeeded Mulliner as master of the boys
at St. Paul's Cathedral ; he wrote many services and anthems,
one of which, *Rejoice in the Lord*, is still in use. Richard
Edwards, also a writer of much Church music, is better known
to us as the composer of the beautiful madrigal *In going to
my naked bed.* Some of the works of Dr. Tye also are still
performed. He formed the idea of making a rhymed translation of the Acts of the Apostles and of setting it to music,
but does not seem to have advanced beyond the fourteenth
chapter.

Tallis was one of the most learned composers in an age

of learning. In proof of this we may point to his canon in
forty parts which is still extant. One of his familiar works is

Fig. 82.—" Music," allegorical picture, after an engraving by Rousselet (seventeenth century).

the well-known tune to 'Bishop Ken's evening hymn, which
contains a canon between the treble and tenor parts. William

Byrd is known to most by his canon *Non nobis Domine*, so often sung as a grace. It has remained a matter of discussion whether Byrd conformed to the Protestant religion or continued in the Romish faith ; but it is certain that he composed several masses. One of these, for five voices, forms the earliest publication of the Musical Antiquarian Society. With Tallis, who was his master, he published a set of *Cantiones Sacræ*, and other sets by himself alone, under similar titles. Of his English works we have *Psalms, Sonets, and Songs of Sadnes and Pietie, Songs of Sundrie Natures, some of gravitie and others of myrth*, and *Psalms, Songs, and Sonnets, some solemne, others joyful, framed to the Life of the Words*. To Tallis and Byrd, and to the survivor of them, was granted by Queen Elizabeth the exclusive right of printing music and of ruling music paper. Tallis died in 1585, and the patent devolved wholly on Byrd, who is believed to have gained largely by it.

We must not pass by Richard Farrant, gentleman of the Chapel Royal, without mention. The beautiful subject of his still favourite anthem, *Lord, for Thy tender mercies' sake*, is alone sufficient to preserve his name from oblivion, although by some it has been attributed to Hilton.

We have now come to the golden age of music in England, a time when its composers will bear comparison with any contemporary writers on the Continent. This period has been happily called the Madrigalian Era, and is covered by a space of exactly fifty years from the year 1588, which is the date of the first collection of madrigals published in this country. The title is worth transcribing :—

"*Musica Transalpina :* Madrigales translated of foure, five, and sixe parts, chosen out of divers excellent Authors, with the first and second part of *La Verginella*, made by Maister Byrd, upon two stanz's of Ariosto, and brought to speak English with the rest. Published by N. Yonge, in favour of such as take pleasure in musick of voices. Imprinted at London by Thomas East, the assigné of William Byrd. 1588."

It will thus be seen that this first collection was almost exclusively, as its title infers, a collection of the works of foreign musicians ; in fact, it contains, among others, four by Palestrina, four by F. di Monte, ten by Luca Marenzio, two by Orlando di Lassus, and fourteen by Ferabosco. In his quaint preface Yonge says :—

"Since I first began to keepe house in this citie, it hath been no small comfort unto mee that ˙a great number of gentlemen and merchants of good accompt (as well of this realme as of forraine nations) have taken in good part such entertainment of pleasure, as my poore abilitie was able to affoord them, both by the exercise of musicke daily used in my house, and by furnishing them with bookes of that kinde yearly sent me out of Italy and other places, which, beeing for the most part Italian songs, are for sweetness of aire verie well liked of all, but most in account with them that understand that language. . . . And albeit there be some English

songs lately set forth by a great master of musicke which for
skill and sweetness may content the most curious ; yet because

Fig. 83.—Woman personifying Hearing (Auditus) and playing the mandora (after an engraving
by Abraham Bosse, seventeenth century).

they are not many in number, men delighted with varietie
have wished more of the same sort."

To the praiseworthy desire so quaintly expressed we are indebted for this collection, which Yonge followed up with a second in the year 1597. From the wording of the preface it was generally supposed that Yonge was a merchant in London ; there seems little reason now, however, to doubt that he was really one of the vicars choral of St. Paul's.

Another collection of foreign madrigals was published in 1590 by Thomas Watson : *The first sett of Italian Madrigalls Englished, not to the sense of the originall Dittie, but after the affection of the Noate.* Whether this introduction of foreign madrigals directed the efforts of our own musicians into that channel we are unable to say, but certain it is that from that time set after set followed each other in quick succession. The principal composers were Morley, with a set for four voices and another for five, besides ballets and canzonets, or *Little Short Aers ;* Weelkes, five sets of madrigals and one of *Ayeres, or Phantastike Spirits ;* Wilbye, two sets, comprising the well-known *Flora gave me fairest flowers* and *Sweet honey-sucking bees ;* Bateson, also two sets ; Ward and Orlando Gibbons each wrote a set. They were among the later representatives of the school. Gibbons' *Silver Swan* is a little masterpiece of dramatic expression. We have selected only the most prominent writers for mention, but together they produced a large body of works mostly of the greatest interest and merit.

There is one set which we have not mentioned, that called the *Triumphs of Oriana*, a collection of twenty-five

madrigals, two of which were by Ellis Gibbons, brother of
Orlando Gibbons ; but, with this exception, each was by a
different composer, and each ended with the same burden in
praise of Oriana, under which title is meant Queen Elizabeth,
who has been accused of having encouraged the delicate flattery.
Certainly it is flattery of which any monarch might be proud.
The work was collected by Morley.

The publication of so much vocal part music supposes a
very wide knowledge of music, and this, we find, was the case.
Every gentleman was expected to be able to take his part.
For instance, in Morley's *Plaine and Easie Introduction to
Practicall Musicke* (1597), Philomathes, the disciple, gives
the following reason for seeking instruction : " Supper being
ended, and musicke-bookes, according to the custome, being
brought to the table, the mistresse of the house presented mee
with a part, earnestly requesting me to sing. But when, after
manie excuses, I protested unfainedly that I could not, euerie
one began to wonder. Yea, some whispered to others, demanding
how I was brought vp. So that, vpon shame of mine ignorance,
I go nowe to seeke out mine olde friende master Gnorimus,
to make my selfe his scholler." To this his friend Polymathes
replies, " I am glad you are at length come to bee of that
minde, though I wished it sooner. Therefore goe, and I praie
God send you such good successe as you would wish to your selfe."

It is much to be regretted that a very small portion only
of all these riches is available for performance, or even for
study. We have already spoken of the rarity of original

copies of music of this character, which was invariably published
in parts, and in consequence is seldom found complete. Some

Fig. 84.—Woman playing the viol (after an engraving by Leblond, seventeenth century).

attempt was made about the year 1840 to remove this reproach
by the foundation of the Musical Antiquarian Society, which

during several years republished, with some luxury, many of
these masterpieces, in score.   Unfortunately, however, after
some time, as too frequently is the case with such undertakings, the work got into arrears, and the subscribers fell
away, and thus the Society came to an end when its work was
but just beginning.   Musical activity has now run into different
channels, and we fear there is but little chance that these
works of the golden age of English music will be ever rendered
accessible.

Many of these madrigals are described as "apt for viols,"
and no doubt formed the principal resource of the instrumental
performers of those days, although Orlando Gibbons wrote a
set of *Fantasies in three parts*, and a few by other composers
exist.   Of some of the foreign madrigals, parts are found without
the words, expressly arranged for instrumental performance.
The year 1611 saw the publication of *Parthenia, the Mayden-
head of the first Musicke that was ever printed for the
Virginals, by the famous masters William Byrd, Dr. John
Bull, and Orlando Gibbons, Gentlemen of his Majesties most
Illustrious Chappell.*   It is said to be the earliest work printed
from copper plates, and is engraved on a double stave of six
lines in each.   The music consists of *preludiums, pavanas*, and
galiardos, and its difficulty speaks well for the executive power
of those days.   Dr. John Bull, whom we have just mentioned,
was a very skilful performer on the organ and a musician of
great attainments, much in favour with Queen Elizabeth.   His
health having given way, he travelled in France and Germany,

being everywhere received with the respect due to his abilities. James I. having appointed him his organist, he returned to England, but starting again on his travels, became organist of Antwerp Cathedral. He must have been a man of a restless disposition, for he died at Lübeck in 1628; some, however, say in Hamburg. To him is attributed, we fear on somewhat slender grounds, the composition of our national anthem *God save the King.*

By the munificence of a citizen of London, Sir Thomas Gresham, provision was made for the foundation of a college to afford instruction in the principal branches of knowledge, among which music had a place. The bequest was not to take effect until the death of his widow, who survived him for some years, so that it was not until 1597 that the scheme could be matured. On the express recommendation of Queen Elizabeth, Bull was appointed the first professor. Precise injunctions were drawn up as to the course to be adopted by the professor. "The solemn music lecture is to be read in manner following; that is to say, the theoretic part for one half-hour or thereabouts and the practical part, by help of voices or instruments, for the rest of the hour." All the other lectures were to be read both in Latin and English; but, in deference to Bull's small acquaintance with Latin, this requirement was waived in the case of the music professor, and this arrangement has continued to the present day. Bull's inaugural lecture is extant; but when his health gave way, Thomas Byrd, a son of William Byrd, seems to have undertaken his duties.

7

It is disgraceful to have to state that the intentions of the founder, at least with regard to the music lectures, were absolutely neglected. The subsequent professors were completely ignorant of the art they undertook to illustrate, and it was not until the present century that a better state of things was inaugurated by the appointment of R. J. S. Stevens, a musician of adequate attainments. In 1609 was published by Thomas Ravenscroft, under the title of *Pammelia*, the first collection of catches, rounds, and canons printed in this country. This was followed in the same year by *Deuteromelia*, which contains the favourite nursery catch *Three Blinde Mice*, and it is worthy of note that it is written in the minor, not in the major, as it is now almost invariably sung. Hilton's *Catch that catch can*, first printed in 1652, was another favourite collection, which was frequently reprinted.

The first attempt to form a collection of cathedral music was made by the Rev. John Barnard, one of the minor canons of St. Paul's, in the year 1641. It comprises both services and anthems by most of the eminent Church musicians who had written before that time. No complete copy of this valuable work is known. It should consist of ten vocal parts. Of these Hereford Cathedral possessed eight, of which several were imperfect; in 1862 the Sacred Harmonic Society, at that time in the height of its prosperity, became the fortunate possessor of eight parts; and, strange to say, these two libraries each had the parts wanting to complete the other set. Soon afterwards one of the missing parts was purchased for Hereford,

and at a later period the Sacred Harmonic Society also
acquired one of the parts which it lacked, so that the two

Fig. 85.—Woman playing on the clavecin (after an engraving by Leblond, seventeenth century).

libraries each possessed nine parts out of ten.   Lichfield has
seven of the parts.   There is strong ground for supposing that
an organ part must also have existed, but this has never been

seen. That an edition of an important work should disappear
so completely is very remarkable, and it is generally thought
that the bulk of the copies must have been destroyed during
the political troubles which resulted in the Commonwealth.
The very valuable library of the Sacred Harmonic Society,
which contains an almost complete collection of the English
madrigals, such as it would be hopeless to try to get together
now, has passed into the possession of the Royal College of
Music. It is not a little remarkable that, in addition to the
printed volumes of Barnard's *Church Musick*, it contains seven
volumes of manuscript collections made by him for this work.

It followed as a natural result of the Reformed religion
that the people asserted their right to take part in the common
praise of the Church, and this impulse found its embodiment
in metrical psalmody. The version that received official sanction
was that by Thomas Sternhold, John Hopkins, "and others."
It was a sorry production. The whole sublimity of the original
was lost in a flood of maundering verbiage. In one or two
instances the versifiers stumbled on a rendering which showed
some rugged dignity, as, for instance, in the hundredth Psalm,
which still is in use, but such examples are apparently due to
a fortunate chance. The first complete edition was dated 1562,
and this contained the melodies of the tunes, which were mostly
derived from German sources. Several editions were subsequently published in vocal parts, one by Est in 1594. The
tunes in this were harmonized by John Douland, Farmer,
Allison, Farnaby, and others, the melody being assigned to

the tenor. voice.   But perhaps the best-known is that published
by Ravenscroft in 1621, in which a melody is assigned to
each psalm.   Some were German tunes which by this time
had become naturalized, others were by Ravenscroft himself,
while among other composers the name of John Milton, the
father of our great poet, appears.

The Psalms were again paraphrased by George Sandys,
and set to music by Henry Lawes, but this version, which
had far greater literary merit, was never adopted for public
use in churches. The "old" version of Sternhold and Hopkins
maintained its position for many long years, till it was supplanted by the equally prosaic productions of Brady and Tate;
in some country places that change had not taken place even
in living memory. Both are now deservedly shelved.

We have now brought down the history of English music
to the time of the civil war, which, we need scarcely add, put
a complete stop to the cultivation of music in this country.
To the ears of the Puritan music was anathema, and its
professors were compelled to seek for some other livelihood.

CHAPTER VI.

THE ORIGIN OF THE OPERA AND ORATORIO.

Influence of the Renaissance—Study of Greek Music—Vincenzo Galilei—Giulio Caccini and Jacopo Peri—Rinuccini's *Euridice* set to Music by both these Composers—Monteverde—His Instrumentation—The Opera in Venice—Origin of the Oratorio—Carissimi—Alessandro Scarlatti—Durante — Pergolesi—Jomelli — Lotti — Marcello—His Psalms—*Il Teatro alla moda*—Porpora—Corelli and his School—Tartini—Frescobaldi—Domenico Scarlatti.

OF all the movements which have affected the intellectual and artistic development of the civilized world there has been none so great in its results as that consequent on the discovery of the remains of classical literature and classical art, which is called the Renaissance. Of that movement Florence was the centre.

One of the natural results of this great impulse was a tendency to attach an excessive admiration to everything descending from classic times. The literary men of the time could appreciate the beauty of the ancient Greek and Roman works which were gradually opened to them. The artists could judge how far the sculptures which were continually being brought to light excelled the works of themselves and their fellows. Finding the ancient nations so greatly in advance both in literature and the plastic arts, it was naturally supposed that ancient music stood at a height of similar pre-eminence ; and this notion was fostered by the accounts which the ancients themselves gave of the effects produced by their own music.

It is not surprising therefore that the thoughts of those interested in music should at that time be directed towards the study of the art as practised in ancient Greece. The subject was one of great difficulty and complication, and the materials then available were insufficient for a solution of the problem. But such considerations generally act as a stimulus to investigation ; of all musical questions none has perhaps engaged more attention, while none has produced less satisfactory results, many points, even in our own day, being still in dispute.

Among those engaged in the investigation of this question was a small body of friends who were in the habit of meeting in constant intercourse at the palace of Giovanni Bardi in Florence. In addition to the host, these consisted of Vincenzo Galilei (the father of the still more celebrated astronomer), a man of great ability and learning, who was a good practical musician, and the author, among other works, of a dialogue comparing ancient and modern music. In this work, which was dedicated to Bardi, he proved to his own entire satisfaction the complete superiority of ancient over modern music. Three short fragments of Grecian music only were known to Galilei ; in fact, these, with another of doubtful authenticity, are all that have been discovered even down to the present day. In the year 1581, when this work was published, Orlando di

Lassus and Palestrina were at the height of their celebrity. The *Missa Papæ Marcelli* had been produced for sixteen years, and yet a man could persuade himself that these scraps of ancient melody proved that modern music was in comparison worthless ! The other members of the society were Pietro Strozzi and Giacomo Corsi, Florentine noblemen ; Rinuccini, a poet ; Giulio Caccini, Emilio del Cavaliere, and Jacopo Peri, all three musicians. All these were burning with the desire to restore the ancient Greek tragedy, with its musically accompanied declamation. The first attempt was a drama by Jacopo Peri, *Dafne*, which was privately performed in 1597. Galilei wrote a cantata on the story of Count Ugolino to exemplify the principles he had enforced, while three dramas were brought out by Emilio del Cavaliere.

None of these works have come down to us. But about the year 1600, or somewhat earlier, the poet of the coterie wrote a libretto on the subject of Euridice ; both Peri and Caccini at once set it to music, and the setting by Peri was chosen to be performed in honour of the marriage of Henri IV. of France with Maria de' Medici. The work of Caccini appears to have never been performed, but both were published in 1600 at Florence. Both are of the utmost rarity. A second edition of Peri's work was brought out in Venice eight years later, and both operas have been reprinted in cheap form by Guidi, of Florence, within the last few years.

This *Euridice* of Peri was the first opera ever represented. It cannot fail to appear remarkable that an attempt

to turn back the current of musical thought into ancient
channels should have developed during the course of years
into the modern Italian opera, but the chain of connection is
continuous. In the preface to his *Euridice* Peri has preserved
the names of his singers and instrumentalists, and he has also
told us what instruments composed the band. This consisted
of a clavecin, a *chitarone*, a large lira or viol, and a great
lute. With the views which the composer was endeavouring
to enforce, it will readily be supposed that the work is mainly
in recitative ; but another composer shortly appeared who
materially developed the operatic style. This was Monteverde,
a musician of the Venetian school, and director of the music
at St. Mark's. In such estimation was he held that on his
election to this post the salary was at once raised from two
to three hundred ducats, and subsequently to four hundred, in
addition to which he received from time to time several valuable marks of favour. No public occasion, either in Venice or
in other towns of Northern Italy, was complete without a work
from his pen. Thus he composed for the Duke of Parma
four interludes on the subject of Diana and Endymion,
a requiem for the funeral of Cosmo de' Medici, Duke of
Tuscany, and other works. He also composed a large number
of madrigals. But it is as a writer of opera that we speak
of him here. In 1607 he composed his opera *Ariana* for the
court of Mantua, which was a great advance on other
works of that kind. "Widely superior," says Fétis, "to Peri,
to Caccini, and even to Emilio Cavaliere as regards invention

of melody, he gave us in that work passages the pathetic
expression of which would even in our own day excite the
interest of artists. . . . In his *Orfeo* he discovered new forms
of recitative, invented the scenic duo, and without any previous
example to serve as a model contrived varieties of instrumentation with an effect as new as it was piquant." He seems
in some measure to have anticipated the *leit-motiv* of Wagner,
in so far that particular instruments were assigned to the
accompaniment of the different characters. Thus two harpsichords played the symphonies and accompaniments of the
prologue, which was sung by a personification of Music ; two
lyres or great viols of thirteen strings accompanied Orpheus ;
two treble viols gave the interludes of the recitative sung by
Euridice ; a large double harp accompanied the chorus of
nymphs ; Hope was announced by two " French " violins and
a harpsichord ; Charon's son was accompanied by two guitars,
the chorus of spirits by two organs, Proserpine by three bass-
viols, Pluto by four trombones, Apollo by a " regal," or small,
organ, and the final chorus of shepherds by a flageolet, two
cornets (which were reed instruments resembling a coarse-toned
hautboy), a clarion, and three muted trumpets. The aim would
seem to have been variety of tone, as the instruments were not
used together. The effect on the musical world of that day was
marvellous, so much so that shortly afterwards we find instruments other than the organ introduced into churches, resulting
in gradual but complete alteration in the character of ecclesiastical
music. Monteverde was, in fact, essentially an inventor. Among

other things due to him is the *tremolo*, a form of accompaniment which his successors have not failed to make use of. But he was still more noticeable for his innovations in harmony, which caused much controversy in his day, one of the foremost of his opponents being Artusi, in a book called *L'Artusi, ovvero delle imperfezzioni della moderna musica* (Bologna, 1600). So radical were the changes which he effected that he may be considered as the father of modern music. Space forbids us to give a complete list of his operas, one of which only, *Orfeo*, has been printed.

In 1637, six years before the death of Monteverde, to whom the opera is so largely indebted, the first theatre for the public performance of opera, which till then had been performed only in the palaces of princes, was built by Benedetto Ferrari and Francesco Manelli at Venice, the former a poet, the latter a musician. It was called the Teatro di San Cassiano. It was opened with a joint work of the proprietors, who had taken Monteverde as model. The veteran composer was at once attracted by the sweets of popular approbation, and several of his works were performed at other theatres in Venice In 1643 he died.

From the year 1637, the date of the building of the Teatro di San Cassiano, there is published a detailed list by Antonio Groppo of all the *drammi in musica* brought out in Venice, which shows how this form of composition at once gained a footing. Two other theatres were soon afterwards opened, with a succession of operas by Francesco Cavalli, Ferrari (who

was a poet as well as a musician), Francesco Paolo Sacrati,
Cesti, and others too numerous to enumerate here.   Opera-houses
were opened in most of the larger Italian cities; the fashion
spread to Germany, and soon extended to France also.

We must now turn our attention to the infancy of a form of
composition with very different aims from those of the opera.

We have already had occasion to speak of the liturgical dramas
of the early days of music.   Of these the oratorio may in
some sort be considered the descendant, although its later
development was due to a desire to make use of the attractions
of music as a means of bringing the people to a discharge of
their religious duties.   In the year 1564 St. Philip Neri united
his disciples at Rome in the religious order called the *Oratorians*,
for the reason that they stood outside their church exhorting
the passers-by to come in to *pray*.   In furtherance of this object,
and especially with the view of gaining the attendance of
youth, St. Philip introduced music of an attractive character,
which he employed Animuccia, a native of Florence, to
compose.   He produced motets, psalms, and other works, both
in Italian and Latin, under the general title of *Laudi Spirituali*, the first book of which was published in 1563.   These
were sung at the conclusion of the regular services.

The range of subject of these compositions was gradually
widened, but the first work on a scale at all corresponding to
that which we now call an oratorio was *La Rappresentazione
di Anima e di Corpo*, by Emilio del Cavaliere, and it was
performed in the Church of Santa Maria della Vallicella in

Rome in the year 1600. The recitatives were composed by
his friend Jacopo Peri. It will be seen therefore that both
opera and oratorio owe their origin to the same composers,
and agree in the date of their first production. From the
place of their first performance this species of composition
acquired its name of oratorio. It appears that Cavaliere's
oratorio was performed on a stage erected in the church, with
action and scenery.

But it is to Carissimi that the development of the oratorio
is chiefly indebted. He was born near to Rome about the
year 1604. It is not known to whom he owed his musical
training. He appears never to have written for the stage, and
but little of his service music is extant ; he devoted himself almost
exclusively to the production of sacred cantatas and oratorios.
In his hands recitative acquired a power of expressiveness which
till then it had not known, and which indeed has seldom been
surpassed. A few only of his works have been published, but
four of his oratorios—*Jephtha, The Judgment of Solomon, Jonah,*
and *Belshazzar*—have been issued in a volume edited by Dr.
Chrysander, the well-known critic and Handel scholar. The
traditions of this fine composer were continued at Naples by
Alessandro Scarlatti, who is by some thought to have been a
pupil of Carissimi. He was a composer of great originality
and learning, excelling both in oratorio and in opera. To him
we are indebted for the invention of *accompanied* recitative,
that is, recitative not simply supported by the harpsichord and
bass or, as in our own day, by the principal violoncello and

contrabasso (a practice, however, which is fast dying out), but
accompanied with the orchestra, the phrases of the recitative
being connected by suitable interludes. Of this form of recitative,
Comfort ye in the *Messiah* is a familiar instance. He also was
the first to make a return to the principal subject of an air
after the second part, a practice which soon became universal
in the music of that period. His fecundity was extraordinary
and inexhaustible. He became director of the Conservatoire
of St. Onofrio at Naples, and there trained many pupils (among
others Durante and Hasse) who formed the glory of the
Neapolitan school.

Durante devoted himself exclusively to religious music,
and excelled more in the treatment and development of his
subjects than in the invention of them, but all the vocal parts
have such "singing" qualities that they have served as models
for vocal writing. Leonardo Leo, who was also one of the
ornaments of the Neapolitan school, wrote both for the church
and for the theatre. He had at his command great majesty
of style, and at the same time knew how to touch the
heart.

The name of Pergolesi, so called from his birthplace, is
perhaps better known at the present day. He also was Neapolitan
by education. The sweetness and charm of his melody have
preserved the popularity of several of his works, among others
his *Stabat Mater* for two female voices. He died of consumption
at the early age of twenty-six, but not before he had written
enough both for the stage and for the church to show how

great was the loss to music. His operetta *La Serva Padrona* may almost be said to keep the stage. The extraordinary excitement caused by its production in Paris will be described later. The mention of Jomelli, who was equally celebrated as a writer both of sacred and of operatic music, will conclude this notice of the Neapolitan school.

We must now return to Venice. Lotti was one of that chain of distinguished men who devoted their services to the cathedral of St. Mark. He served the successive offices of second and first organist and of director of the music, and in these capacities he composed much sacred music, written in a clear, simple, and expressive style. His operas, which were humorous, are somewhat wanting in dramatic power. He composed much vocal music for the chamber, among which is the madrigal *In una siepe ombrosa*, to which we shall have to refer when we come to speak of Bononcini. Lotti's song *Pur dicesti* is well known even in the present day. His pupil Galuppi, although wanting in science, hit the taste of the Venetian public in his light and sprightly operas. He also became musical director at St. Mark's. On the invitation of the Empress Catherine II. of Russia, he was induced to visit St. Petersburg, but he found the orchestra wretched, and was soon glad to return to his native city, which he continued to delight with his works, preserving to an advanced age the gaiety of his disposition.

We have still to speak of one other distinguished Venetian musician : Benedetto Marcello. He was born in the year 1686, of a noble family, and received, under his father's supervision, the most solid and brilliant education it was possible to obtain. Among other accomplishments, he was taught the art of music, learning first the violin. The mechanical difficulties of this instrument he had not the perseverance to overcome, and he shortly abandoned it in favour of singing and composition, but even the serious study of the latter was somewhat irksome to him. His musical tastes soon began to absorb all his energies, and his father, who wished him to devote his time to the study of law, sent him into the country, to be out of the reach of all musical influences. The passion was too deep-seated to be subdued. His father had to yield, and dying soon afterwards, his son returned to Venice.

There he pursued his calling of advocate, receiving several public appointments, leading the life of a brilliant man of the world, and availing himself to the full of all those pleasures which the light and easy society of the theatre offered. Such was Marcello, when a remarkable circumstance entirely changed the direction of his thoughts. He was attending service at the Church of the SS. Apostoli, when a stone which covered a grave gave way beneath him, and he fell to the bottom of the tomb. He was uninjured ; but he looked on the circumstance as a providential warning, and from that time changed his habits of life, broke away from his old associates, and almost renounced his taste for music.

The work by which Marcello is best known is his setting of Giustiniani's paraphrase of the first fifty Psalms. Of these the first twenty-five were published at Venice in 1724, under the title of *Estro Poetico Armonico, Parafrasi sopra i primi venticinque salmi*, the following twenty-five being brought out in 1726 and 1727. They are written for one, two, three, or four voices, with figured bass for the organ, sometimes with *obbligato* string parts. The variety which they show testifies to the great powers of their composer; in fact, they are a mine of beauty which in the present day has been lost sight of. Several editions were brought out in Venice, and an excellent one, with English words, in London by Avison, organist of Newcastle-on-Tyne, whose name has lately been brought before the public by Mr. Browning in his *Parleyings with Certain People*. Avison was an enthusiast for the works of Marcello, having written an *Essay on Musical Expression*, the main purpose of which was to exalt Marcello at the expense of Handel.

But Marcello has other claims to notice. In addition to his musical works, he was the author of a brilliant little satire, *Il teatro alla moda*, the first edition of which was published in 1727,—possibly earlier. It professes to give instructions in their duties to all the persons engaged in a theatre, much in the style of Swift's *Directions to Servants*, the publication of which (1745) it preceded by several years. For example, it is by no means necessary that the virtuoso should be able to read or write, or that he should pronounce his vowels well, or that he should understand the meaning of the words, but very desirable that he should jumble up sense, letters, and syllables, in order to show his taste in shakes, etc. He must always take care

8

to say that he is not in voice, that he has a toothache, or a headache, or a stomach-ache, and that the music is not written for his voice. The prima donna will make a point of absenting herself from most of the rehearsals, sending her mother instead to make her excuses, etc., etc., and in this style through all the persons employed about a theatre.

A word of mention also must be given to Porpora, a composer of many operas, but still better known as the most eminent master of singing who ever existed. Among others, he trained the great singers Farinelli and Caffarelli.

A few remarks on the progress of instrumental music in Italy will close this chapter. The skill of the Italian instrument-makers had definitely settled the forms of the instruments of the violin family, when a musician appeared who was qualified to turn them to the best account in the person of Arcangelo Corelli (fig. 86), who was born in 1653. He was a pupil of Bassani, but his great powers were the fruits of genius, and there can be no doubt that he was the greatest performer of the time in which he lived. Nothing could exceed the amiability and modesty of his character. He found a protector in Cardinal Ottoboni, in whose palace he passed the greater part of his life, leaving it only to make a journey to Naples, which did not conduce to his happiness. In fact, he was of so retiring a nature that he does not appear to have done himself justice before strangers nor in unusual surroundings. Of him is told the characteristic anecdote that, playing on one occasion to a large company, he found they were all talking, on which

he put away his violin, fearing, as he said, to interrupt conversation.   His works are well known (or, at least, *used* to
be) to all violinists.   They consist of four sets of sonatas for
two violins, violoncello and figured bass for the harpsichord,
which formed a model for much similar music by his successors,

Fig. 86.—Arcangelo Corelli.

a set of sonatas for violin and bass, which even now are a
capital study for the violinist, and a set of concertos for two
violins and violoncello, with two *ripieni* violins, viola and bass.
Of these, No. 8, written for the night of the Nativity, is
especially charming.   A school of violin-players was the result

of his teaching. Among these were Veracini, Alberti, Albinoni, Geminiani, who passed the greater part of his life in England, Locatelli, and Vivaldi. The latter modified the concerto. In his hands it became more similar to that which we now understand by a concerto: a principal and leading part for the first violin, the other instruments forming an accompaniment.

Giuseppe Tartini was one of those whose genius irresistibly surmounted the obstacles of their education. His father intended him for a monk, but this being distasteful to him, he was sent to Padua to study law. His quickness rendered this study so easy to him that he found ample time to devote to the art of fencing, into which he threw himself with great enthusiasm. Having secretly married a young lady at Padua who was related to the Bishop, he was compelled to fly, and sought an asylum in a monastery at Assisi. Here he devoted himself with equal ardour to the study of the violin. At the end of two years the anger of the Bishop was appeased, and he was enabled to return to Padua and to his wife, who had been left there without any knowledge of the place of his refuge. Shortly after this, being with his wife in Venice, he chanced to hear Veracini. His remarkable playing convinced him that he had still much to learn, and he retired once more for a lengthened period to Ancona, devoting himself, with that singleness of purpose which seemed part of his nature, to further studies, the management of the bow receiving great attention. He came forth from his retirement a violinist of the first rank, for whom difficulties as understood at that time did not exist. He composed much for his instrument, and his works show how greatly he had advanced on the mechanical skill of Corelli. One sonata of his may still be heard in our own day, that known as *Il trillo del diavolo*, which derives its name from the circumstance that the devil appeared to him in a dream and performed a piece of music of a difficulty which to Tartini appeared impossible. He was fortunately at once able to write it down and preserve it for posterity. Tartini was also much occupied with the scientific aspect of music. To him we are indebted for the discovery of the "*third sound;*" that is, when thirds or fifths are played on a violin or other instrument capable of sustaining the sound perfectly in tune, and with some force, a resultant sound will be heard which is an octave below the lowest of the notes sounded. This phenomenon, which had not previously been observed, has received the name of "Tartini's tones." Tartini trained many excellent pupils, the most famous among whom was Nardini.

The organ seems in Italy never to have obtained that prominence which was accorded it in Germany. Its use was restricted mainly to the accompaniment of the services. Even at the present day St. Peter's at Rome possesses no instrument at all worthy of the church, those in use being wheeled about from place to place as convenience dictates. Among the few organists who have attained to eminence as such must be named the two Gabrielis, uncle and nephew, both organists of St. Mark's at Venice (Andrea 1510—1586 ; Giovanni 1557--

1613). To the latter is attributed the first use of the term "sonata." A man of greater eminence was Girolamo Fresco-

Fig. 87.—Girolamo Frescobaldi (1587—1654).

baldi (fig. 87) (1587—1654), who was not only a great performer, but an eminent composer for his instrument. The principal part of his life was passed in Rome as organist of St. Peter's, and so great was his celebrity that it is related that thirty thousand persons assembled on the occasion of his first performance there.   He published much for his instrument, and it may be interesting to add that, as originally printed, the part for the right hand is engraved on a stave of six lines, while that for the left has eight lines.   It would be difficult to find any one at the present day ready to undertake to play from the original copies.

Domenico Scarlatti (1683—1757), son of Alessandro Scarlatti, of whom we have already spoken, was also celebrated as an organist, adding another to the eminent men who filled that post at St. Peter's at Rome.   He was somewhat fond of wandering, and filled this office for a short time only.   But he was still more eminent as a performer and composer for the harpsichord ; in fact, he was the most eminent player of those days. His works for that instrument are distinguished by much grace and variety ; they are also exceedingly difficult, and would tax the skill of many a pianist of the present day.   He made much use of the practice of crossing the hands, which he was able to do even in rapid passages with great skill and neatness. It was observed, however, that in his later works this practice was much less frequently indulged in, the explanation being that the composer had become so immoderately fat that this method of execution had become quite impossible to him.

CHAPTER VII.

THE RISE OF THE OPERA IN FRANCE.

Chapel Music of the Kings of France—Clément Marot's Psalms—*Ballet Comique de la Royne*—Claude Lejeune—E. de Caurroy—Italian Singers brought into France by Mazarin—Skill of Louis XIV. in Music—Introduction of French Opera by Perrin and Cambert—Jean Baptiste Lully—His Career and Influence—Colasse—Desmarest—Campra—Destouches—Cultivation of Instrumental Music—Descartes—Père Mersenne.

MANY of the early kings of France showed an interest in music, and maintained a body of musicians attached to their chapel for the dignified performance of the rites of religion. The names of some of these are recorded, but the first of any eminence was Jehan Ockenheim, who entered the service of Charles VII. as chaplain or director of the choir, another testimony to the acknowledged pre-eminence of the Flemish school. We have already spoken of the relations between Louis XII. and the director of his music, Josquin des Prés ; under him the King's chapel was considered to be the best in Europe. Francis I. and Henri II. aspired to be considered composers, and Charles IX. had an even greater passion for the art. " At mass," says Brantôme, " King Charles would often rise and, in imitation of the late King Henri, his father, go to the lectern and sing, and he sang the tenor and the upper part very well, and he was very fond of his singers, and especially of Etienne Leroy, who had a very beautiful voice." Among other proofs of his attachment to music was the patronage he extended to Antoine de Baif (fig. 88), a very inferior poet who also cultivated the sister art. He obtained from the King letters patent for the establishment of an academy of poetry and music at his own house, where the concerts which he gave soon became very popular among people of fashion ; but the vogue did not last long, and poor Baif died forgotten. Marguerite

Fig. 88.—Portrait of Antoine de Baif (1512—1589, after Leonard Gaultier

de Valois also patronized music and its professors, giving concerts in the gardens of her chateau of Issy, to the accompaniment of a fountain, which her courtiers called the fountain of Castalia (fig. 89), in recollection of the one running at the foot of Parnassus, consecrated by the Greeks to the Muses.

In those parts of France where Protestantism was in the ascendant, metrical psalmody was introduced. The first fifty Psalms were translated into French verse by Clément Marot, and the work was completed by Theodore Beza. The

translation was carried out at the express desire of Calvin, and
popular melodies were adapted to the words by Guillaume

Fig. 89.--The "Fountain of Castalia," of marble and coloured lead, formerly in the Château d'Issy.

Franc, but without harmony. Calvin's views on the subject of
sacred music are well expressed in his letter "to all Christians

and lovers of the word of God" prefixed to Marot's translation. "Among the various things which are suitable for man's recreation and pleasure music is the first, or one of the foremost, and leads us to the belief that it is a gift of God set apart for this purpose. . . . It is always necessary to be careful that the song be not light nor flighty, but that it have weight and majesty, as says St. Augustine, and therefore that there be a great distinction between the music designed to delight men at table and in their houses and the Psalms which are sung in church in the presence of God and His angels."

In spite of the political and religious struggles which were agitating France during the latter part of the sixteenth century, the amusements of the court were carried on with great gaiety. Among the most popular of these were ballets, a form of diversion introduced from Italy, in which the highest personages themselves took part. Among the most famous of these was the representation known as the *Ballet Comique de la Royne*, on the subject of Circe, which was performed on the occasion of the marriage of the Duc de Joyeuse with Marguerite de Vaudémont de Lorraine, sister of the queen of Henri III. of France. The words and music, illustrated with engravings of the different characters and decorations, were published by Adrian le Roy in the year 1582, and we are thus able to judge of the magnificence and disregard of expense with which the work was mounted. The general design of the work was due to Baltasar de Beaujoyeulx, an Italian musician who had been induced to come to France by the Maréchal de Brissac,

Fig. 90.—The *Ballet Comique de la Royne*, performed before Henri III. and the court (facsimile of the frontispiece of that work, 1582).

where he became director of the music to Catherine de' Medici,
but the music in it was actually composed by two French
musicians, Beaulieu and Maistre Salmon.   The performance
took place at the Château de Moustier, and it lasted from ten
o'clock at night until four o'clock the next morning, the Queen

Fig. 91.—Tritons playing on instruments of music (from the *Ballet Comique de la Royne*, 1582).

and her sister both taking part in it.   In this work occurs the
melody so popular a few years back under the title of the
gavotte of Louis XIII.   We give a general view of the
appearance of the hall (fig. 90), and also of a group of tritons
performing on various musical instruments, both extracted from
the original work, which is now of great rarity (fig. 91).

The fashion having been thus set by the court, ballets at once became the favourite amusement of the upper classes; and it is worthy of note that much of the pleasure consisted in taking part in the actual performances, which was thought by no means inconsistent with the dignity of the highest in the land, for even Henri IV., Louis XIII., and Louis XIV. loved to appear in them. Nor was the practice confined to France alone. It was in consequence of his reflections on Henrietta Maria, who had engaged in similar entertainments at Somerset House, that Prynne drew on himself the cruel sentence of the Star Chamber for his *Histrio-Mastix.* It must be borne in mind that these ballets consisted not simply of dancing, but that they also comprised much vocal as well as instrumental music. While mythology furnished the subjects for a large number of them, the choice was by no means restricted, and we find such titles as *Les Grimaceurs, Les Barbiers, Les Coqs, Don Quichotte, La Délivrance de Renaud,* the latter arranged from Ariosto, in which Louis XIII. represented the demon of fire. We give the whimsical dresses of some of the performers (fig. 92). This was a work on a large scale, and had received the care of three several composers: Mauduit, who conducted a concealed chorus of sixty-four singers, accompanied by twenty-eight viols and fourteen lutes; Guesdron, who was in charge of ninety-two voices and forty-five instruments; these two composers had written the vocal music, while the dance music was the work of Belleville who directed ¡that department.

Claude or Claudin Lejeune was in the service both of
Henri III. and Henri IV. as composer of the chamber, and at the
same time Eustache de Caurroy was director of the chapel.
To him is assigned the composition of the popular air *Vive
Henri IV.* (fig. 93), and also of *Charmante Gabrielle.*

Public performances of music, in distinction to those given

Fig. 92.—Figures in the ballet of the *Délivrance de Renaud* (1617), printed and published by
Pierre Ballard, music-printer to the King.

The characters are, from left to right—(1) the demon of the fools (M. de Gondy, Count de
Joigny); (2) a monster; (3) the demon of avarice (M. de Chalais); (4) a monster; (5) the
demon of the Moors (M. de Brantes).

at the houses of the rich for the entertainment of their friends,
were as yet unknown. The first company of Italian singers
which was heard in France was induced to visit that country
by Cardinal Mazarin during the regency of Anne of Austria,
whose tastes his own interests prompted him to study. The
Italians gave their first performance on the 14th December,
1645, in the Salle du Petit-Bourbon, with the piece *La finta*

Pazza, which was partly spoken and partly sung ; but one of the great attractions was the mechanical effects, which had been arranged by Torelli, an Italian architect with special gifts in that direction, who formed one of the company. A singer, Margarita Bertolazzi, won golden opinions, but the entertainment does not seem to have commended itself to French

Fig. 93.—The air *Vive Henri Quatre* (sixteenth century).

tastes. Of this there are interesting evidences in the *Mémoires* of Madame de Motteville, quoted by M. Chouquet. She says, " Those who are judges think very highly of the Italians. For my part, I find the length of the performance takes largely away from the pleasure, and that verses repeated in a simple manner represent conversation more naturally and touch the heart more deeply than the singing pleases the ears." Later on, however, she tells us, " On Shrove Tuesday" (1646) "the Queen had a performance of one of her musical comedies in the small hall of the Palais-Royal. We were only twenty or thirty persons in the place, and we thought we should die of cold and *ennui*." It is possible therefore that discomfort may have warped the lady's critical judgment.

The sums squandered by Mazarin on these amusements were enormous. The Italian company was again brought over during the years 1647 and 1648, and during February of the former year they produced the tragi-comedy of *Orfeo*, in mounting which it is said Mazarin expended the sum of 500,000 livres. The composer of this work is not known ; it has been suggested that it may have been the work of Monteverde, but the contemporary descriptions do not seem to agree with the existing score.

Although, in spite of the advantages resulting from such powerful support, the Italian company appears to have aroused no enthusiasm, there can be no doubt that their example was the means of turning the thoughts of French musicians into a similar channel. With a view of utilizing the expensive stage machinery which was constructed for *Orfeo*, Corneille was employed to write a comedy for music ; he chose the subject of Andromeda, to which the music was composed by D'Assoucy, no part of which is now to be found. The Italians continued their visits until the troubles consequent on the " Fronde" interrupted them for a time.

The musical education of Louis XIV. seems to have been directed with some care. When very young, a child of his own age, born of Swiss parents living in Rome, named Antonio Bannieri, who was the possessor of a soprano voice of remarkable beauty, was placed in attendance on the young King, that he might have the advantage of profiting by so good an example. The boy was plain and deformed, so that he had to be placed on a table to sing, but the marvellous beauty of his voice atoned for all such defects. The King appears to have continued his protection, and he died in 1740 at the advanced age of a hundred and two years. Mazarin also brought for the King from Italy a master for the guitar, on which he learned to play with remarkable skill, and it has also been claimed for him "that he played the violin in a way that no one has ever approached," but for this statement some allowance must no doubt be made for the proverbial flattery of a courtier. As a composer he does not appear to have equalled Louis XIII., his father; at least, no specimens appear to be preserved of his skill in that direction.

There can be no doubt that the true creation of opera in France was due to the fortunate combination of the powers of poet and composer in the persons of Perrin and Cambert. The former, always known as the Abbé Perrin, in obedience to a literary affectation of the day, although he held no Church preferment, filled the post of introducer of ambassadors to the Duke of Orleans, but after the death of the Duke and of Mazarin, who extended his protection to him, he appears to have become little better than a literary hack. At the least he deserves the credit of perceiving that the heroic verses of the fashionable poets of the day lent themselves with difficulty to musical treatment. On a hint from Mazarin, he wrote *La Pastorale.* Cambert was at that time master of the music to Anne of Austria, having been a pupil of Chambonnières, one of the most famous harpsichord-players of that time. From the position he held there can be no doubt that he was a capable musician. To him therefore Perrin applied to write the music for his new drama. The result justified the choice. The piece, *La Pastorale, première comédie française en musique* as it was entitled, was performed at Issy, in the house of M. de la Haye. It received no advantages of scenic splendour, but the success was nevertheless prodigious. So great was it that Louis XIV. commanded a performance at Vincennes. The authors followed up their triumph by another work, *Ariane; ou, Le Mariage de Bacchus,* which was in rehearsal at Issy when the death of Mazarin unfortunately put a stop to the performance.

The favourable reception which these works had received in the circle of the court led Perrin to entertain the idea that the public would be disposed to support him in similar performances. A considerable sum of money would be necessary to carry on so ambitious an enterprise, and Perrin was at all times impecunious, but he succeeded in finding a financier, Champeron, who was disposed to advance the necessary funds. After much scheming he at last, in 1669, obtained the required

patent granting him the privilege of establishing throughout the
whole kingdom "academies of opera or musical representations"
in the French language.   One thing alone was wanting—a
suitable locality in which to give the performances.   After much
search a tennis-court was found, known as the "Jeu de Paume
de la Bouteille," in the Rue Mazarine, and in this it was
decided to begin the enterprise, but of course many alterations
were necessary to fit it for its new purpose.   With Perrin,
Cambert, and Champeron had become associated the Marquis
de Sourdéac, a man who had developed a peculiar talent for
stage mechanism, to whom therefore this department was assigned.   At last all was ready.   On the 19th March, 1671, the
new theatre was opened with the joint work of Perrin and
Cambert, as poet and composer, the opera *Pomona;* and this
was the first occasion on which the public were admitted by
payment to such a performance.   The poem does not seem to
have pleased, and indeed it must be admitted that Perrin was
a very poor poet, but the public were delighted with the music
of Cambert, as well as with the splendour of the spectacle
which the ingenuity of Sourdéac had arranged.   The spectators
were in rapture; the house was full to overflowing night after
night, although the prices of admission were very high, a
pit ticket costing as much as ten livres, a sum equal to about
thirty francs of the present day.   The piece ran for eight con-
secutive months, during which the partners made a net profit
of 120,000 livres.   So great was the struggle for places that
the police had to be called in to maintain order.   Unfortunately

no complete copy exists of this work, which is really a land-
mark in the history of dramatic music in France ; an engraved
copy of a portion of the score is in the National Library in Paris,
but this contains forty pages only, comprising the first act and
a fragment of the second. The manuscript copy at the
Conservatoire stops at the same place, as does also that in
the library of the Opéra. One is forced to believe that the
engraving of the work was never completed, and indeed
circumstances soon arose which may have led to this result.

In spite—or perhaps in consequence—of the financial success
of the undertaking, it was not long before differences took
place between the partners in it. Perrin, always needy, had
before the opening of the theatre borrowed money from time
to time of the Marquis de Sourdéac. He was probably lavish
as well as thriftless, and, in spite of the large amount of his
share in the profits, was unable or unwilling to repay these
advances, with the result that he was refused admission to
the theatre which owed its existence to him. Law pro-
ceedings naturally followed. Sourdéac was already provided
with another poet, named Gabriel Gilbert, and to him
was entrusted the preparation of a pastoral poem in five
acts, called *Les Peines et les Plaisirs d Amour*, the music for
which Cambert set to work at once to compose. It was produced in November, 1671. Of this work also a few fragments
only have been preserved, but there can be no reason to
doubt that its popularity bade fair to rival that of its predecessor.

While these attempts at the foundation of a lyric drama were going on, another musician was pushing his way to the

Fig. 94.—Jean Baptiste Lully (after the portrait by Mignard, engraved by Roullet, seventeenth century).

front, whose abilities and good fortune were to throw those of Cambert into the shade. This was Jean Baptiste Lully (fig. 94).

He was by birth an Italian, having been brought from Florence by the Chevalier de Guise, who was pleased with the spirit and vivacity of the boy, then twelve or thirteen years of age. The Chevalier had promised Mademoiselle de Montpensier to give her a little Italian boy, and, in accordance with this promise, the young Lulli—or Lully, as the name was always spelled in France—was handed over to this lady, who had no better employment for him than to make him a scullion. But genius will always assert itself. A visitor having by chance heard him playing on the violin, urged his mistress to provide him with proper instruction, and he proved so apt a pupil that in a short time he was admitted among the number of the Princess's musicians. Gratitude was not a prominent feature of his character, and having been guilty of setting to music a copy of scurrilous verses against his mistress, he was turned away in well-merited disgrace.

But his talents both as a performer and as a composer had already gained him some reputation, and secured his ready admission into the band of Louis XIV. He had the honour of playing some of his own compositions to the King, who was so pleased with them that he appointed him inspector of his violins, and soon afterwards created for him a new band, with the name of the " Petits Violons du Roi." Under Lully's guidance these became the best in France, for in that time there did not exist a single musician able to play his part if he had not previously learned it by heart !

Attached to the court,· he assisted in the composition of

the ballets in which the King took part, and subsequently
wrote entire works of this nature.   He was an excellent mimic,
and frequently performed in these ballets, and having become
intimate with Molière, he wrote the incidental music to several
of his comedies, among them *L'Amour Médecin, M. de
Porceaugnac,* and *Le Bourgeois Gentilhomme,* in all of which
he appeared on the stage with great success.   The King was
greatly amused with his buffooneries, and from that time over-
whelmed him with favours, and would listen to no other music
than his.

In this enviable position Lully found himself at the precise moment when the strife between Perrin and his associates
broke out.   No scruples of conscience ever stood in the way
of the realisation of any project on which he had set his
mind.   He at once formed the resolution to oust Cambert and
his friends and to get the management of the opera into his
own hands.   The privilege had been granted to Perrin, who
had sufficient reasons for entertaining no lively feelings of
friendship towards his late partners.   There seems little doubt
that Perrin was induced to cede this privilege, which was for
twelve years, to Lully for a sum of money, of which he had
always need.   The influence of Lully with the King had
become so great that he had little trouble in obtaining a new
privilege, securing to himself the exclusive right to carry on
such an enterprise.   The patent was not registered without some
litigation, but eventually Lully, backed by the King's favour,
triumphed.   The   person   most   injured   was   the   composer

Cambert, who found his occupation gone; he ultimately came
to this country, and entered the service of Charles II., as we
have stated elsewhere.

Duly provided with his privilege, Lully began his search
for a home worthy of the Académie Royale de Musique.
He found at last another tennis-court in the Rue Vaugirard,
near the garden of the Luxembourg, which, with the assistance
of an Italian architect named Vigarani, he transformed into a
theatre.   He got together some of the scattered members of
Perrin's troupe, and the new house was opened in May, 1672, with
the *Fêtes de l'Amour et de Bacchus*, a pasticcio made in haste
from the fragments of the incidental music written to Molière's
comedies.

From that time his fortune was made.   He allied himself
with the poet Quinault, whose reputation is mainly due to the
celebrity he acquired as librettist to Lully.   The first opera
specially written for the new theatre was *Cadmus*, which at
once placed him in the foremost rank as a dramatic composer.
Others followed in rapid succession, to the number of nineteen;
all were received with the greatest favour, and were published
in a style of considerable magnificence, as the specimens of
the titles which we give (figs. 95—97) will show.   His works
prove the possession of great dramatic power, and he was in
addition an excellent director of a theatre, training singers,
band, and chorus to perform their parts in a manner which had
not been known before in France.

The King would listen to no other music, and loaded the

composer with favours, even going to the length of making
him one of his secretaries, to the disgust of the other members

Fig. 95.—Title of the opera *Alceste, ou Le Triomphe d'Alcide*, by Lully, with a view of the Tuileries (after the drawing by Chauveau, 1674).

of the body. With his great genius, he was sordid and
avaricious, grovelling to the great, overbearing to those under
his command. He married a daughter of a musician named

Lambert, who brought him some fortune and every disposition
to second him in his desire to accumulate wealth.

Fig. 96.—Title of *Atys*, tragedy set to music by Lully, published by Christ. Ballard in 1676
(drawn by Chauveau and engraved by Lalouette).

He was a man of considerable wit.   During an illness his
confessor required him to burn the score of *Armide*, which he

was then writing. The Prince de Conti, visiting him the same day and hearing what had passed, exclaimed, "Surely, Lully, you cannot have burned so fine a work!" "All right!" replied Lully; "I knew what I was about. I had another copy in my drawer!" His death was caused by what may have seemed to be a trifling accident. In conducting a new work he hit his foot with his stick. He was in bad health, and an abscess was the result, followed by graver symptoms. He was advised to have the toe, then the foot, and finally the leg, amputated, but he fell into the hands of a quack who undertook to cure him without resorting to such desperate remedies, and in a short time he died, in his fifty-fifth year, on the 22nd of March, 1687. His operas kept the stage for many years ; the last performance of one of them, *Thésée*, took place in 1778, *i.e.*, one hundred and three years after its first production.

In addition to his operas, on which his fame mainly rests, he composed much Church music, including a large number of motets and other larger works. Although an instrumental performer himself, he seems to have paid but little attention to the scoring of his works. His practice was to write the vocal parts and the figured bass, handing the orchestration over to one of his pupils, Lalouette or Colasse.

The animosity which his overbearing behaviour had aroused showed itself in several works which were published after his death, and in none with more bitterness than in a curious little book with the title *Lettre de Clément Marot à Monsieur de * * * touchant ce qui est passé à l'arrivée de Jean*

Baptiste Lully aux Champs Elysées.   The author was Antoine
Bauderon, Sieur de Sénecé, who had a grudge against Lully on

Fig. 97. Title of the opera *Armide*, by Lully (engraved by J. Dolivar, after a drawing by
Berain), published by Christ. Ballard, 1686.

account of the composer's rejection of a libretto which he had
written.   In it Cambert is made to appear covered with wounds

and accusing Lully of having caused him to be assassinated in England. For this accusation there are no grounds whatever.

During the lifetime of Lully the composer's jealousy allowed no one else to occupy the stage ; but he had no reason to fear any rivalry. For many years after his death each new work was but a feeble reflection of the style of the master. For some time his favourite pupil, Colasse, who had scored most of his operas and had also acted as assistant conductor, was the composer most in request. His operas reached the number of ten, the only one which achieved any popularity being *Les Noces de Thétis et de Pelée* (fig. 98), for he was in truth completely wanting in genius, and it is said that the most successful portions of his works were, in fact, airs written by Lully and cast aside as unsuitable, which his pupil had been careful to preserve. Late in life he abandoned music for the search after the philosopher's stone, and ultimately became imbecile. The two sons of Lully, Louis and Jean Louis de Lully, were also composers, and together wrote the opera *Zéphyre et Flore*. The younger died at the age of twenty-one, his career was therefore short, but his brother produced several operas alone or in conjunction with Colasse or Marais ; but these young men possessed the name only, and not the genius, of their father.

Desmarets was among the most able of the immediate successors of Lully, several of his operas having been well received. The circumstances of his life were romantic. Having been "page of the music" to the King, he tried to obtain the appointment of one of the *maîtres de chapelle*, and was passed over on account of his youth alone, the King granting him a pension to compensate for the disappointment. In 1700, while on a visit to a friend at Senlis, he made the acquaintance

Fig. 98.—*Les Noces de Thétis et de Pélée* (scene from the opera of Colasse, with a view of the Pont Neuf, designed and engraved by Sebastien Leclerc, 1689).

of, and married secretly, the daughter of a high official, who set the law in motion, with the result that Desmarets was condemned to death. He was compelled to seek refuge in Spain, where he became chapel-master to Philippe V., and although Louis XIV.

had been well disposed towards him and admired his abilities, he refused to pardon him, and it was not until the Regency that he was allowed to return to France and his marriage was declared valid.

Fig. 99.—André Campra, A. Danchet (author of most of Campra's librettos), and Bon Boullogne (after a picture by the latter, seventeenth century).

The only musician of the time who showed any disposition to break away from the stereotyped monotony of the ruling style was Campra (fig. 99), who, although not a genius, was a musician of great ability, and the composer of a score at least of operas which were very popular, as they were

characterized by a greater vivacity and a more strongly marked
rhythm than was then usual.   Campra was educated as a
Church musician, and it was while in office at Nôtre Dame in
Paris that he produced his first two operas, which had in
consequence to be brought out under the name of his brother,

Fig. 100.—Mademoiselle Journet in the character of Mélisse in *Amadis de Grèce*, by Destouches
(Académie Royale de Musique, 1699).

a musician in the band of the Académie de Musique.   He
was also favourably known as a writer of Church music, five
books of motets of his composition being extant.   We must
also mention Destouches, who began life with a voyage to
Spain in company with the Jesuit fathers, a body which he

10

proposed to join. On his return, however, the profession of arms had greater attractions; this he abandoned for the pursuit of music. His opera *Issé* was performed in 1691, and it pleased by its natural melody. But his knowledge of music was so small that he was only able to compose his melodies, and was therefore obliged to call in assistance to score it. Sensible of his deficiencies, he went to Campra for instruction. Unfortunately an increase of knowledge seems to have destroyed his originality; and although several of his operas were played, he never renewed his first success (fig. 100).

It may be interesting to mention that nearly all the operas of this time were published in score, in which the violin parts were invariably printed in what is called the French violin clef, with the G clef on the *first* line in place of the second line, in accordance with present practice. We may also note the fact that the contrabasso was first introduced into the French orchestra by Montéclair, in his opera *Les Festes de l'Eté*, in the year 1716.

Instrumental music appears to have received increased attention in private circles. The guitar became very popular, which may in part have been the result of the King's skill on it (fig. 101); but a more remarkable outbreak of fashion was the adoption of the musette, which was taken up by both sexes alike (fig. 102). An excellent and handsomely illustrated guide to this instrument was published at Lyons in 1672 by C. E. Borjon, an amateur, a learned advocate, who was the author of several works on jurisprudence.

During the reign of Louis XIII. the study of musical
theory began to attract the attention of men of science. Descartes, at that time barely twenty-two years of age, published
in 1618 his *Compendium Musicæ*, a work not altogether free

Fig. 101.   Lady of quality playing the guitar (from an engraving by H. Bonnart, 1695).

from error, of which the author indeed seems to have been
conscious, as he would not allow it to be reprinted during his
lifetime, although it was more than once republished afterwards,
having been translated into French by Père Poisson, and into

English by Lord Brouncker, the first President of the Royal Society and an able mathematician, under the title of *Renatus Descartes Excellent Compendium of Musick: with Necessary and Judicious Animadversions Thereupon. By a Person of Honour.* A few years after, Père Mersenne, who enjoyed the intimacy, although he shared but little of the philosophic spirit, of Descartes, began his investigations in the field of music. Among the earliest of his writings was his commentary on Genesis —a work which, although it extended to twelve hundred pages folio, only allowed space for the consideration of the first seven chapters. The text "His brother's name was Jubal; he was the father of all such as handle the harp and organ," was an opportunity which he could not resist, and he entered on a disquisition on music in general and on that of the Jews in particular which takes one hundred pages at least. But he had long meditated a large work which should embrace the whole field of musical knowledge. It was some time before he was able to put this idea into practice. Probably no publisher was willing to undertake so vast a speculation. The delay he filled up by the issue of certain trial portions, some in French, some in Latin. Among these is the curious and characteristic *Préludes de l'Harmonie Universelle*, in which he discusses not only the temperament most suitable for a musician, but also the horoscope necessary to produce the perfect artist. At last in 1636 his great work, *L'Harmonie Universelle*, which is in the French language, appeared—a vast folio of upwards of fifteen hundred pages, full of woodcuts, copper-plate engravings, and musical

examples.   The cost of producing it must have been enormous, and
the outlay can never have repaid the publisher, Cramoisy.   The

Fig. 102.—A player on the musette (engraved by Leblond, after C. David, seventeenth century).

erudition it contains is immense, but the critical faculty of
the author was defective.   For the history of music the work

is of great interest, as it contains many specimens of compositions which it would be difficult to find elsewhere, as well as particulars about their authors. It is to be presumed that the sale of the book was small, for the book is one of great scarcity.

CHAPTER VIII.

MUSIC IN GERMANY.

The "Stadt-pfeiffer "—The Bach Family—J. S. Bach—His Sons and Pupils—Foundation
of the Gewandhaus Concerts—The Opera in Germany—Reinhard Keiser—Early
Career of Handel—Johann Mattheson—Hasse—Graun—Musical Journalism—Marpurg
—Music in Vienna—J. J. Fux—Gluck—His Musical Reforms.

In the first half of the seventeenth century Germany was
suffering from the horrors of the Thirty Years' War. Such
a period was most unfavourable for the fostering of one of the
most peaceful of arts. A few eminent musicians had survived
from happier times, among whom may be mentioned Adam
Gumpelzhaimer (fig. 103), famous both as a theorist and as a
writer of sacred music, and Michael Prætorius (Schultz), whose
Syntagma we have already spoken of at p. 83. But it was
of necessity a time of but little musical activity, Froberger,
Pachelbel, and Buxtehude being among the few writers of
any celebrity. Such musical life as existed was preserved
among the "Stadt-pfeiffer," or town musicians, a body of men
who were not held in great estimation either for their musical
powers or for their private worth. The town musicians were
the privileged performers on all occasions of public and private
rejoicing. They formed a close body, like the company of

minstrels in France, to which admission was gained by a regular term of apprenticeship, and the privilege of belonging to the

Fig. 103.—Adam Gumpelzhaimer (1560–   ?).

body had a natural tendency to be perpetuated in the same family.   In the year 1653 a desire to protect their common interests impelled the town musicians of some of the larger places in Northern and Central Germany to unite in the formation of a scheme of united action, in furtherance of which a series of rules was drawn up and submitted to the Emperor Ferdinand III., whose approval it received. Many of these rules are very quaint, for instance—

" III. Inasmuch as Almighty God is wont marvellously to distribute His grace and favours, giving and lending to one much and to another little, therefore no man may contemn another by reason that he can perform on a better sort of musical instrument.

" V. No man, whether he be master, assistant, or apprentice, shall divert himself by singing or performing coarse obscenities or disgraceful and immodest songs or ballads, inasmuch as they greatly provoke the wrath of Almighty God and vex decent souls, particularly the innocence of youth.

" VIII. No man shall dare to perform on dishonourable instruments, such as bagpipes, sheep-horns, hurdy-gurdies, and triangles, which beggars often use for collecting alms at house doors, so that the noble art would be brought into contempt and disgrace by them."

These, and other rules which are too long to transcribe here, prove that in their ranks were some anxious to improve the status of a body of men at that time held in scant respect. Among the most respectable musicians of the Society were several members of one family named Bach, all of whom followed the musical calling with enthusiasm. They traced their descent from a certain Veit (*i.e.*, Vitus) Bach, a baker and miller of Wechmar, in Thuringia, who died in 1619. His chief delight was to play on his cithern while the corn was grinding, and so great was his love of music that he sent his son Hans to Gotha to be instructed by Caspar Bach, another member of the family, who was town piper. Hans combined the occupations of carpet-weaver and musician, and died of the plague in 1626, but not before he had brought up three sons, out of his large family, to the profession of music. From that time this course became traditional. The Bachs had large families, all of whom were devoted to music, and thus it came about that in the towns of Thuringia—Arnstadt, Erfurt, Gotha, and Eisenach—they seem to have monopolized the offices of organist and town musician. The Bachs became a musical power, the name being considered as almost synonymous with "musician," and it is an interesting evidence of their family unity that they were all in the habit of meeting together once a year in Erfurt, Eisenach, or Arnstadt for social and musical intercourse, the meetings always opening in simple and pious fashion by the singing of a chorale.

In 1685 was born at Eisenach Johann Sebastian Bach (fig. 104), a great-grandson of Hans Bach, who was destined to raise the fame of the family to the highest pitch, and to become one of the greatest musicians of all time. As a child his father taught him the violin, but both his parents died before he had reached his tenth birthday. His elder brother, Johann Christoph, was organist of Ohrdruf, and he undertook the charge of the orphan boy, grounding him thoroughly in music, teaching him the clavichord (for he had himself been a pupil

Fig. 104.—Johann Sebastian Bach.

of Pachelbel), and sending him to the Lyceum, where he was instructed in Latin and Greek, acquiring a fair knowledge of the former language. This went on till he reached his fifteenth

year.   He had exhausted his brother's teaching, and with a
school companion he travelled to Luneburg, in which place
they both joined the choir of the Church of St. Michael, where,
in addition to musical instruction, his general education was not
neglected.   The organ was already his favourite instrument.
In 1703 he left Luneburg to join the band of Prince Johann
Ernst at Weimar, but in the same year was appointed organist
at Arnstadt.   The fame of Buxtehude, a Dane, who was organist
at Lübeck, induced him to make use of his first month's holiday
to visit him, walking the whole distance of fifty leagues.   The
musical attraction of Buxtehude's playing was so great that
his one month's leave extended to three ; on his return the
authorities at Arnstadt naturally demanded an explanation.   In
short, his position ceased to be comfortable ; and he was glad,
on an early opportunity, to transfer his services to Mühlhausen,
a position of greater importance.   On the strength of this
preferment, he married, and shortly after received the appointment
of organist and court *musicus* at Weimar, a post which was
very congenial to him, for both the Duke and his brother took
much pleasure in music.   He was called on to write a number of
Church compositions, and acquired great celebrity as an organist,
and thus was frequently invited to different towns to give
performances.   On one occasion he visited Dresden, where at
that time was living a harpsichord-player of great skill, a
Frenchman named Marchand (fig. 105).   The friends of the
rival musicians arranged a trial of skill in the house of one of
the ministers.   At the appointed time Bach was ready.   Marhcand

did not appear. After waiting some time a messenger was sent to his house; and it appeared that, dreading the result, he had left Dresden that morning.

For what reason is not ascertained, but in 1717 Bach

Fig. 105.—Louis Marchand.

left Weimar to enter the service of Leopold, Prince of Anhalt-Coethen, himself an enthusiastic musician. While here he lost his wife, but after a year and a half married again. His second wife, Anna Magdalen Wülken, who was court singer, was an excellent help to him. She was an admirable singer, and in addition wrote a fine hand, which enabled her to be of great use in copying his manuscripts.

But the circle of his influence at Coethen was a narrow one, and a vacancy occurring in the post of "Cantor" of the Thomas-schule at Leipzig by the death of Kuhnau, he offered himself, and was selected from several candidates, among whom was the celebrated Telemann. He was installed into his new office on the 31st May, 1723. It went somewhat against the grain with him to give up the title of "Capellmeister" for that of "Cantor," but the position offered a much wider field for his artistic activity. It did not prove altogether a bed of roses. The Thomas-schule was both a choir school and a grammar school, and his duty required him to teach Latin, although for this he was allowed to pay a deputy. He had to superintend the services at two principal churches, to each of which a choir of boys had to be sent, as well as to two subsidiary churches in the town. The school had been neglected, and was under the superintendence of the town council. There were thus all the elements of much heart-burning. In his own family Bach was a man of easy and amiable character, but in his public capacity he stood on his dignity. He seems to have been one of those men who rather enjoy an atmosphere of strife, and although he made one or two appeals to friends to obtain for him some more peaceful appointment, he continued to fill this office to the day of his death. The salary was seven hundred thalers—say £105 per annum—with apartments and some few fees —no very high pay for so great a genius. This was the time of his greatest activity. His fame continued to increase. He had always been fond of making journeys to the larger towns, both to hear and to be heard, but as age crept on these became less frequent. His son Emmanuel had

Fig. 1c6.—Jchann Joachim Quantz.

become chamber musician and accompanist to Frederick the Great, who was an enthusiastic musician and a creditable performer on the flute; for this instrument Quantz (fig. 106) was his master; he was in the regular service of the King, and it was part of his duty to write a constant succession of new compositions for him, a lofty pile of which may still be seen reposing in a cabinet at Potsdam. Frederick was most anxious to make the acquaintance of the great master. At last he was persuaded to start for Potsdam, where he arrived on Sunday, May 7th, 1747. A concert took place every evening from seven to nine. The King was about to begin a solo on the flute when the daily list of the strangers who had arrived was handed to him. He turned to the band with some excitement, and said, "Gentlemen, old Bach is come!" His flute was laid aside, and Bach was at once sent for, not being allowed time to change his dress. Much conversation then ensued, especially on the merits of Silbermann's pianofortes. The King had several, and Bach was carried from one to the other to test their merits and to improvise on them. The next day Bach performed on the organ in the church, and in the evening he played a six-part fugue to the King's great satisfaction.

The closing years of his life were clouded by a gradually increasing blindness, which did not yield to the attentions of an oculist living in Leipzig, who performed two operations without success. The medical treatment shook his constitution, and he died on July 28th, 1750, surrounded by his family and friends, at the age of seventy-five years.

Bach was a man of great industry, producing a constant succession of new works in all departments of musical composition. Of these his organ works will probably be considered his most enduring monument. His thoughts moved naturally in polyphonic forms of composition, and the strict rules of fugue seemed to him to be no trammel. As a performer on the organ he stood in the first rank. He was well acquainted with its mechanical details, and was frequently employed in trying new instruments, when his first act was to draw all the stops to see that the supply of wind was ample. As director of church choirs, he produced much music for religious worship, comprising among other works five complete sets of cantatas for every Sunday and holy day of the ecclesiastical year. In Germany it is a common practice to sing during Holy Week music appropriate to that sacred season, under the title of Passion music. It consists of solemn music illustrative of the Gospel narrative, interspersed with chorales, in which the congregation are expected to join. Of these Bach produced five, the one according to St. Matthew being that on the largest scale and probably the best known. He also wrote a similar work suitable for Christmas.

It may seem strange that a Protestant, and one whose abilities were devoted to the service of a Protestant Church, should have become the composer of masses. It would appear, however, that in Leipzig the form of worship had retained many Catholic practices, and even the occasional use of the Latin language. The B minor mass was probably intended for Dresden —at least, parts of it were certainly written with that destination—where the court was, and still continues to be, of the Romish Church. This is a work of great power and elaboration, on a scale hardly suited to the purposes of public worship, but it is well known in the present day by several careful performances of it which have been given by the Bach choir.

For the harpsichord he wrote much ; in fact, he may be said to have revolutionized the art of playing on that instrument. In those days the fourth finger was used but sparingly, the thumb not at all, being allowed to hang down in front of the keys in the way which one used to see affected by old-fashioned organists in our own time. Bach used the thumb equally with the other fingers. He wrote two sets of *suites*, one called the English *suites*, the other the French. The *suite* was a composition consisting of a succession of movements written in the rhythm of the dances of the period—the Allemande, Saraband, Gavotte, Minuet, Bourrée, Gigue, etc.—arranged in such order as to contrast in style. The *suite* was destined to develop into the sonata, of which we shall speak presently.

But the best known of his instrumental compositions is probably the *Wohltemperirte Clavier*, or *Well-tempered Harpsi-chord*. To explain this title, it is necessary to understand that in an instrument having fixed tones it is only possible for one key to be perfectly in tune. For convenience of performance the same note is made to do duty for $C\sharp$ and $D\flat$, and so on throughout the scale ; but this is not theoretically correct. In the days before Bach, the practice was to make the key of C in accurate tune, leaving the rest to their fate, and this fate was unbearable if the key involved several sharps or flats. This was still more the case where the sound was capable of being sustained, as in the organ, and it was therefore necessary to avoid remote keys altogether. A distribution of the error among all the notes of the octave is called the system of equal temperament. No one key is of course in *perfect* tune, but all diverge so little from accuracy that the difference is only perceptible to those of extreme nicety of ear. It is not claimed for Bach that he invented this system, but he was the first to bring it into practical use, tuning his harpsichords himself with great care. To enforce this system, he wrote the *Wohltemperirte Clavier*, or forty-eight preludes and fugues, in all the keys, major and minor. Many of these keys had *never* been used before, and the performance of them was only possible by means of his improved method of fingering.

He also wrote for stringed instruments : concertos for violins and other instruments ; sonatas for harpsichord and violin, and also for violin alone. One is tempted to look on the latter as technical exercises ; it is difficult to believe that the violin-player existed in those days who could execute them.

A few only of his works were published during his lifetime ; in fact, the expense was so great a bar to their publication, that he actually engraved with his own hand his *Art of Fugue*. It is in our own time only that the greater part of his works have seen the light, or indeed that his powers have been fully appreciated. This reproach, however, may be withdrawn, as the Bach Gesellschaft is bringing out a splendid and complete edition of his compositions, which is already well advanced.

His sons sustained the family reputation. They all received

a careful and thorough musical training from their father. The eldest and most able of them, Wilhelm Friedemann, unfortunately was a man of an irritable and restless disposition, so that he led a wandering and purposeless life and did no justice to his great abilities. The next son, Carl Philip Emanuel (fig. 107),

Fig. 107.—Carl Philip Emanuel Bach.

entered the service of Frederick the Great at Berlin as accompanist, subsequently removing to Hamburg. He adopted a much lighter and more graceful style of writing than his father, and there is no doubt that his works formed the model of the pianoforte compositions of Haydn and Mozart. To him and to

Schobert may be attributed the settlement of the form of the sonata. He was an excellent performer on the harpsichord, and the author of an admirable treatise on the art, which undoubtedly paved the way for the modern school of pianoforte-playing. Friedemann and Emanuel were sons by the first wife, and to them were entrusted the manuscripts left by their father. Most of those which fell to the share of Friedemann were lost in his many wanderings; those in the possession of Emanuel were carefully preserved. The youngest son, Johann Christian, after visiting Italy and marrying a singer, settled in England, where he brought out many operas and composed much instrumental music, dying here in respect, while a son of *his* fourth son died so recently as 1846, in his ninety-third year, in Berlin, where he filled the post of court musician. With him, at least as regards music, the annals of this remarkable family cease.

In addition to his sons, Bach trained many pupils, among others J. F. Agricola; Altnikol, who married his daughter; J. C. Vogler, who was looked on as one of the best organists of his time; Ludwig Krebs, one of his favourite pupils; and Kirnberger, who became famous as a writer on the theory of music.

From very early days the organ had been much studied in Germany (fig. 108). J. P. Sweelinck (fig. 109), a Dutchman, who, after visiting Venice and sitting at the feet of Zarlino, became organist of the principal church in Amsterdam, may be looked on as the father of the great school of German organists which became so famous and received its highest

Fig. 108. – German musician playing on a portable organ (facsimile of an engraving by Israel van Meekenen, end of the fifteenth century).

development in the person of J. S. Bach. To that country we are indebted for most of its improvements, and especially for the addition of pedals, a resource opening a wide field to the powers of the composer, of which Bach and his followers availed themselves so ably.

Fig. 109.—Jon Peter Sweelinck.

Every town of importance possessed at least one fine instrument, which was in the hands of a competent performer. Many of the finest instruments were built in those days. Among builders the family of the Silbermanns was especially eminent, as they were also for their improvements in the harpsichord.

Telemann, who had competed with Bach for the appointment of Cantor of the Thomas-schule in Leipzig, formed a
choral society in that place, of which he was conductor. But
the first subscription concert in Leipzig took place in 1743,
under the direction of Doles. The series was interrupted by
the Seven Years' War, but they were subsequently resumed by
J. A. Hiller, a musician of great attainments, who was the first
to perform Handel's *Messiah* in Germany. In 1779 and 1780
the disused Cloth Hall (Gewandhaus) was turned into a concert-room ; to this room the concerts were transferred in 1781.
They have since then been known as the Gewandhaus concerts,
and for more than a century have maintained a character as
the foremost, as they are now the most venerable of all
associations for the performance of classical music.

The Germans were by nature a grave and serious people,
and thus the opera was for a long time an exotic among
them. The eminent scholar Reuchlin arranged a comedy
with music, under the title of *Scenica Progymnasmata*, for
performance by the scholars of the Gymnasium in Heidelberg,
so far back as the year 1497, which, from the number of
editions it went through, may be supposed to have attained to
considerable popularity, but the title of opera can scarcely be
claimed for it. Certain Passion plays, with music, were also in
vogue. The first real opera was composed by Heinrich Schütz
or Sagittarius, more celebrated for his sacred music (fig. 110),
to a translation of Rinnucini's *Dafne*, but this was for a
court performance at a royal wedding. The first public

Fig. 110.—Heinrich Schütz.

performance was given at Hamburg. It was by Johann
Theile, on the story of Adam and Eve, and it was followed

by other similar works, and thus Hamburg became the cradle of opera in Germany. A facile composer appeared in the person of Reinhard Keiser, whose first opera, *Basilius*, was hailed with enthusiasm by the inhabitants of that town. He followed up his success with commendable industry, opera after opera flowing from his pen for a space of forty years. During this time he brought out upwards of a hundred operas, a few only of which have been printed (fig. 111), some existing in manuscript, but all distinguished by an inexhaustible fund of bright and sparkling writing.

At this time appeared a composer who was destined to raise the opera to a pitch of excellence till that time undreamt of, but who was to be even more famous from the sublimity of his compositions in a still higher department of art. George Frederic Handel was born at Halle in 1685—the same year, and within a short distance of the place, which saw the birth of Germany's other great musician, John Sebastian Bach. His father was originally a barber, but had developed, as was usual in those days, into a surgeon, who by a fortunate second marriage with the widow of another surgeon acquired a good practice and a position of esteem. His son showed a musical disposition ; the father aimed to make him a lawyer. The boy was possessed of much firmness of purpose, and practised his music in secret, till at last a fortunate chance brought his powers under the notice of the Duke of Weissenfels, who impressed on his father that it was absolutely sinful to check such talent. The result was that on his return home he

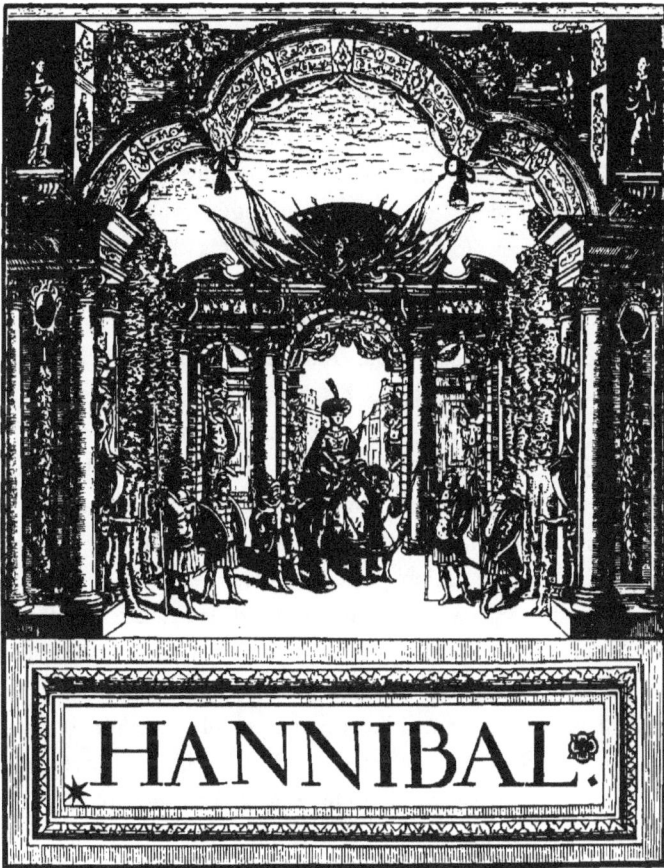

Fig. 111.—Title-page of Keiser's *Hannibal*.

was put under the care of Zachau, organist of the Frauenkirche in Halle, a musician of no great depth, but a pleasing com-

poser and, what was more to the purpose, the possessor of a
large and well-selected library of scores, which proved a happy
hunting-ground for his earnest pupil. Many of these he
copied, and it is supposed that half-unconscious recollections of passages in these scores may account for the
curious coincidences (to use no stronger word) which have
undoubtedly been found in some of his later works. His
industry was unbounded, for, in addition to his theoretical studies,
he acquired great skill on the organ, as well as some command
of the violin and oboe, which remained a favourite instrument
with him. After three years his master had to confess that he
could teach him no more. He was then sent to Berlin, where
he had the opportunity of increasing his experience by hearing
works of the Italian school and by making the acquaintance of
Ariosti and also of Buononcini, subsequently to be his most
serious rival. The King was delighted with his precocious
abilities, and proposed to send him to Italy, but to this his
father would not listen, insisting on his return. His father
survived this return but a few months. His mother, a woman
of excellent sense, kept him to the regular studies of youth,
while music was not neglected, and he acquired a reputation
something more than local. He was at the age of seventeen
appointed organist of the Schloss and Domkirche at Halle,
where he had a fine organ at his command. This post he held
while still studying at the university, and he also found time
to form a choir of his old schoolfellows for the practice of
sacred music, as well as to write several important compositions.

But the bent of his genius was essentially dramatic, and he was naturally drawn by the attractions of the Hamburg Opera. In the year 1703, therefore, he threw up his appointment at Halle, and started for Hamburg in pursuit of fortune, which came to him in the very modest guise of *ripieno* second violin in the orchestra of the opera. While there he made the acquaintance of Johann Mattheson, who was at that time singing as principal tenor at the opera. He was a man of great and varied accomplishments, as will be seen later, and to him we are indebted for many details of the great composer's life. Among others, we learn that the two friends went on a journey together to Lübeck, where Mattheson had been invited to become successor to the eminent Dieterich Buxtehude. They tried together every organ in the place, and heard the veteran Buxtehude also. It appeared, however, that the acceptance of the post involved marrying the daughter of the retiring organist, a condition which neither was willing to adopt ; the appointment therefore went to a more compliant candidate.

One result of this friendship was to introduce Handel to society, and among other houses to that of Sir Cyril Wich, the English representative, to whose son he gave lessons on the harpsichord. Subsequently, however, Mattheson became tutor to the boy, supplanting Handel in his engagement as harpsichord-master.

While engaged in the orchestra the fortunate absence of the harpsichord-player gave Handel the opportunity of dis-

tinguishing himself, and he also produced a Passion oratorio
for performance in Holy Week. This, Mattheson, who was
of a jealous disposition, criticised with some bitterness. Further
differences arose. Mattheson had composed an opera called
Cleopatra, which was produced in the ensuing winter season,
the composer taking the principal tenor part, Antonius, while
Handel was at the harpsichord. Antonius dying early in the
action, Mattheson was not engaged on the stage, but insisted
on taking Handel's place at the harpsichord. Handel refused
to yield, and a quarrel ensued, ending in a box on the ear
given by Mattheson. Such an insult in those days could of
course only result in a duel, which was at once fought out
before the opera-house, in the midst of a crowd of spectators.
Fortunately Mattheson's sword broke against a button on
Handel's coat, which terminated the encounter, or the world
might have been all the poorer. By the intervention
of friends, the combatants were reconciled, and became as
good companions as ever, and we find Mattheson taking the
principal tenor part in Handel's first opera, *Almira*, which
was produced on the 8th January, 1705.

It seems almost incredible, but opera in Germany retained
so much of its Italian origin that it was performed in a mixture
of the two languages. This was the case with *Almira*. As a
question of art the custom was absurd, and it is difficult to
see what practical advantage was gained by it. The reason
was not ignorance of German on the part of the singers,
for to several of them are allotted airs in both languages

The custom, however, was not confined to Germany, for it was introduced both into France and England.

The opera had considerable success, running for nineteen or twenty nights. The music has come down to us in an imperfect copy which has been published in the German Handel Society's edition. In it is a saraband which was subsequently very popular when set to the words "Lascia ch' io pianza" in the later opera *Rinaldo*. Its success served to arouse the jealousy of Keiser, who shortly afterwards set the same libretto without the effect which the composer intended.

Handel's second opera, *Nero*, was produced the same year, but after three performances the theatre closed its doors, Keiser and his partner Drüsicke being compelled to fly from their creditors. Handel seems to have occupied himself for a time with teaching. He had been careful in his habits, and had saved a sufficient sum to enable him to visit Italy, where he arrived in the early part of 1707. It is supposed that his first resting-place was Florence, but at Easter he was undoubtedly in Rome, then and for long after the goal of so many musicians at that season. His mind during this visit seems to have been receptive rather than productive, and after a few months he returned to Florence, where he brought out his first Italian opera, *Rodrigo*, in which he used up much of the material of his Hamburg operas, the overture, for instance, being in many parts the same as *Almira*. The Grand Duke of Tuscany, whose brother had made Handel's acquaintance in Hamburg and had been instrumental in inducing him to visit Italy, was so pleased · with the work that he presented the author with a service of plate and a purse of a hundred sequins.   The prima donna, Vittoria (probably Vittoria Tesi), a young lady of very impulsive disposition, fell madly in love with him.   Whether the passion was returned is not certain, but in 1708, when Handel produced his *Agrippina* in Venice, she obtained consent to go there for the purpose of singing the principal part, and the work was received with great favour.

The spring of 1708 found him again in Rome, where he produced his first oratorio, the *Resurrezione*, for the Marchese Ruspoli, in whose house he lived.   He also wrote *Il Trionfo del Tempo e del Disinganno*, a cantata which in after-years served as the foundation of *The Triumph of Time and Truth*. It is *apropos* of the overture of this work that the well-known story of Corelli is told.   His quiet style of playing did not suit the spirited passages of this overture.   Handel made several attempts to instruct him in the way he wished them rendered. At last he lost his temper (which, in truth, seems not unfrequently to have happened), and snatching the violin from Corelli's hand, himself played the passages.   Corelli's sweetness of disposition did not desert him.   He replied, " Ma, caro Sassone, questa musica è nel stile Francese, di ch' io non intendo " (" But, dear Saxon, this music is in the French style, which I do not understand ").   Eventually Handel modified it so as to be more in accordance with the Italian style.

While at Rome Cardinal Ottoboni arranged a trial of skill

both on the organ and on the harpsichord between Handel and Domenico Scarlatti. On the latter instrument their merits were considered nearly equal, with a slight preference for Scarlatti; but on the organ there was no room for question. Scarlatti himself acknowledged the superiority of Handel, and said that before that time he was unacquainted with the capabilities of the instrument. Domenico Scarlatti took great delight in the society of Handel; and when people praised him for his great execution, he would cross himself and speak of Handel.

In July, 1708, he left Rome and visited Naples, where he remained for more than a year, much courted by the best society. Here he wrote much, although no work of great importance; and late in 1709 he prepared to leave those scenes through which he had made almost a triumphant progress. His route lay through Venice, and he there renewed his intimacy with the Abbate Steffani and Baron Kielmansegge, in whose company he started northward. As a good son, his first care was to visit his mother. He then proceeded to Hanover, where, through the kind offices of Steffani, he was appointed Kapellmeister, with liberal arrangements as to leave of absence. His intention was to visit England, and he arrived in this country towards the close of the year 1710. It may be truly said that this formed the beginning of his real career. The history of the rest of his life will fittingly find a place in another chapter.

We have noticed the fact that Sebastian Bach and Handel were born at no great distance apart, and in the same year.

It is not a little remarkable that these two great musicians never met. It was the wish of Bach's life to make the acquaintance of his great rival. On two separate occasions he made the attempt. In 1719, hearing that Handel was staying with his mother in Halle, Bach started from Coethen, arriving in Halle only to find that Handel had started the day previous for London. On the second occasion, in 1729, Bach, being himself unwell, sent his son Friedemann from Leipzig to Halle with an invitation to Handel to visit him. On this occasion time did not allow him to accept his brother-musician's invitation, and thus these two great men, so well qualified to understand each other, and whose careers ran parallel for sixty-five years, never met.

Mattheson's last appearance on the stage was in Handel's *Nero*. We have seen that he had become tutor to the son of the English ambassador ; and, by his patron's influence, he was soon after appointed secretary of the Legation. He was a man of very great and varied abilities. When only nine years of age, he was able to undertake the organ in several churches, and he soon acquired great proficiency in languages. He wrote several operas, and a great deal of music for the harpsichord, all of which is now forgotten except by antiquaries. It is as a writer on music that his fame is preserved, and he was without doubt the foremost critic of that time ; in fact, it may almost be said that he was the inventor of musical criticism. His *Critica Musica*, the first attempt at a journal specially devoted to music, was commenced in 1722 and continued till 1725. Another work of the same character was started by him in 1728, under the title of *Der Musicalische Patriot*. The German writing of that day was distinguished by great pedantry ; certainly Mattheson's was no exception, and in addition he was very bitter and overbearing in controversy, never entertaining any possibility of error on his own part. He was a most indefatigable writer, and a large number of his works are controversial, but he also wrote many of a didactic nature, one of the best known of which, *Der Vollkommene Kapellmeister*, for many years kept its place as a text-book.

Among the numerous ways in which his literary activity broke out, he conceived the fortunate notion of collecting the Lives of the most eminent German musicians of those days, as far as possible from information supplied by themselves, under the title of *Grundlage einer Ehrenpforte*, or *Foundations of a Triumphal Arch*. This book was published in 1740, and, with the *Lexicon* of Walther, published a few years earlier (Leipzig, 1732), forms the main source of our knowledge of the earlier German musicians. It contains a Life of himself written with delightful self-satisfaction. Handel was of course invited with the rest to furnish particulars of his career for the work, but this, modesty or want of time forbade him to undertake. Mattheson's knowledge, however, was sufficiently intimate to enable him to supply the necessary details. Later on, in 1761, he brought out a second and distinct Life of the great master, some of the statements in which are difficult to reconcile with the previous Life. This second work was soon translated into English by the Rev. John Mainwaring, and for a long series of years remained the only Life of the great musician in the language of the country which he had honoured by making his home.

Another composer, whose reputation was at one time enormous, but who is now almost forgotten, is Hasse (fig. 112). He was born near to Hamburg in 1699, and made his first appearance as a tenor singer at Dresden in 1718, where Keiser, whose acquaintance we made at Hamburg, was conducting the opera. It was not till 1723 that he found the means of producing his first opera, *Antigone*, at Brunswick, with success; but he himself recognized that he had much to learn, and, with the object of completing his musical education, he started for Italy in 1724, and having arrived in Naples, he placed himself under Porpora. His ambition was to have lessons from Alessandro Scarlatti, but he feared that the master's terms would be beyond his modest means. Fortunately the young man had the good luck to meet Scarlatti, and to please him by his skilful performance on the harpsichord, with the result that the veteran proffered his assistance. Several minor works having met with favour, he was entrusted with the composition of an opera, *Sesostrate*, which was performed at the Royal Theatre in 1726. Its success was perfect, and from that day Hasse was known in Italy by no other name than "il caro Sassone."

In 1727 Hasse went to Venice. In this city was performing Faustina Bordoni, a singer endowed with a soprano voice of great beauty and with the most extraordinary skill in the management of it, her execution being truly remarkable; in

short, she was one of the greatest singers of that time. This
great artist Hasse married, and she continued for many
years to take the leading part in the constant succession of
operas which he produced for many of the principal cities of
Europe. He fixed himself mainly in Dresden. The number

Fig. 112.—Johann Adolp Hasse.

of his works was enormous, his operas alone exceeding fifty.
He had in contemplation a complete edition of his works, but
during the siege of Dresden in 1760 the whole of his manuscripts
were destroyed, with other property. The Seven Years' War
left the country so impoverished that the court was compelled

to discontinue the opera. Hasse and his wife were pensioned, and they settled in Vienna, where he still continued to compose. His last opera was written for Milan, on the marriage of the Archduke Ferdinand. For this occasion also the boy Mozart, then thirteen years of age, wrote his first opera, *Mitridate*. Hasse heard it, and exclaimed, "This child will cause us all to be forgotten." The prophecy has been verified ; there is probably no one in the present day who is acquainted with a single air of Hasse, great as was his reputation during his lifetime.

Graun (fig. 113) was more fortunate than Hasse, for one of his works has kept its place in public estimation, at least in Germany. He was born near Dresden in 1701, and was the youngest of three brothers, all of whom followed the profession of music. Early in life he had the opportunity of hearing the greatest singers of the day ; and as he was the possessor of an excellent tenor voice, he profited by the example, while he was still prosecuting his studies in composition. He was in the service of three successive princes of Brunswick, from the last of whom he was begged by Frederick the Great of Prussia, then only Crown Prince ; but when he came to the throne, he confirmed Graun in his musical appointments, which he retained till his death in 1759. He composed no less than thirty operas, but the work by which he is best known is his oratorio *Der Tod Jesu*, which stands in much the same estimation in Germany as Handel's *Messiah* with us, and is frequently performed in churches during Holy Week. A Te Deum, with chorus and orchestra, is also well known. His music

shows much dramatic power, joined to a grace of melody no
doubt partly owing to the Italian influences of his early life.

The example set by Mattheson of a periodical publication
devoted to music soon found imitators. Lorenz Mizler's

Fig. 113.—Carl Heinrich Graun.

Neu-eröffnete Musikalische Bibliothek was started in 1736 and
continued at uncertain intervals till 1754 ; almost at the same
time Scheibe began his *Kritischer Musicus*, which appeared
weekly in Hamburg during the years 1737-8. In 1750 the
eminent theorist Marpurg brought out the first number of a

similar work. As it was published in Berlin, and to distinguish it from the last-named, he called it *Der Kritische Musikus an der Spree*, after the muddy river on which that city is situated. As fifty numbers only were published, Marpurg's efforts do not seem to have received the support they deserved. He made another attempt, however, in 1754 with his *Historisch-kritische Beytrage zur aufnahme der Musik*, and with this he was more fortunate, as it was continued, although irregularly, till 1762. During the progress of this work he started another weekly periodical, called *Kritische Briefe über die Tonkunst*, which went on from 1759 to 1764. The rarity of the later numbers of all these works indicates a gradual falling away of the subscribers. J. A. Hiller, of Leipzig (fig. 114), a successor of Bach in the appointment of Cantor of the Thomas-schule, of whom we have before spoken, was next in the field; and from that time Germany was never without a paper devoted to musical matters, and in this it was far in advance of any other country.

Marpurg's compositions were not numerous. It is as a theorist that he is best known. His *Handbuch bey dem Generalbasse* and his *Abhandlung von der Fuge*, both reprinted more than once, and translated into several languages, were looked on as forming the basis of a sound musical education. The mathematical questions involved in the study of music, such as temperament, etc., also engaged his attention, and formed the subject of several of his works.

The golden age of music in Vienna belongs to a later

period than that contained within the scope of this volume.
The intercourse between that city and Italy had been for a
long time intimate. Apostolo Zeno and Metastasio had been
successively welcomed as poets-laureate by the Austrian court,
and for most of its musicians it depended on the same country.

Fig. 114.—Johann Adam Hiller.

Many names of some celebrity will be found in the list of
court musicians, among whom may be mentioned Antonio
Draghi, J. B. Buononcini, P. F. Tosi (whose *Treatise on
the Florid Song*, originally published in Italian, gives so much
information on the science of singing as then practised, and

also many interesting particulars of the great singers of those days), Antonia Caldara, and others.

But there was one musician filling the post of Capellmeister at Vienna who deserves a more extended notice, for his celebrity was European. This was Johann Josef Fux, who was court composer from 1698 to 1740, serving under the three emperors Leopold I., Joseph I., and Charles VI. He was born in the year 1660 in Styria, and but little is known of his education beyond the fact that he appears to have travelled in France, Germany, and Italy to increase his knowledge and experience. In 1675 he was already settled in Vienna. All three of the sovereigns whom he served were well versed in music, and testified for him the greatest esteem. He attempted with success all kinds of musical composition : instrumental, sacred and operatic. As an example of the footing on which he stood with the Emperor Charles VI., it is related that, having composed an opera in honour of the birthday of the Archduchess, aunt of the Emperor, the latter was so delighted with the work that, as a special mark of esteem, he himself accompanied it on the harpsichord at the third performance. Fux was placed at the side of the Emperor, and turning over the leaves of the score for him, was so struck with his skill that he exclaimed, " What a pity your Majesty should not be a capellmeister ! " " There is no harm done," replied the Emperor ; " things are very well as they are ! "

On the coronation of Charles VI. at Prague in 1723 as king of Bohemia, Fux wrote an opera, *Costanza e Fortezza*, for the occasion. The whole staff of the Imperial chapel was sent to Prague to unite with the principal musicians of that city and others who came from Italy in the performance of the opera. Fux was unfortunately overcome with an attack of gout. That his presence might not be wanting on so great an occasion, the Emperor had him conveyed the whole way on a litter, and at the performance ordered the composer's chair to be placed at the side of his own. He received the congratulations of the many distinguished people, artists and others, who were gathered together for such an important event, and it was a great triumph for him.

Nearly all his compositions have remained in manuscript, and are now entirely unknown. But every one has heard of the great work of his life, his *Gradus ad Parnassum.* The publication of this treatise formed another opportunity for the Emperor to show his admiration for his capellmeister, as he undertook the entire expense of its publication. The style in which the work is printed shows that no expense was spared to make the externals of the book worthy of its contents. It was published at Vienna in 1725 in the Latin language, but was soon translated into German by Mizler, and subsequently into Italian, French, and English, and for many years it formed the indispensable handbook to the higher branches of a musical education.

The master died in Vienna in the year 1741, at the age of eighty-one years. He was one of the eminent men to whom Mattheson gave a niche in his *Ehrenpforte,* and whom he requested to supply the necessary information. Mattheson had previously criticised some of his theoretical views roughly, as was usual with him, and that in a work which, with a strange want of delicacy, he dedicated to Fux. The latter replied with some dignity that "modesty forbade him to give details how he had received advancement in the offices he held which would be to sound his own praises. It was sufficient to say that he had been found worthy of being first capell-meister to Charles VI." Thus unfortunately most of the particulars of his life are wanting to us.

Up to this time the opera was looked on as a vehicle for the display of the skill of the singers engaged rather than as a dramatic composition to be developed in musical language. The number of airs and their character were each laid down and ordered according to certain fixed rules. Early in the eighteenth century appeared a musician who could think for himself, and who was destined to sweep away all these arbitrary restrictions. His name was Christopher Willibald Gluck. He was born in the year 1714 in Bohemia. His father was in the service of Prince Lobkowitz, and was in a position to give him a good general as well as musical education. When a young man, he made his way to Vienna, where still lived A. Caldara, J. J. Fux, and other musicians of eminence. While there he had the good fortune to meet, at the house of Prince Lobkowitz, the Prince Melzi, who was so struck with his abilities that he took him back to Milan and then put him under G. B. Sammartini, a composer of merit. He shortly began to compose operas on his own account, which were received with much favour, and caused their author to be looked on as one of the best composers. So great was his reputation that in 1745 he was invited to London to compose two operas for that city. During his residence here, he found time to pay a visit to Paris, in order to hear the operas of Rameau—another musician who thought for himself. After various wanderings in fulfilment of his engagements, he returned to Vienna. He was now forty-four years of age. His reputation had gradually increased ; his operas showed an advance in dramatic power, but he was content to work on the same lines as the other dramatic composers of his day. In 1762 he brought out in Vienna his *Orfeo*, in which he made a bound forward ; indeed, it is a masterpiece. He had allied himself with Calzabigi, a poet who carried out the composer's views of dramatic treatment. Almost every one knows the magnificent air *Che faro senza Euridice*, which for depth of feeling is unsurpassed. This opera showed the development of his principles, but in the year 1767 he brought out his *Alcestis*, in which he claimed to revolutionize the art of writing for the theatre. To the score of this work, published in Vienna in 1769, is prefixed a dedicatory epistle, in which he sets out the principles which guided him in its composition. This preface is of such deep interest that we give a translation of the principal passages. "When I undertook to set *Alceste* to music, I proposed to myself to avoid all the abuses which the ill-restrained vanity

of singers, or the too great compliance of composers, had
introduced into Italian opera, which, from being the most
dignified and the most splendid of entertainments, had become
the most ridiculous and the most tedious. I endeavoured to
confine music to its true office of adding force to poetry by
the expression and the introduction of melody, without interrupt-
ing the action or chilling it by the introduction of useless and
superfluous ornament. I thought that it should act in the
same way as cheerful colour and the contrast of light and
shade do to a well-arranged drawing, that it should animate
the design without altering the outline. I had no desire to
interrupt an actor in the warmth of a dialogue to listen to
a tedious *ritornello*, nor to stop him in the middle of a speech
upon a favourable vowel, either for the sake of his displaying
his fine voice in a long ornamented passage, or to wait while
the orchestra gave him time to take breath for a cadenza. . I
did not believe that the second part of an air should be
passed over rapidly when it was the most important, in order
to repeat the words, according to rule, four times over, nor to
finish the air where the sense did not finish for the purpose
of giving the singer the opportunity of showing to his own
satisfaction how capriciously he could vary a passage. In
short, I endeavoured to restrain all those abuses against which
for a long time both good sense and reason had cried out in
vain.

"I supposed that the overture should give the spectators
a foreshadowing of what was to be presented, and form, so to

speak, the argument. . . . I thought also that my great aim should be a noble simplicity; and I have avoided making a show of difficulty at the expense of clearness. I have not sought after novelty which did not arise naturally out of the situation or the sentiment; and there is no customary rule which I have not thought it my duty to sacrifice willingly in favour of effect.

"Such are my principles. . . . Success has justified them, and universal approval in so enlightened a city has shown clearly that simplicity, truth, and natural expression are the great principles in all the productions of art."

The soundness of these principles will be admitted, as well as the dignity and straightforwardness with which they are enforced. It appears, however, that the popular approval was not so complete as he claimed. Many of the public took the opposite view, those who were in entire accord with the composer being the court party, headed by the Emperor, who was a good musician. *Alceste* was followed up by *Paride ed Elena*, in the dedication of which he further developed his views.

He was not, however, completely satisfied with the reception that these works received at the hands of the Viennese public. He formed the idea, possibly from his recollections of the operas of Rameau, that the French stage was more suitable for carrying out his designs. There was at that time (1772) living in Vienna, attached to the French Embassy, the Bailli du Rollet, a man of considerable acquirements. To him Gluck expounded his views, with the result that a libretto was arranged from the *Iphigénie en Aulide* of Racine. The work was at once put in hand, and some preliminary rehearsals of it were gone through.

Du Rollet was much impressed by what he heard, and lost no time in trying to induce the administration of the Opera in Paris to engage Gluck to produce his work in that city. In furtherance of this scheme, he addressed a letter, expounding the new principles, to the *Mercure de France*, which appeared in October, 1772. It proved to be a declaration of war. The administration was strongly opposed to these novelties. Gluck, however, had been the music-master of the Dauphiness Marie Antoinette. She threw her influence into the scale, with the result that Gluck left Vienna for Paris, and the opera was put in rehearsal and produced in 1774. The extraordinary strife which broke out on its production belongs to another chapter. Gluck was now sixty years of age, and he remained in Paris until the end of 1779, when an attack of apoplexy induced him to return to Vienna, and in that city he died in 1787.

Gluck attempted instrumental music, composing several symphonies; but in this style of music he was not so successful. Dramatic situations were requisite to bring out his greatest powers. Instrumental music, however, enjoyed great popularity in Vienna. Among the composers most sought after for such works was Giambattista Sammartini, of Milan (who must not be confounded with Padre Martini, of Bologna, the eminent historian and theorist). So highly was he in fashion, that several amateurs, among whom was Prince Esterhazy, combined in giving a commission to a banker at Milan to buy every symphony he produced at a fixed price. These have now all been forgotten, although many of them have been published at Paris, and some of his compositions in London ; but there can be no doubt that they exercised an important influence on the development of that style of music, and especially on the composer Haydn, whose symphonies have deservedly enjoyed such great celebrity. Haydn, it is well known, was in the service of Prince Esterhazy, and thus must have become well acquainted with them.

With the exception of dramatic music, in which he did not excel, Haydn impressed his individuality on most forms' of composition.   Both the symphony and the quartet owe their settled form to him.   From his days Vienna became for a long time the home of all that was greatest in musical art. Mozart settled there as soon as he decided on freeing himself from the trammels of the Bishop of Salzburg's court ; and there lived during the greater part of his life Ludwig van Beethoven, attracted there in the first instance by the desire of obtaining the advice of Haydn.

13

CHAPTER IX.

MUSIC IN ENGLAND AT THE TIME OF THE RESTORATION.

Discouragement of Music during the Commonwealth—The resumption of the Cathedral Service—"Captain" Cooke—Matthew Lock—The "Salmon and Lock" Controversy—. —Pelham Humfrey, Blow, and Wise—The "Verse" Anthem—Jeremiah Clarke and Croft—Henry Purcell—Boyce's "Cathedral Music"—The Progress of Organ-building in England—"Father Smith" and Renatus Harris—The Temple Organ—John Play-ford, the Music-publisher—Christopher Simpson—Mace's *Musick's Monument*—Tom d'Urfey.

NOTHING could well be more depressing than the outlook of music in England at the time of the Restoration. Cathedral service throughout the land had been put a stop to. The choirs had been dispersed, the service books burnt or torn in pieces, and in many cases the organs had been destroyed. Cromwell is believed to have been fond of music, and it is certain that his Latin secretary, Milton, was a good musician and the friend of Henry Lawes—the "Harry whose tuneful and well-measur'd song" is celebrated in his well-known sonnet, and who in happier times had set the music to the poet's work of *Comus*. But any appreciation of music was exceptional. The Scriptural injunction "Is any merry? let him sing psalms," was obeyed implicitly, and no other music was tolerated.

When therefore the King "enjoyed his own again," the

whole machinery for the decent performance of Divine worship in "choirs and places where they sing" had to be reconstructed. Henry Lawes, who during the troubles had managed to support himself by teaching, still survived, and on him devolved the duty of composing the anthem for Charles II.'s coronation.

Among those who had adhered to the Royalist cause was Henry Cooke, formerly a chorister of the Chapel Royal. At the outbreak of the Rebellion his duties ceased, but he followed his royal master in his troubles, and turned soldier, behaving with such bravery that he received a captain's commission. At the Restoration, possibly in reward for his services, he received the appointment of master of the children of the Chapel Royal. He continued to be called Captain Cooke, under which title he is frequently referred to by Pepys in his diary, for instance, under December 21st, 1665, "Captain Cooke and his two boys did sing some Italian songs, which I must in a word say I think was fully the best musique that I ever yet heard in all my life." Pepys was not blind to one of his failings, for he says elsewhere, "A vain coxcomb he is, though he sings so well."

At first it was so difficult to find boys with any musical training whatever, that all sorts of expedients were necessary in order to perform the music at the Chapel Royal. Matthew Lock tells us, "For above a year after the opening of His Majestie's Chappel, the orderers of the musick there were necessitated to supply superior parts of the music with cornets and men's feigned voices, there being not one lad for all that time capable of singing his part readily."

The appointment of Captain Cooke, whatever may have been the motives which prompted it, seems to have been a happy one, as he possessed remarkable skill in the training of boys, and he was, moreover, very fortunate in the material he had to work upon. Of those who first came under his tuition, three—Pelham Humfrey, John Blow, and Michael Wise—soon distinguished themselves. To supply the places of the men was not so difficult. Dr. William Child, Dr. Christopher Gibbons (son of the famous madrigal-writer Orlando Gibbons), who had both been "children" of the Chapel Royal during the reign of the late King, and Edmund Lowe, formerly of Salisbury, were appointed organists, while twenty men-singers were collected possessed of some experience. For the coronation Matthew Lock (well known by name to most people in the present day as the reputed composer of the music to *Macbeth*, although by many it is attributed to Purcell), who had been a choirman at Exeter, was employed to write some triumphal music for performance during the King's progress from the Tower to Whitehall, which was so much appreciated that he was appointed composer-in-ordinary to the King. Lock was a fine example of the musician militant; he was always engaged in controversy. In a service which he wrote for the Chapel Royal he set each response to the Commandments in a different way. This was of course an innovation, which has not commended itself to subsequent practice, and in those days it was looked on with great

MUSIC IN ENGLAND AT THE TIME OF THE RESTORATION. 197

disfavour. Lock published his setting, with a preface in which he roundly abused his opponents, under the title "*Modern Church Musick, Pre-accused, Censur'd, and Obstructed in its Performance before His Majesty, April 1st*, 1666 Vindicated by the Author, Matt. Lock, Composer-in-ordinary to His Majesty."

In 1675 he published "*The English Opera; or, The Vocal Musick in 'Psyche,' with the Instrumental Therein Intermix'd.* To which is adjoyned the Instrumental Musick in the *Tempest*," also preceded by an aggressive preface.

But it was in a discussion known as the Salmon and Lock controversy that his quarrelsome disposition showed to the greatest disadvantage. A young clergyman, the Rev. Thomas Salmon, was fired with the desire of simplifying musical notation—a desire which has possessed many both before and since. His plan was, in the words of the title of the pamphlet which he published in 1672, "the advancement of musick, by casting away the perplexity of different cliffs, and uniting all sorts of musick—lute, viol, violin, organ, harpischord, voice, etc.—in one universal character." His scheme consisted in calling the five lines of the staff invariably *g*, *b*, *d*, *f*, *a*, and signifying their actual pitch by the letters *T*, *M*, and *B*, standing for Treble, Mean, and Bass, placed at the beginning of each line. The plan had the merit of apparent simplicity. Lock at once made an onslaught from the height of his professional position, apparently surprised that any amateur should presume to attempt to abolish the time-honoured difficulties of the old notation. His reply showed all his native truculence. Mr. Salmon ought to have felt himself annihilated. Instead of this, he returned to the charge with a *Vindication* of his essay, which took the form of a letter addressed to Dr. John Wallis, the eminent mathematician, who had done good service to the cause of music, especially by publishing the treatises of Ptolemy and Bryennius. It was not surprising that, after the treatment he had received at the hands of Lock, the author should begin to show signs of failing temper. Of course Lock replied, waxing even more abusive. To his pamphlet is added *Duellum Musicum; or, The Musical Duel, by John Phillips, Gent.*, who was a nephew of Milton. Why he meddled in the fray is not apparent. He shows but little knowledge of the question, confining himself to vulgar personalities. The controversy was wound up by John Playford, whose common-sense stands out to great advantage in this wordy warfare. Lock also brought out in 1673 a book called *Melothesia; or, Certain General Rules for Playing upon a Continued Bass.* Becoming a Roman Catholic, he resigned his appointment at the Chapel Royal, and was appointed organist to the Queen at Somerset House.

Anything that savoured of dulness was very distasteful to the King. During his enforced residence in France he had learned to admire the lighter style of Church music which was popular at the court, where Lully had introduced the seductions of instrumental music into the services. To one who had for a long time become accustomed to such variety, the accompaniment of the organ alone seemed monotonous, and the severe and solemn compositions of the older masters tedious. The King determined to form his own chapel on the model of that at Versailles. Twenty-four instrumentalists were engaged, who were first brought into requisition on Sunday, September 14th, 1662. Need it be said that Mr. Pepys was not absent on so important an occasion? He reports as follows :—

"To Whitehall Chapel, when sermon almost done, and I heard Captain Cooke's new musique. This the first of having vialls and other instruments to play a symphony between every verse of the anthems, but the musique more full than it was last Sunday, and very fine it is."

Michael Wise, who was, as we have seen, one of Captain Cooke's early pupils, was born in Salisbury, and in 1668 became organist of the cathedral of his native city, being then about twenty years of age. He was in great favour with King Charles, who appointed him his organist. Unfortunately he was a man of hasty temper, which led to his losing his life in a chance medley with a watchman in the streets of Salisbury. He wrote several services and anthems of great beauty and power of expression, which are still sung, especially *The ways of Zion do mourn*.

Pelham Humfrey was probably the most precocious of the three young choristers, for while still singing as a boy in the choir he had already composed several anthems. His quickness, joined

to a certain charm of manner, seems to have commended him to
the King, who, when his voice broke, sent him to France to have
the advantage of studying under Lully.   He remained abroad for
three years, and returned to find that he had already been appointed a "gentleman of the Chapel Royal." Pepys, who had
characterized him as "a pretty boy" before he left England,
speaks thus of him on his return :—

"Home, and there find, as I expected, Mr. Cæsar and little
Pelham Humfreys, lately returned from France, and is an absolute
mosieur, as full of form and confidence and vanity, and disparages
everything and everybody's skill but his own.   But to hear how
he laughs at all the King's musick here ; at Blagrave and others,
that they cannot keep time or tune, nor understand anything ;
and at Grebus, the Frenchman, the King's master of musick, how
he understands nothing, nor can play on any instrument, and
so cannot compose, and that he will give him a lift out of his
place, and that he and the King are mighty great."

"Grebus, the Frenchman," was M. Grabu, who was certainly
a dull musician.   His only title to fame was the composition,
towards the end of Charles II.'s reign, of an opera called *Albion
and Albanius.*   The words of the piece were by Dryden, and
the satire which they contained gave the work an importance
which the music alone would never have acquired, except
perhaps to the ears of Dryden, who in his preface exalted
the composer at the expense of Purcell.

Of the brilliancy of Humfrey's attainments there can be
no doubt, and the foreign experience which he had acquired

rendered his style peculiarly acceptable to the King, who, on the death of Captain Cooke in 1672, appointed him Master of the

Fig. 115.—Dr. John Blow (from the frontispiece of his *Amphion Anglicus*, drawn and engraved by R. White, 1700).

Children, and soon afterwards composer-in-ordinary for the violin to his Majesty. Several of his sacred compositions are still in use. His secular works, not being readily found in available form, are less known. Unfortunately his career was cut short at the early age of twenty-seven.

Dr. John Blow (fig. 115) was a man of an entirely different character. Nothing could exceed his modesty, which actually went so far as to prompt him to resign the post of organist of Westminster Abbey in favour of a pupil whose genius he recognized as exceeding his own ; this pupil was Henry Purcell. Blow was without doubt a man of genius. Much of his Church music has come down to us, some of which is still heard, and deserves to continue to be heard. His best-known anthems are *I beheld, and lo! a great multitude* and *I was in the Spirit*, which in many cathedrals is always sung on Whit-Sunday. He was also the composer of much secular music, a collection of which he made and published under the title of *Amphion Anglicus*, containing songs which could well bear resuscitation. He died in 1708, in his sixtieth year.

To these composers of whom we have been speaking is to be attributed the introduction of the *verse* anthem. Up to the time of the Restoration anthems had consisted entirely of chorus. They were now interspersed with passages written for a single voice to a part. This was called "verse," for what reason is not obvious. The introduction of solos naturally followed.

Another innovation is also due to this period—the introduction of what are now known as "Anglican" chants. On the resumption of the cathedral service, Edward Lowe, originally a chorister of Salisbury, but at that time organist of Christ Church, Oxford, at the request of that university, drew up a *Short Direction for the Performance of Cathedral Service.* This was based on the old plain-song. But the more florid style of music which had come into vogue for services and anthems was not in keeping with the severity of the ancient music, and the result was the invention of the well-known Anglican chant, which was soon followed by the double-chant.

If Captain Cooke was fortunate in finding three boys of the capacity of Wise, Humfrey, and Blow, the latter, who had been appointed Master of the Children in the year 1674, in succession to Humfrey, was still more so, for he had as pupils Jeremiah Clark, William Croft, and Henry Purcell.

Jeremiah Clark was much esteemed as a composer of Church music, some of his anthems still being in use ; but he distinguished himself more by his songs, many of which are to be found in the collection published by Playford and D'Urfey. The circumstances of his death were so romantic that we must give them here. He formed a hopeless attachment for a lady of a higher rank in life than himself. His misfortune induced great despondency. We give the sequel in the words of a contemporary : " Being at the house of a friend in the country, he took an abrupt resolution to return to London ; his friend, having observed in his manner marks of great dejection, furnished him with a horse and a servant. Riding along the road, a fit of melancholy seized him, upon which he alighted, and giving the servant his horse to hold, went into a field, in a corner whereof was a pond, and also trees, and began to debate with himself whether he should then end his days by hanging or drowning. Not being able to resolve on either, he thought of making what he looked upon as chance the umpire, and drew out of his pocket a piece of money, and tossing it into the air, it came down on its edge, and stuck in the clay. Though the declaration answered not his wish, it was far from ambiguous, as it seemed to forbid both methods of destruction, and would have given unspeakable comfort to a mind less disorganized than his own. Being thus interrupted in his purpose, he returned, and mounting his horse, rode on to London, and in a short time shot himself.'' This occurred in the year 1707, when Clark was thirty-eight years of age.

Croft became a chorister at the Chapel Royal in 1685, and in 1699 was appointed organist of St. Anne's, Soho. In 1700 he was admitted a gentleman of the Chapel Royal, as well as to the reversion of the post of organist jointly with Clark, at whose decease he succeeded to the full place. On the death of Blow, in the following year, he was made organist of Westminster Abbey. He wrote many anthems, and some services, which are still much admired ; for instance, *God is gone up* and *We will rejoice* are frequently heard. The best known of his works, however, is his Funeral Ser-vice, the dignity and solemnity of which are in such perfect keeping with its intention that no other music is likely to displace it.

The third of these young men was Henry Purcell, a

name which must ever be held in reverence by English musicians, for he was without doubt the greatest of our modern composers.

Fig. 116. Henry Purcell (from the engraving by Zobel after Klosterman's portrait in the possession of the Royal Society of Musicians).

Henry Purcell (fig. 116) was born in 1658, in a house almost under the shadow of Westminster Abbey, in which his father was a singing-man, in addition to being a gentleman of the Chapel Royal, Master of the Boys at the Abbey, and music copyist to that church, and a member of the Royal Band, so that the future composer entered on life surrounded by an atmosphere of music. When he was just six years old, his father died; and in proof that the boy had already acquired some musical knowledge, he was at once admitted a chorister of the Chapel Royal. He was committed to the charge of his uncle, Thomas Purcell, also an esteemed musician, who honestly did his best by the child.

Captain Cooke was still Master of the Boys, and under him Purcell advanced with rapid strides. On Cooke's death Pelham Humfrey was appointed to his post, and was able to initiate Purcell into the French style of Lully; but he was soon carried off, and Blow was put in his place. Purcell was now sixteen years of age, and must naturally have lost his soprano voice, and have become no longer useful in the choir; it seems, however, that boys who appeared to possess exceptional ability were retained, and this was the case with Purcell. He had already written several works which showed the possession of great talent; and, on the recommendation, as it is believed, of Blow, he was appointed copyist to Westminster Abbey, a post formerly held by his father. It is probable that the music known as Locke's music to *Macbeth* was actually written by Purcell in these early days, and it is certain that he composed music to Dryden's *Aureng-Zebe*, as well as to two plays by Shadwell, in one of which, *The*

Libertine, occurs the well-known chorus *In these delightful, pleasant groves.*

At the time of which we are writing there was a minor canon of Canterbury Cathedral, the Rev. John Gosling, who possessed a bass voice of extraordinary depth and power. He was on very intimate terms with the Purcell family, and Henry Purcell wrote more than one anthem specially to show off his lower notes. Of one of these the following story is told. Charles II. was very fond of Gosling, and took him with him on the trial trip of a new yacht. Off the North Foreland a violent storm arose, and the ship was in such great danger that the King and the Duke of York had to work like common sailors in helping to manage the vessel. Fortunately the lives of all on board were saved, but Mr. Gosling was so affected by the dangers they had gone through, and so thankful for their preservation, that he selected from the Psalms the words of an anthem which he requested Purcell to set to music. The result was the well-known *They that go down to the sea in ships,* in which the bass is made to go down to the low D.

In 1680 Dr. Blow performed an extraordinary act of modesty and generosity in resigning the appointment of organist of Westminster in favour of his pupil Purcell, who was then twenty-two years of age. In the same year Purcell composed his opera *Dido and Æneas,* which, strange to say, was written for "Mr. Josias Priest's boarding-school at Chertsey," and "performed by young gentlewomen." It was presumably a fashionable place of education, as the epilogue on the occasion was spoken by "the Lady Dorothy Burk." The book was by Nahum Tate. The music was in advance of the time, for the work was a true opera, not songs interspersed with dialogue, but set to music throughout. The composer seems never to have repeated the experiment.

In 1681 he married, and in 1682 received the further appointment of organist of the Chapel Royal. In the fulfilment of the duties of his Church appointments, he wrote much sacred music, both services and anthems, some with orchestral accompaniments, as his *Te Deum* and *Jubilate*, composed for St. Cecilia's Day, 1694, which for many years successively were performed at St. Paul's Cathedral on the occasion of the festival of the "Sons of the Clergy."

But he was equally industrious in secular composition. Although he attempted no other opera, he wrote incidental music to many dramatic pieces. That for *The Tempest* is well known, for it contains *Come unto these yellow sands* and *Full fathom five*, which are as beautiful as they are familiar. This was followed by *Dioclesian; or, The Prophetess*, adapted by Betterton from Beaumont and Fletcher, *Amphitryon*, by Dryden, and many others which we cannot mention here. *King Arthur*, however, also by Dryden, cannot be passed over, for in it is the solo for tenor, with chorus, *Come if you dare*, which possesses all the attributes of a patriotic song, and still holds its place. In it is also the celebrated frost scene, now no longer heard, but which used to freeze our ancestors in the days of the "antient concerts," of which we shall have a word to say later. We must also mention *The Indian Queen*, with its *Ye twice ten hundred deities* and the exquisite song *I attempt from love's sickness to fly*. Purcell also wrote two sets of sonatas for two violins and bass, which no doubt were the works from which Corelli formed the high opinion he is known to have held of him. It is even said that Corelli proposed to visit England for the express purpose of making the acquaintance of his brother-composer, a decision which he abandoned on hearing of Purcell's death, just as he was on the point of starting.

It was an excellent custom in those days for the "friends of musick" to meet on the feast of St. Cecilia, November 22nd, to celebrate the patron saint of the art they practised— a custom which might well be revived in our own day. The members attended Divine service at St. Bride's Church, in Fleet Street. The service, it need hardly be said, was choral ; the anthem was generally composed for the occasion ; and a sermon in praise of music was preached, some of which have been published and come down to us. The religious part of the ceremony performed, the members assembled in some public room, where a special ode in praise of music was performed, which, as becomes Englishmen, was followed by a dinner.

There are some reasons for believing that the meetings were instituted earlier than the time of Purcell, but the first recorded celebration took place in 1683, when Purcell set to

14

music three separate odes, two in English and one in Latin ; but it seems that one only was performed : certainly only one was published. The ode for 1684 was composed by Blow, as was also that for 1691. The political changes of 1688 interrupted the meetings, and it was not till 1692 that Purcell was again employed. The words of the ode were the production of Nicholas Brady, Tate's associate in the new version of the Psalms. This work met with great success, and was frequently performed, and was published in our own day by the Musical Antiquarian Society. In 1694 the Church service was performed with unusual magnificence, Purcell's *Te Deum* and *Jubilate* in D, with orchestra, of which we have already spoken, being written for the occasion. The intention appears to have been to have repeated its performance at the next festival, but for some unassigned reason this did not take place, a similar work by Dr. Blow being substituted. It will have been seen that this festival was associated with many of Purcell's triumphs. The feast of St. Cecilia in 1695 was a day of mourning for all who had taken part in these celebrations, as well as for all who loved music. On the eve of the festival, within earshot of the Abbey in whose services he had so frequently borne a part, the illustrious composer died, not having completed his thirty-seventh year—an age which has been fatal to several great musicians. He was buried most fittingly in Westminster Abbey, beneath the organ which he had so worthily played, and on a pillar close by may still be read one of those few epitaphs which seem worthy of the occasion :—

"Here lies Henry Purcell, Esq., who left this life, and is gone to that blessed place where only his harmony can be exceeded."

Comparatively a small portion only of his works was published during his lifetime. In fact, he seems to have shown almost an antipathy to printing them. To the best of her powers his widow made it her pious duty to repair this omission. The most important collection was published under the title of "*Orpheus Britannicus:* A Collection of all the choicest Songs for one, two, and three voices, composed by Mr. Henry Purcell;" and this work must have been well received, as a second edition was called for.

His master, Dr. Blow, survived him several years, living until 1708. Croft was younger than Purcell, and nobly maintained the traditions of sacred music till the year 1727, and in this he was assisted by Weldon, Greene, and Boyce. The latter has further claims on our gratitude, for, in addition to his numerous compositions—among which is the well-known *O where shall wisdom be found?*—he published a collection of anthems and services by the most eminent of our Church musicians. The work was originally projected by Greene ; but his engagements not allowing him to carry out his design, he bequeathed his materials to Boyce. It was the first attempt to bring out such a collection in score, the only previous work of the kind, Barnard's, having been in parts. The work, which is in three   lio volumes, is of the greatest value, and is so much appreciated that it has been twice reprinted in our own days.

These names comprise the greatest among our cathedral composers. Their work was continued by men who were well-instructed and capable musicians. We may mention William Hayes and his son Philip Hayes, who succeeded his father both as organist at Magdalen College, Oxford, and as Professor of Music in the university—each of whom aimed too openly at catching the ear—Charles King, Nares, Travers, Jackson of Exeter—a man of many accomplishments, whose well-known *Te Deum* shows how feeble a man of some talent can be— Dupuis, Benjamin Cooke, and John Battishill, whose greatest triumphs however, were obtained in secular music.

The destruction of organs during the Civil War had been so general that there was no lack of work for organ-builders at the Restoration. Among the first builders in the field was Bernard Schmidt, better known in England as " Father Smith," who came over from Germany with two nephews. The first commission given to him was an organ for the Chapel Royal at Whitehall, which was completed in 1660, for evidence of which we appeal again to Mr. Pepys.

" July 8th (Lord's Day). To Whitehall Chapel, where I got in with ease by going before the Lord Chancellor with Mr. Kipps. Here I heard very good musique, the first time that ever I remember to have heard the organs and singing-men in surplices in my life."

This first effort does not seem to have been entirely satisfactory, but it was built against time. Smith, however, soon had further employment, for in 1662 he built an organ for Westminster Abbey, and subsequently others for St. Giles's-in-the-Fields and St. Margaret's, Westminster. He was in great favour with the King, who gave him rooms in Whitehall. The organs he built are very numerous. The quality of tone he produced was very beautiful, but in mechanical arrangements he was not so successful, his touch being bad and the interior work ill arranged.

But he was not allowed to have a monopoly. He had only been a few months in England when Harris, with his son René or Renatus, arrived from France. For some time Smith retained the greater part of the work, but the elder Harris died in 1672, and Renatus turned out to be a man of great ability and resource, proving a formidable rival to his competitor. In one instance this led to a memorable and well-known struggle. At the end of the reign of Charles II. the Societies of the Inner and Middle Temple determined to build for their well-known church the best organ they could obtain. The authorities appear to have been in treaty with Smith on the subject, when some of the Benchers of the Inner Temple brought forward Harris. As a settlement of the matter it was proposed that each of the builders should set up an organ in one of the Halls, and that the best should be chosen from the two for erection in the church. Smith demurred to this arrangement, affirming (and bringing forward some proof of his affirmation) that the work had been already entrusted to him. He was compelled, however, to fall in with the proposal, and after a time the two organs were completed, both being erected in the church itself.

Dr. Blow and Purcell performed on Father Smith's organ on several occasions, and it proved so excellent that the belief that it would be chosen was general. Harris's instrument had not been heard. He availed himself of the services of Baptist Draghi, organist to the Queen at Somerset House, and a well-known performer. This instrument proved to be of equal excellence. The committee were quite unable to decide between the rival merits of the two organs. Public opinion was aroused, and war was declared between the adherents of the two builders. The strife continued for a twelvemonth, when Harris challenged Smith to add certain reed-stops, such as the Cremona and Vox Humana. The stops were unknown in England, and delighted the public ear, but the difficulty of deciding on their excellence was as great as ever. The Benchers of the Middle Temple at last lost patience, and passed a resolution affirming "the organ made by Bernard Smith to bee in their Judgments, both for sweetnes and fulnes of Sound (besides y° extraordinary stopps, quarter Notes, and other Rarityes therein), beyond comparison preferrable before the other of the said Organs made by Harris, and that the same is more ornamentall and substantiall, and both for Depthe of Sound and Strengthe fitter for the use of the said Church ; . . . and for that the organ made by the said Harris is discernably too low and too weake for the said Church, their ma^r. pp^{es}. see not any Cause of further Delay or need of any reference to Musicians or others to determine the Difference, but doe for their parts unanimously make Choise of the said Organ made by Smith." No one can doubt what followed. The Inner Temple was dissatisfied that any such decision should have been arrived at without consulting them, and declared that it was "high time and absolutely necessary" that impartial judges, who were good judges of music, should be nominated by both Houses to determine the controversy, at the same time appointing a committee to confer with the Benchers of the Middle Temple. Both sides stuck to their colours, the Middle Temple strong in the opinion that they had made the best selection, the Inner, leaning possibly to the side of Harris, making no selection themselves, but anxious to call in skilled judgment to decide. It required no little judgment to come to any arrangement whatever, and at last the question was referred for decision to Lord Chief Justice Jefferies. The authority for this statement is Dr. Burney. He seems a curious umpire to have chosen, but possibly it was a legal rather than a musical opinion that he was asked to give. His decision was in favour of Smith, but the difficulty which the best judges had found in deciding on the merits of the instruments was so great that Harris's reputation did not suffer. His organ was divided, part of it going to Christ Church Cathedral, Dublin, and the remainder to St. Andrew's, Holborn

The contest appears to have been carried on with extra-

ordinary virulence by the partisans of the respective competitors.
The Hon. Roger North in his *Memoirs of Music* says that they
" proceeded to the most mischievous and unwarrantable acts of
hostilities, and that in the night preceding the last trial of the
reed-stops the friends of Harris cut the bellows of Smith's
organ ; " and he adds that " *Smith and Harris were but just
not ruined.*"

Smith's reputation now stood on the firmest basis, and
he was at once employed, among other commissions, to build
organs for Durham and for St. Paul's Cathedral, where he
was much hampered by the size of the case, which Wren would
not allow to exceed certain dimensions, complaining that the
building was already spoiled by the " box of whistles."

It will have been noticed that the Benchers of the Middle
Temple in their resolution refer to "quarter-notes." When writing
of Bach, we spoke of the practice which prevailed of tuning
organs by unequal temperament, so that they could be employed
in a few keys only. In the Temple organ an attempt was
made to overcome the difficulty by supplying more than twelve
sounds to the octave. With this view the black key between
G and A was divided, as was also the one between D and E,
so that separate sounds existed for G♯ and A♭ as well as for
D♯ and E♭. The division was made in the length of the key,
the back part being raised as much above the front, as the
front was above the naturals. It will be seen that this extended
very considerably the resources of the instrument, the keys of
E♭ and A♭, A and E, being all available. The practice of tuning

organs by equal temperament was long before it gained ground
in this country, many organists even in our own day having
been violently opposed to the change.

The most active music-publisher of those times was John
Playford.   Among the works he brought out was his own
Introduction to the Skill of Musick, which was first published
in 1655—a single copy has been found with the date 1654—a
work which went through nineteen numbered editions, and
four or five to which no number was attached, tending to show
that the art of music was assiduously cultivated.   The twelfth
edition was revised by Purcell, who almost rewrote the part
which treats of the art of descant.   The later editions claim
to be "done on the new Ty'd-Note;" *i.e.*, the tails of quavers
and smaller notes forming groups were joined, instead of each
note being separate.   This was a great improvement both in
appearance and ease of reading.   Playford had his shop in the
Temple, and was a man of great worth, being known as "honest
John Playford."   At his death his son Henry continued the
business.   Many important works issued from this establishment,
including most of Purcell's published during the lifetime of the
composer : also *The Treasury of Musick; The Theater of
Musick*, containing airs by Lawes, Purcell, Blow, and others ; and
Harmonia Sacra, consisting of sacred works principally by the
same writers.

Another very popular handbook of those days was
Christopher Simpson's *Compendium of Practical Musick*, of
which nine editions appeared.   The author of it was a skilful

player on the viol. At the Revolution, his occupation at an end, he served in the army of Charles. After the defeat of the Royalists he found an asylum in the house of Sir Richard Bolles, who, in Simpson's own words, afforded him "a cheerful maintenance, when the Iniquity of the Times had reduced me (with many others in that common calamity) to a condition of needing it." He gives a sad account of the state of music : " That ͵innocent and now distressed muse, driven from her Sacred Habitations and forced to seek a livelihood in Streets and Taverns, where she is exposed and prostituted to all pro-phaneness, hath, in this her deplorable condition, found a chaste and cheerfull Sanctuary within your Wals." He was charged with the musical education of the son of his protector, who became the most skilful amateur of the day. For his pupil he composed a work entitled *The Division Violist ; or, An Introduction to the Playing upon a Ground*, which at that time was the fashionable way of showing the performer's skill. Second and third editions were subsequently brought out, which each contained a Latin translation in parallel columns.

Another very remarkable book was published about this time : *Mace's Musick's Monument ; or, A Remembrancer of the Best Practical Musick, Both Divine and Civil, that has ever been known to have been in the world.* The author was chapel clerk of Trinity College, Cambridge, but seems to have given up his post and settled in London to follow his favourite art. The book treats in the first part of music in churches, both parochial and cathedral. The second part gives instructions for playing the lute, with particular directions for executing repairs and keeping it in order, for which purpose he recommends it to be put during the daytime into a bed that is constantly used, between the rug and blanket! The third part contains a scheme for a music-room. But the mere statement of the contents gives a feeble notion of the book. The style is quaint in the highest degree, and must be read to be appreciated. So remarkable is it that Southey has made long extracts from it in his *Doctor*.

The tastes of Charles II. and his court sanctioned great freedom and licentiousness in the songs of the day, most of the collections of which have now to be kept on the most inaccessible shelves of the library. Among the greatest offenders was Tom d'Urfey, who was said to have been so good a companion that it was considered an honour to have been in his company. He was a great favourite of the King, who, according to the *Guardian*, would lean on his shoulder and hum tunes with him. His *Wit and Mirth ; or, Pills to purge Melancholy*, the well-known collection of his songs, is sufficiently rare and "curious" to have been thought worthy of reprinting in our own time. It is not surprising that this licentiousness should have had the effect of setting the faces of members of the religious world against music and its professors. A similar tendency in France brought forth a treatise "contre les Danses et les Mauvaises Chansons ;" here the Rev. Arthur Bedford, of Bristol, but subsequently chaplain of Aske's Hospital in Hoxton, published his *Great Abuse of Musick*, which he dedicated to

the Society for Promoting Christian Knowledge, then recently
founded.   Bedford was himself a great lover of music, and a
few years later brought out his *Temple Musick*, the object of
which was to prove that the cathedral service was directly
derived from that in use in the Temple at Jerusalem. Without
doubt his *Great Abuse* was called for, but the intense seriousness of it makes the book very amusing.

CHAPTER X.

THE RISE OF OPERA AND ORATORIO IN ENGLAND.

Early Attempts at English Opera—Celebrated Singers of that Time—Addison's Criticisms—Arrival of Handel in England—His Success in Opera—Story of his "Water Music"—Enters the Service of the Duke of Chandos—His First Oratorio, *Esther*—*Acis and Galatæa*—The "Royal Academy of Music"—Buononcini and Ariosti—The Singers Francesca Cuzzoni and Faustina Bordoni—Collapse of the Royal Academy of Music—The Beggar's Opera—Handel's Partnership with Heidegger and Resumption of Italian Opera—First Public Performances of Oratorio —Buononcini's Rival Opera—His Disgrace—Heidegger's Perfidy—Handel joins Rich—His Illness—Further Failure of Opera—Handel's Oratorios—*Saul*—*Israel in Egypt*—*The Messiah*—Its Success in Dublin—*Samson*—Dettingen *Te Deum*— *Belshazzar*—His Bankruptcy—*Judas Maccabæus*—*Joshua*—*Solomon*—His Blindness and Death.

IT has been seen that the music written for the stage in England was rather in the form of incidental music than of regular opera. Among the foreigners attracted to the English court was Cambert, the first to produce opera in France, whom the jealousy of Lully had succeeded in driving from his own country. Charles II. made him master of the second company of musicians, and, with the assistance of his countryman Grabu, his opera *Ariadne* was arranged for performance in English; but its success was small, and Cambert is supposed to have died of vexation at its failure. It has even been said that he

was murdered by assassins employed by Lully. For this im-
probable statement there is no evidence whatever; but that
it should have been made at all is a proof of the character for
vindictiveness which Lully had acquired.

The opera established itself in England very slowly.
Arsinoe, Queen of Cyprus, an opera then popular in Italy,
was translated and set to music by Thomas Clayton, a man
of feeble powers, and brought out at Drury Lane Theatre in
1705. This was followed by *Camilla*, which was translated
and adapted to the original music by Marc Antonio Buononcini,
brother of the more celebrated Giovanni Buononcini. These
works were afterwards diversified by the production of
Thomyris, Queen of Scythia, an opera of the same character.

The favourite female singers were Mrs. Mary Davis, Mrs.
Cibber, Mrs. Bracegirdle, and Mrs. Tofts, all Englishwomen;
but in 1692 an advertisement appeared in the *Gazette* announcing "the Italian lady that is lately come over that is
so famous for singing." This was the celebrated Margherita
de l'Epine, who, having acquired a fortune by her singing,
afterwards married Dr. Pepusch, of whom we shall have to
speak later. The rivalry between the admirers of Mrs. Tofts
and Mademoiselle de l'Epine divided the world of fashion
into two warlike camps, and even produced a disturbance in
the theatre.

Mrs. Tofts produced great effect in the character of
Camilla. While the piece was running there was a further
arrival on our shores of Italian singers. The result was that

they received engagements in *Camilla*, performing their own parts in Italian, while the English performers retained the use of their own language. " At length," says Addison in the *Spectator*, " the Audience grew tired of understanding Half the Opera ; and therefore, to ease themselves intirely of the Fatigue of thinking, have so ordered it at present that the whole Opera is performed in an unknown Tongue. We no longer understand the Language of our own Stage, insomuch that I have often been afraid. when I have seen our *Italian* Performers chattering in the Vehemence of Action, that they have been calling us Names, and abusing us among themselves ; but I hope, since we do put such an entire Confidence in them, they will not talk against us before our Faces, though they may do it with the same Safety as if it were behind our Backs."

There have been people unkind enough to affirm that the strong feeling which Addison shows against Italian opera was caused by his own want of success in writing for the lyric stage. He wrote the libretto for an opera entitled *Rosamund*, on the subject of Queen Eleanor and Fair Rosamund. It is admitted that the poem is pleasing enough, as might be expected from such a master of style ; but it was deficient in dramatic power, and the author confided the composition of the music to Clayton, who proved wholly unequal to the task, and the work was received with but little favour. It is only fair, however, to add that when, later, the poem was again set to music by Dr. Arne, the result was much the same ; we are thus justified in believing that Addison had miscalculated his powers, which, in spite of the success of his tragedy *Cato*, were not dramatic.

It must be admitted, however, that the opera, whether performed wholly in Italian, or in the ridiculous medley of Italian and English, was a very fair butt for the gentle satire which, in his own transparent style, he heaps upon it from time to time in the pages of the *Spectator*, and in these opinions he was joined by Steele in the *Tatler*. It was, in fact, a period of great dulness ; Henry Purcell, the hope of our English school of musicians, had been removed by an early death, and no composer had appeared of sufficient power to lift the opera above the position of a mere fashionable pastime.

But this reproach was to be removed. In 1711, being then in his twenty-seventh year, Handel first landed on these shores, bringing a great reputation with him. Thenceforth for many years the history of music in this country was the history of Handel's life. Great impatience was manifested to hear an opera from his pen, and he was at once engaged by Aaron Hill, director of the Haymarket Theatre (Her Majesty's Theatre of our day), to compose for him an opera on the episode of Rinaldo from Tasso's *Gerusalemme Liberata*, which was translated into English by Hill, and then re-translated into Italian by a poet named Rossi. The work was composed in a race against time between poet and musician, but Handel, always an impetuous composer, was an easy winner. The poor poet was left panting behind, with

no opportunity of polishing up his verses, so that he was
fain to crave the indulgence of the critics in the following

Fig. 117.—George Frederick Handel.

preface to his libretto :—" Indulgent reader, . . . Herr Handel,
the Orpheus of our time, hardly gave me time to write

15

while composing the music; and I saw with stupor an entire opera set to harmony with the highest degree of perfection in one fortnight. Let this hurried work therefore satisfy you, and, if not deserving of your praise, do not withhold at least your compassion, which indeed will be only justice to the limited time in which it was accomplished."

The new opera took the town by storm, and it was at once seen that a master had appeared. It was put on the stage with great magnificence. In the garden of Armida living birds flew from tree to tree, at which Addison does not fail to make merry. The work was indeed full of beauties — *Cara sposa, Augelletti che cantate, Il tricerbero umiliato*—the march—which were all new. Other numbers had been used in previous works, and among them was the most popular air of them all: *Lascia ch' io pianga*. The Italian opera of the day contained but little concerted music; in *Rinaldo* there are three duets only. The voices required were three sopranos, three altos, and one bass, which unite their forces at the end of the opera, forming the only chorus.

Walsh, who had then become the leading publisher, brought out a volume of songs from *Rinaldo*, by which he is reported to have cleared £1,500, inducing Handel to say that Walsh should write the next opera, and that he would sell it.

But his duties as Capellmeister called him to Hanover, from which place, however, he returned as soon as he could obtain leave of absence. In the meantime the directorship of the Opera had passed into the hands of McSwiney. Handel was at once prepared with a new work—*Il Pastor Fido*—which was produced in November, 1712. Its success was doubtful. *Teseo*, which was brought out in January, 1713, was more fortunate; but McSwiney, unable to meet his expenses, became bankrupt and absconded. The management now fell into the hands of Heidegger, whose ugliness was his greatest claim to celebrity.

The Peace of Utrecht was celebrated by a solemn service at St. Paul's in July, 1713. For this Handel was commanded to write a *Te Deum* and *Jubilate*. He seems to have taken for model Purcell's *Te Deum* with orchestra, but it is the first of his works in which he reveals his power of dealing with choral masses. Queen Anne was kept away by illness, but she conferred on the composer a life pension of £200 a year.

In the following year the Queen died, and the Elector, whose Capellmeister Handel was, came to England to be crowned as George I. Handel remembered, only too late, that he had long outstayed his leave of absence. The court were assiduous attendants at the Opera, *Rinaldo* was revived, *Amadigi* was produced, but the King took no notice of his erring Capellmeister. At last a good friend in the person of Count Kielmansegge interfered to put an end to the awkwardness of the situation. At a grand water-party attended by the court he engaged Handel to compose special music for the occasion. This was performed in a boat which followed the royal barge, Handel himself conducting it. The King was pleased with the music, which was new to him, and inquired who was the author. Kielmansegge informed the King, and apologized in Handel's name for his misconduct. The composer was once more taken into favour, and this was the origin of the celebrated Water Music. It is only right, however, to say that Handel's most recent biographer, Dr. Chrysander, throws some doubt on this story.

In July, 1716, Handel returned for a time to Hanover in the suite of his royal master, but early in the following year we find him again in England. The favourite *Rinaldo* was once more revived, to be followed by *Amadigi*. But this was the period of wild speculation consequent on the South Sea scheme, which engrossed popular attention, so that the opera languished, and indeed for a time came to a full stop.

At this crisis Handel was fortunate enough to meet with a patron of unexampled magnificence. The Duke of Chandos had just built for himself a palace at Cannons, near Edgware, at an enormous cost, in which he maintained an almost regal state, one of the manifestations of which was a private chapel, for the services in which he kept up a large choir, supported by a band of instruments. Of this magnificence the chapel is the only remaining evidence. No vestiges of the house are to be traced; but the chapel is now the parish church of Whitchurch. The Duke's first musical director was Dr. Pepusch, but in 1718 Handel was appointed in his place.

For performance in this chapel he composed a series of twelve anthems, written on a large scale, with instrumental accompaniments, all but one preceded by a regular overture, assuming, in fact, the proportions of a cantata.   In addition to these, he composed two separate settings of the *Te Deum*, also with instruments.

But his residence at Cannons had a still more important result.   At that place he wrote his first oratorio, *Esther*, which was produced there on the 20th of August, 1720.   The Duke was so delighted with the success of his musical director that he presented him with £1,000.   It cannot be doubted that in after-years Handel made great advances on his first attempt at this sort of composition, but it is a foretaste of the great works he was to give to us subsequently.   The overture was one of the most popular he ever wrote.

Still another form of composition owes its origin to this busy time.   At Cannons also he produced his pastoral, *Acis and Galatea*, one of those delightful works which surely can never grow old.   Who can forget the charming tenor air *Love in her eyes sits playing*, or Galatea's *Hush, ye pretty warbling choir* and *As when the dove*, or Polyphemus's recitative *I rage, I melt, I burn*, followed by the popular *O ruddier than the cherry?*   Nor are the choruses less delightful ; witness *O the pleasures of the plains*, *Wretched lovers*, *Happy we*, and *Galatea, dry thy tears*.   The words of this work were supplied by the poet Gay.

While at Cannons he also published his *Suite de Pièces*

pour le Clavecin, impelled to do so by the fact that un-
authorized persons were circulating incorrect copies.   The law
of copyright was unsettled in those days, and Handel was a
frequent sufferer from its uncertainty.   In this set of lessons
is the famous composition known as the *Harmonious Blacksmith*, although its author gave it no such title.

During Handel's sojourn at Cannons the public began to
feel the want of an opera in London, and several noblemen
and lovers of this form of entertainment united to raise a fund
to put the opera on a firm basis.   A capital of £50,000 was
raised, the King giving £1,000 a year and his consent that
the undertaking should be called "The Royal Academy of
Music."   A body of directors was to be chosen annually from
the contributors, but the virtual manager was Heidegger.
Handel, apparently with the consent of the Duke of Chandos,
was appointed composer, and was sent abroad to get together
a suitable company of singers, among whom was engaged the
famous Senesino.   The King's Theatre in the Haymarket was
opened on the 2nd of April, 1720, with an opera by Giovanni
Porta, entitled *Numitor*, which was only produced to give
time for the rehearsals of an opera by Handel.   After being
postponed by command, *Radamisto* was produced on the 27th
of April, amidst a scene of the greatest excitement.   The
struggle for places was so great that ladies were carried away
fainting, and their dresses torn to shreds.   Forty shillings
were in vain offered for tickets for the gallery, and this excitement was caused purely by a desire to hear the music, for the

great singers whom Handel had engaged had not arrived, as they were not yet free from their other engagements. The opera continued to be performed to crowded houses till the 30th of May, when D. Scarlatti's *Narciso* took its place. It was performed five nights, and a single performance of *Radamisto* and one of *Numitor* closed the season with great success.

With Handel as chief composer had been associated Giovanni Battista Buononcini and Attilio Ariosti. The latter, who had been a Dominican monk, but released from his vows by the Pope, was a respectable composer ; the former was something more than respectable. The new season opened with an opera by Buononcini : *Astarto*. The singers engaged by Handel had now arrived, and Senesino, Signora Durastanti and Broschi, with others, took part in it. The directors then announced that they were about to produce a work the joint production of the three composers. The libretto of an opera, *Muzio Scevola*, had been prepared by Paolo Rolli, the poet of the establishment; Ariosti undertook the first act, Buononcini the second, and Handel the third. To ensure fairness as far as possible, each act was to be preceded by an overture. It was an ill-judged scheme, and could not fail to produce unsatisfactory results, but it served to excite the curiosity of the public. Of course, Handel carried off the palm. Ariosti was a man of gentle character, but Buononcini was of a jealous disposition, and this feeling was fomented by his friends, causing the ill-starred rivalry to become the source of much subsequent bitterness.

During 1721 Handel definitely gave up his appointment
at Cannons, with the duties of which his operatic pursuits
must have greatly interfered. On the 9th of December he
brought out his *Floridante*. During the following season one
of Handel's most beautiful operas, *Ottone*, was produced for
the *début* of the eminent soprano Francesca Cuzzoni. She was
a woman of a difficult temper, and gave much trouble at
rehearsal, refusing to sing the beautiful air *Falsa immagine*.
Handel was the last man to brook treatment of this sort. He
addressed her thus : " I know, madam, that you are a very
she-devil ; but I will let you know that I am Beelzebub, the
prince of the devils ! " Thereupon he took her in his arms,
and swore he would throw her out of window. Finding her
master, she consented to sing the song, and achieved one of
her greatest triumphs in it.

Space does not suffice to give the details of all Handel's
operatic successes, which followed each other without a check.
We content ourselves with naming *Flavio, Giulio Cesare,
Tamerlano, Rodelinda,* and *Scipio,* the march in which is still
so popular as the parade march of the Grenadier Guards, in
which regiment there is a tradition that it was originally
written for them and afterwards introduced into *Scipio*.

This brings us to the season of 1726. Although outside
speculators had made large sums by trafficking in tickets, the
direction of the Royal Academy had never succeeded in making
both ends meet, in spite of the fact that the house was
always full. This being the case, it seems remarkable that

they should have added largely to their working expenses, and still more to their difficulties, by engaging another soprano of the first rank in addition to Cuzzoni. This course, however, they adopted by the engagement of Signora Faustina Bordoni, afterwards, as we have already related, the wife of the composer Hasse. The new-comer was a woman who possessed great beauty and charm of manner, in addition to a voice clear, sweet, and flexible. As to vocal acquirements Cuzzoni seems to have been her equal, but she was far from beautiful, and did not atone for this deficiency by any charm of manner. To give a notion of the terms which in those days were thought liberal for singers of the first rank, it may be mentioned that each of these ladies received £2,000 per annum. It needs but a slight acquaintance with artistic susceptibility to form a judgment of the difficulties the directors were creating for themselves. When *débutantes*, these rivals had sung in the same piece at Venice, and Handel determined that they should do so again. With this view he composed the opera *Alessandro*, in which neither singer was favoured at the expense of the other. The peculiar style of each was carefully studied. Each in turn had an air which brought out the full beauty of her voice and manner. Each had a duet with Senesino, and in the duet which they sang together the parts were so carefully balanced that neither could claim a victory. Exhibitions of this sort are exhilarating to the audience, but bad blood is engendered, with the result that the public become partisans. The rivalry was continued

in *Admeto*, produced on January 31st, 1727, in which the two
queens of song were persuaded once more to unite their powers.
But Handel, with all his energy, was unable to keep the peace.
The admirers of the respective singers waxed uproarious, and
from the free use of the legitimate means of showing their
opinions proceeded to introduce cat-calls and other noisy
methods of enforcing their views, the presence of royalty in
the person of the Princess of Wales acting as no restraint.
" The town " was divided into two hostile camps, and the season
was brought to an abrupt close, amid the lampoons and caricatures
of the wits of the day.

Handel had been naturalized in 1726 as a preliminary
to receiving the appointment of "Composer of Musick to the
Chapel Royal," which could only be held by an Englishman;
and he was also nominated composer to the court. In this
capacity he was called on to compose the anthem for the
coronation of George II. He interpreted his commission so
liberally that he wrote four—*Zadok the Priest, Let thy hand
be strengthened, The king shall rejoice,* and *My heart is
inditing*—and they were all performed on the occasion.

In October, 1727, peace had been sufficiently patched up
between Cuzzoni and Faustina to allow of their united appearance
in *Ricciardo Primo* and *Siroe*. But the disgraceful scenes of
the last season began to produce their natural results. The
more respectable part of the audience stayed away, although
the new works presented real attractions. Handel was not to
be daunted, but produced his *Tolomeo* in April to diminishing

audiences, when an overwhelming attraction elsewhere proved too powerful. The season came to an end. A meeting of the directors was held to consider their position. It appeared that the whole of the £50,000 originally subscribed had been lost in the lavish expenditure of the management ; and, in face of so serious a state of affairs, it was decided to abandon the enterprise.

The superior attraction of which we have spoken was the celebrated *Beggar's Opera*, which was produced at Lincoln's Inn Fields in January, 1728. It is said to owe its origin to a remark of Swift to Gay that "a Newgate pastoral might make an odd, pretty kind of thing." Gay acted on the hint. The opera professed to hold up to reprobation highwaymen, thieves, and their associates ; but under a thin disguise Walpole and other prominent characters in the world of politics, as well as the frivolities of fashionable life, were satirized. Its success was complete. The upper classes enjoyed the satire ; the people were content to look no deeper than the surface of the story. Although professing to have a moral purpose, it really exalted highwaymen into heroes. None of the music was original. It consisted principally of English and Scotch ballads, many of great beauty, selected and arranged by Dr. Pepusch. Even Handel was laid under contribution, his march in *Rinaldo* being set to the words *Let us take the road.* The fickle public, which had been wrangling over the respective merits of Cuzzoni and Faustina, deserted in a body to the new attraction. Walker, the original Macheath, was so courted by

the young men of fashion that he fell into habits of
dissipation, which shortened his days. The original Polly
Peachum was Miss Lavinia Fenton, who so captivated the
Duke of Bolton in the part that he ran away with and subsequently married her.

The Academy at an end, Handel was without occupation.
But his energy was enormous. He at once entered into
partnership for three years with Heidegger, and made a journey
to Italy to get together a company in order to resume the
performance of Italian opera. Among those he engaged was
Signora Anna Strada, an excellent soprano, who was always
a favourite with him. The theatre opened with *Lotario* in
December, 1729, which was handed to the copyist, rehearsed,
and produced in the short space of a fortnight. Strada had
no pretensions to beauty—in fact, she was commonly called
" *the Pig*"—and thus at first made but little way with the public ;
but she had much capability and willingness, and developed
into an excellent artist.

Partenope followed, but the public gave but a lukewarm
support to the undertaking. To revive the interest, Senesino
was engaged, for whom *Scipio* was remounted. *Poro*, *Ezio*,
Orlando, succeeded, but the fortunes of the house did not
revive.

The success of the *Beggar's Opera* had awakened interest
once more in works set to English words. Strange to say,
it occurred to Rich to produce at Lincoln's Inn Handel's *Acis
and Galatea*. It was a wretched performance ; but the same

work was given by Arne, father of Dr. Arne, with English
singers, the soprano being Miss Arne (afterwards Mrs.
Cibber), at the "Little Theatre" in the Haymarket, which had not
been long opened. These performances seem to have struck
Handel as worthy of imitation, and on June 10th, 1732, he
also gave *Acis*, made up of his English composition of that
name and partly of an earlier work which he wrote at
Naples: *Aci, Galatea, e Polifemo*. It was performed by a
mixed company of Italian and English singers, each using his
or her own language, with scenery and dresses, but without
action.   Shortly afterwards *Esther* was performed in the concert-room in York Buildings, Villars Street, by Bernard Gates,
Master of the Children of the Chapel Royal. It then occurred
to Handel that he also might participate in its success, and
he therefore brought out a revised version of *Esther* at the
King's Theatre on the 2nd of May, 1732. The advertisement announced, "There will be no acting on the stage, but
the house will be fitted up in a decent manner for the
audience." The singers were all Italian, Strada and Senesino
both appearing, and they sang their parts in Italian.

The success of the performance so greatly surpassed expectation, that he was persuaded to renew the attempt, and in March of
the following year he brought out his *Deborah*. Several numbers
were adaptations from his previous works, while some of the
choruses were double.   Handel and Heidegger, with whom
he was still in partnership, were ill-advised enough to raise
the prices, which caused great dissatisfaction; but, apart from

the ill-feeling thus raised, the work was only moderately successful.

In the meantime the operatic efforts of the partners had been far from flourishing. The season of 1732 opened with an opera by Leonardo Leo—*Catone*—and in January, 1733, *Orlando*, by Handel, was produced. This opera contains the last song which Handel wrote for Senesino, who was a man of a scheming disposition. Although receiving an enormous salary, he probably found Handel rather a hard taskmaster. Buononcini, Handel's old rival, had lost no opportunity of making powerful friends, among whom he found a warm patroness in the person of Lady Henrietta Churchill, daughter of the famous Duke of Marlborough. She had married Earl Godolphin, but on the death of her father, without male issue, the title descended to her, and she became Duchess of Marlborough. She manifested the greatest interest in Buononcini, took him into her house in the Stable Yard, St. James's Palace, and settled on him a pension of £500 a year. When differences arose between Senesino and Handel, she and other partisans started a scheme for the establishment of a new opera at the theatre in Lincoln's Inn Fields, and they succeeded in wiling away all Handel's best singers, with the exception of Strada, who was faithful to the master to whom she owed so much. The assistance of Cuzzoni was also obtained, and Porpora was engaged to conduct the performances.

As far as the personal triumph of Buononcini was concerned, it was of short duration. Some three years previously he had produced as his own a madrigal entitled *La Vita Caduca;* just at this time a printed volume of music, by the well-known Antonio Lotti, was received in this country, and in it occurred the madrigal *La Vita Caduca.* The music as well as the words, beginning *In una siepe ombrosa*, were identical with the composition brought forward by Buononcini, who asserted in such a positive manner his ownership of the composition that the "Academy of Ancient Musick" entered into correspondence with Lotti. The latter produced ample testimony on oath, by a number of gentlemen by whom he was well known, that the music was written by him in the year 1705. The evidence was complete, and Buononcini's misconduct was triumphantly proved. A pamphlet was drawn up embodying the facts, with the result that Buononcini left this country, never to return. He quitted England in company with an adventurer who had persuaded him that he possessed the secret of the philosopher's stone. The spell was of short duration, and he had to revert to music for a living, dying at last at Venice, at an advanced age, in a state of destitution.

The rival opera, arrogating to itself the name of the "Opera of the Nobility," opened its first season at Lincoln's Inn on the 29th of December, 1733, with an opera on the subject of Ariadne, composed for the occasion and conducted by Porpora. Handel had been beforehand, opening on the 30th of October, with no great attraction. But he was the last man to fold his hands under the pressure of difficulties, and on the 4th of December he was prepared with an artist who was in every way competent to take the place of Senesino. This was Giovanni Carestini, who, after a preliminary appearance in a pasticcio, made a great effect in a new opera by Handel on the same subject as Porpora's. But Handel's troubles were only beginning. His partnership with Heidegger terminated on July 6th, 1734, and the latter was actually mean enough to let the King's Theatre to the rival undertaking. On the 5th of the following October, Handel, in partnership with Rich, opened the Lincoln's Inn Fields Theatre with a reproduction of *Arianna ;* on the 29th their opponents opened their season at the King's Theatre with Hasse's *Artaserse.* In addition to the talent already at their command, they had secured the services of the most renowned artificial soprano in Europe : Carlo Broschi, better known as Farinelli.

The odds against Handel were terrible, but he was one of those who do not know when they are beaten. The new theatre of Covent Garden, which also was the property of Rich, was just completed, and to it Handel removed in December. His energy was enormous. Old works were resumed, new ones written and mounted. In this way *Ariodante* and *Alcina* were produced. During Lent performances of oratorio were given. But his efforts were unavailing. Farinelli had monopolized the popular ear. The royal family remained faithful to Handel, but the public stayed away so completely that at one of the oratorios Lord Chesterfield left at the beginning, explaining that he felt it best to do so " lest he should disturb the King in his privacies."

Handel was on the verge of bankruptcy, and at this crisis Carestini, annoyed by the popularity of Farinelli, abandoned the master. His fertility continued, and in 1736-7 *Atalanta*, *Giustinio*, *Arminio*, and *Berenice* were put on the stage. In the meantime he had filled up the vacancy caused by Carestini's defection by the engagement of a young soprano, Gioacchino Conti, better known as Gizziello.

With this weight of trouble on his shoulders, he found time to write *Alexander's Feast*, to Dryden's well-known words, which he produced at Covent Garden on the 19th of February, 1736. To this period also belong his organ concertos, in which he delighted the public by playing the organ part himself. In June, 1737, the opposition opera scheme broke down, the death-blow being given by the secession of Farinelli. Its supporters had lost £12,000, and the speculation collapsed completely. Handel's losses were but little less serious. He kept his theatre open for a fortnight longer than his rivals, but the savings of an honourable life—about £10,000 — had disappeared, and he was obliged to give his creditors bills for part of their claims ; it is pleasant to be able to add that these bills were all honourably paid. The only objection to this arrangement proceeded from the husband of Signora Strada, but a benefit arranged by his friends enabled him to surmount it.

There arrives a time, however, when the strongest will and the most vigorous constitution give way. The constant anxiety was beginning to tell both on his body and on his mind. A stroke of paralysis deprived him of the use of his right side.

16

His temper, always easily roused, became ungovernable, but this irritability was varied by fits of torpor, from which he could with difficulty be roused. By the advice of his physicians, he went for a time to Aix-la-Chapelle, where, by a 'heroic per_ sistence in the use of vapour baths, he was once more restored to health.

On his return to London he found that Heidegger had once more opened the King's Theatre with opera. The manager made him the offer of £1,000 for two operas, and he at once set to work on the score of *Faramondo*. The work was interrupted by the death of his staunch supporter Queen Caroline. For her funeral he composed the beautiful anthem *The ways of Zion do mourn*—a worthy tribute of his gratitude. *Faramondo* was followed by four other operas, one of which was a pasticcio. The last was *Deidamia*, in 1740. Heidegger's renewed attempt proved no more successful than its predecessors, and Handel bade a final farewell to a form of composition in the advancement of which he had struggled so manfully and suffered so deeply.

He was now fifty-four years of age, and one is tempted to say that he was only just discovering his true powers. Fine as his operas are, they belong to a style of art which can never be revived. Certain extracts will no doubt continue to delight the musician, but they alone would have been insufficient to place their composer on the pinnacle of fame which he occupies. This position he claims in virtue of that grand series of oratorios which he was now to produce. We have seen that he had already brought out a few such works during his operatic management ; and while Heidegger's last ill-starred attempt was in progress on the feast of that saint (November 22nd), the. ode for St. Cecilia's Day was performed, with *Alexander's Feast*. The " ode " contains three magnificent choruses : *The trumpet's loud clangour, As from the power*, and *The dead shall live*. This was followed by *L' Allegro, Il Penseroso, ed il Moderato*, with the favourite *Oft on a plat, Sweet bird*, accompanied by the flute, and the air and chorus *Haste thee, nymph*, which still retain their charm when performed at a Handel festival. But now began the great series of oratorios. In January, 1739, he took the Opera House for a series of twelve weekly performances of oratorio. He had composed two new oratorios as yet unproduced. *Saul* had occupied him two months and three days ; *Israel in Egypt* was written between the 1st and the 28th of October! *Saul* was the first brought out, with very moderate success, although such a chorus as *Envy, eldest-born of Hell*, and the Dead March should have secured it. *Israel* too was received with coldness. No doubt the succession of choruses was found monotonous, for at the second performance it was announced that "the oratorio will be shortened and intermixed with songs." " Intermixed with songs " it remained for many a long day, and it was only in our own time that it was performed as the composer originally intended. Surely *Israel*, with its magnificent series of double choruses, is one of the most stupendous monuments of choral writing that the world has seen!

This colossal work was followed by one which the universal consent of mankind has considered one of the greatest of

musical compositions : his immortal *Messiah*. Handel had been
invited to visit Dublin by the Duke of Devonshire, then Lord
Lieutenant.   Three charitable societies—one for the relief of
imprisoned debtors, Mercer's Hospital, and the Charitable
Infirmary—had united in requesting him to write a work to be
performed on behalf of their funds.   He looked on the idea
with favour, especially as an excellent violinist, Matthew Dubourg,
who was a friend of his, had settled in Dublin and would
superintend the necessary musical arrangements.   During the
late summer of 1741, he set to work on the *Messiah*, the oratorio
destined for this purpose.   His friend Mr. Charles Jennens
made the selection of the words, which were all from the
Holy Scriptures, and, it must be added, with judgment.   He
began the composition on the 22nd of August.   By the 14th
of September the whole work was completed—that is, in twenty-
four days !   His practice was most methodical, always writing
in the date of the beginning and end of each act or part ; and
as an excellent facsimile of the original score is readily obtainable
those who are interested can almost, as it were, see him at
work.

The Charitable Musical Society of Dublin had recently
opened an excellent music-room, and in it Handel's performances took place.   The *Messiah* was not produced till
April 13th, 1742.   The advertisements announcing the
performance wind up with an appeal to the ladies "not to
come with hoops this day," and the gentlemen are desired
to come without their swords.   The occasion was evidently

looked on as important ; the work produced abundantly
justified the opinion. Handel and the whole of his singers
gave their services, the room was crowded, and a sum
approaching £400 was available for the purposes of the
charities. The oratorio at once took hold of the public, and
it has never since lost it. One person alone was not satisfied.
This was the compiler of the words. He informs a friend
that he will show him "a collection I gave Handel, called
Messiah, which I value highly. He has made a fine entertainment of it, though not near so good as he might and
ought to have done." We will not insult our readers by
supposing that they do not know every note of this immortal
work—the "sacred oratorio," as Handel always termed it.
One of the greatest testimonies to the power of music is
the fact that at the first performance of the work in London
the whole audience, with George II. at its head, rose with
one consent at the Hallelujah Chorus, and the custom survives
to the present day.

The work having been originally devoted to the purposes
of charity, Handel appears to have considered such a destination of it to have had some claim on him, for after the
year 1750 he performed it annually, sometimes more than
once, for the benefit of the Foundling Hospital, to which
institution he bequeathed copies of the score and parts. For
some such sacred purpose it has on numberless occasions
been performed since his death ; certainly no other work can
have produced so large a result in the cause of charity.

Eight days after the completion of the score of the *Messiah*, Handel was at work at *Samson*, the words of which had been arranged for him by Newburgh Hamilton from Milton's *Samson Agonistes*. It contains, among others, the well-known choruses *Then round about the starry throne, Fixed in His everlasting seat,* and *Let their celestial concerts all unite*. The solos are equally fine, for they comprise the broad contralto song *Return, O God of hosts, Total eclipse,* one of his most pathetic airs, and the brilliant *Let the bright seraphim,* with trumpet obligato, which is so effective that it is taken up by many sopranos not otherwise Handelian in their predilections.

Handel's stay in Dublin was extended to nine months. While absent his importance had become more completely recognized, and his return was welcomed. Both *Samson* and the *Messiah* were performed, and in 1743 he wrote his well-known *Te Deum* to celebrate the battle of Dettingen. This was followed by *Belshazzar*. He announced a series of twenty-four oratorios, but the attendance was so small that the scheme collapsed at the sixteenth. He had no reserve of capital to fall back upon, and he again became bankrupt. An interval now occurs in his activity, but in the year 1746 he reappeared with the *Occasional Oratorio*, which was partly a pasticcio. The overture is still a favourite.

Handel now looked more to the general public for support, and abandoned having a subscription. His next work, *Judas Maccabæus*, was fortunate in hitting popular taste, and proved remunerative.   It still remains one of his most popular oratorios.   This was followed by *Alexander Balus* and *Joshua*, and in 1748 by *Solomon* and *Susanna*. *Solomon* is one of his finest works, and is distinguished by its double choruses, which compare even with those in *Israel*. *From the censer curling rise* and the series beginning *May no rash intruder* require only to be mentioned.

In March, 1749, appeared *Theodora*. The work was a favourite with the author, but the song *Angels ever bright and fair* alone keeps its place. *Jephtha*, his last oratorio, came out in February, 1752.   This contains the recitative *Deeper and deeper still* and the song *Waft her, angels*, which have been associated with the names of our great English tenors Braham and Mr. Sims Reeves.   But a sad affliction was attacking him,—strange to say, the same from which his contemporary Bach was also suffering.   He was losing his sight. Three times he was operated on without success, and he became totally blind. His spirits gave way for a time, but his marvellous energy reasserted itself, and he was still able to preside at the organ in the performance of his works. A touching story is told that at such a performance of *Samson*, Beard, his favourite tenor, had been singing with great feeling the song—

> "Total eclipse ! no sun, no moon ;
> All dark amid the blaze of noon !"

the sadness of the old master's fate impressed the hearers so powerfully that many were affected to tears. After a few years his strength visibly failed. On April 6th, 1759, he directed a performance of his masterpiece, the *Messiah*. He returned home to take to his bed, expiring near midnight of Good Friday, April 13th, which was the anniversary of the first performance of the *Messiah* in Dublin. He was buried in Westminster Abbey. During his last years fortune had been kinder to him. He had honourably paid off all his liabilities, and had acquired a fortune amounting to £20,000.

CHAPTER XI.

FURTHER HISTORY OF MUSIC IN ENGLAND.

Dr. Arne—Lampe's *Dragon of Wantley*—Henry Carey—Thomas Britton, "the Musical Small-coal Man"—Ballad Operas—Charles Dibdin—Early Concerts—Foundation of the "Concert of Antient Musick"—Cultivation of Part-singing—Catches—Samuel Webbe and the Glee-writers—The Catch Club and its Secretary, E. T. Warren Hall—The Histories of Burney and Hawkins—Visit of Mozart to England.

THE death of Handel left a great void in the musical life of England. The most prominent musician was Dr. Arne, a writer with a distinct and charming vein of melody, which, to do English composers justice, is a merit they have generally possessed. Arne was the son of a prosperous cabinet-maker in King Street, Covent Garden, and, like Handel, was destined by his father for the law. Indeed, their early histories have much in common, for the youthful Arne was also compelled to practise secretly on a muffled spinet in a garret. One night his father, being a guest at an entertainment given by a friend, found, to his surprise, his son installed as conductor of the music, and he was at last compelled to acknowledge the uselessness of opposing so strong a predilection. Arne composed a couple of oratorios, but in these he had to contend with a giant, and they have been long forgotten. As a writer of operas he had great success. He composed about thirty, the best-known

of which was *Artaxerxes*, now out of date, although for many
years it enjoyed great popularity, the overture forming one of the
stock pieces of our grandmothers.   *Water parted from the sea,
Where the bee sucks, Blow, thou wintry wind, Under the greenwood tree, The soldier tired,* even now keep their hold on the
popular taste, while *Rule Britannia* will last as long as the
English nation. His wife was the greatest English singer of
the time. As Miss Cecilia Young she had been the pupil of
Geminiani, from whom she had received an excellent training.

A sister of Mrs. Arne's married J. F. Lampe, a German
musician settled in this country, who acquired great celebrity
by the composition of an opera called *The Dragon of Wantley*.
The libretto was by Henry Carey, and both it and the music
were written in avowed burlesque of the Italian opera, and
this was carried out with evident enjoyment by both poet and
musician, their aim being to "display in English the beauties
of nonsense so prevailing in the Italian operas." It is not
surprising, therefore, that the work had enormous success, and
the satire is so admirably carried out that it richly deserved it.
Henry Carey, who has just been spoken of as writer of the
words, was also a musician of some ability. Much obscurity
rests on his life ; it is supposed that he was a natural son
of George Savile, Marquis of Halifax. He composed the music
of many songs introduced into the theatrical pieces of the day ;
these he subsequently collected in a publication called the
Musical Century. Among them is the charming air *Sally in
our alley*. He was one of those popular men of pleasure who

are always behindhand with the world, and at last his circumstances became so desperate that he destroyed himself. The composition of our National Anthem has been claimed for him, apparently on insufficient grounds.

Fig. 118.—Dr. Arne, from a sketch by Bartolozzi.

An account of music in England during the eighteenth century would be incomplete without mention of Thomas Britton, the "musical small-coal man," who was indeed a power in the musical world. He carried on his business in Aylesbury Street, Clerkenwell, in a sort of stable, and was to be seen struggling about the neighbourhood daily under the weight of sacks of coal. The loft of his stable he had fitted up as a sort of concert-room, which was resorted to weekly, not only by the most eminent musicians of the day, including Handel himself, but also by many members of the nobility, who paid a yearly subscription of ten shillings. He had acquired an excellent knowledge of music, and had collected a considerable musical library. His end was as curious as his life. A gentleman who was in the habit of attending his concerts one evening brought with him a ventriloquist, who in joke foretold his approaching death. The poor man was so alarmed by what he took for a supernatural announcement that in a few days he died.

Italian opera had been no more than a fashionable amusement in England, and after the death of Handel no original works of the kind were produced in England. Those which met with success abroad were brought over, and English gold secured a succession of the most eminent performers to support them. Composers of celebrity were sometimes induced to visit this country to superintend the production of their works. Thus Gluck visited England in 1745. Unfortunately the Rebellion had just broken out, and the Lord Chancellor shut up the Opera House, but was persuaded to open it again for Gluck's *Caduta de' Giganti*, a piece specially written in honour of the Duke of Cumberland, who had subdued the rebels. Still later—in 1784—Cherubini came for a similar purpose. His death did not take place till 1842, and his widow survived till 1864! Arne's *Artaxerxes* 'was an attempt at writing an opera in English on the Italian plan; that is, the whole action was carried on in music, no spoken words being used. This plan, however, was soon abandoned in favour of ballad operas, in which the musical pieces were connected by *spoken* dialogue. These were produced by a succession of facile composers, who aimed rather at immediate success than at lasting reputation : Linley, whose *Duenna* had a most remarkable success—the words were by R. B. Sheridan, who had married Linley's beautiful and accomplished daughter,— Dibdin, Shield, and lastly Storace. The latter was the son of an Italian musician settled in England. With his sister, who became a famous dramatic singer, he was sent abroad to complete his musical education ; during this time they made the acquaintance of Mozart, who esteemed them both. He wrote fifteen or sixteen operas, among which are *The Haunted Tower*, *The Siege of Belgrade*, and, perhaps the most popular of all, *The Iron Chest*. He was ill during the preparation of the last work, but insisted on being conveyed to the theatre in blankets to superintend the final rehearsals. He thus caught cold and died at the age of thirty-three, cutting short a career of great promise. The quartet *Five times by the taper's light* is still familiar.

Charles Dibdin, whose name we have mentioned, became still more celebrated as a writer of sea songs, the spirit and patriotic feeling of which did much to inspire the bravery of our sailors during the great war. He knew how to be rollicking and how to show real feeling ; take for example the familiar *Jolly Young Waterman* and the beautiful and pathetic *Tom Bowling.*

Till the oratorio performances were started by Handel the general public had but few chances of hearing music of a high character; in fact, it was not until the present century that concerts to which the public could obtain admission by payment became general. The first series of concerts on record in England were given by John Banister, a violinist, in his house in Whitefriars. These went on from 1672 to 1678, and the admission was one shilling. This attempt was followed up by Britton, the "small-coal man," of whom we have already spoken. In 1710 a number of noblemen and gentlemen organized a scheme on a broader scale under the title of the Academy of Antient Musick, which was spirited enough to give commissions for the composition of new works, Astorga's *Stabat Mater* having been written for the Society. It does not appear, however, to have received adequate support, in spite of a pamphlet appealing to the public, which ended with the words " Esto perpetua !" and in the year 1776 a new society, under a very similar title—namely, the " Concert of Antient Musick "—was founded. To this Society there can be no doubt that the art was greatly indebted, as it served to perpetuate the traditions of performance of many great works, especially those of Handel, which for some years formed the principal material of their programmes. The Society was exclusively aristocratic. To be a member it was necessary to be

" in society ;" even to be introduced as a visitor at a concert
the name had to be submitted to the directors. One of the
rules provided that no work composed within twenty years
could be performed. It may be possible to be too much
carried away by novelty, but a rule of this character was
obviously absurd in a society whose object was to further
art. The noblemen and gentlemen who formed the body of
directors took it in turn to select the programme, and on
their " night " entertained their brother-directors as well as
the conductor at dinner before the concert, and this duty
kings and royal dukes performed in their turn. The first
professional conductor was Joah Bates, and on his death he
was succeeded in 1779 by Greatorex. The concerts were up
to 1795 held in the " New Rooms, Tottenham Street," on the
site which in our days became well known as that of the
Prince of Wales's Theatre, after that in the concert-room
of the Opera House, and in 1804 they were moved to the
Hanover Square Rooms, which · had been constructed by Sir
John Gallini, a well-known teacher of dancing. Considering
that the management was amateur and the expenditure lavish,
it is wonderful that the Society continued its work so long.
Its existence was continued till the year 1848, but for some
time it had been carried on with difficulty ; its exclusiveness
was no longer in accordance with the spirit of the times ;
and other societies—notably the Sacred Harmonic Society—had
arisen which were able to perform complete oratorios on a
more fitting scale. One of its good actions is still continued.

Michael Festing, an esteemed violinist of the last century, having had a case of distress in the family of a professor of music brought under his notice, was instrumental in founding the Royal Society of Musicians, for the benefit of decayed musicians and their families. To support this Society the "Ancient Concerts" were in the habit of giving annually a performance of the *Messiah*, at which all gave their services gratis, as stipulated in the performers' engagement for the season. This performance is still kept up for the benefit of a most deserving institution.

The fondness for part-singing had never quite died out in England. The Madrigalian Era, extending from 1588 to the time of the Revolution, was, as we have seen, the golden age of the English school of composition. The love of "social harmony" after the Restoration had been mostly kept alive by means of the "catch," a species of composition consisting of a canon or round for three or four voices, generally so arranged that when sung, the words, by the union of the different voices, acquired a different meaning from that apparent on a simple perusal of them. To quote a familiar example in explanation, the well-known one by Callcott—

> "Ah ! how, Sophia, could you leave
> Your lover, and of hope bereave ?
> Go fetch the Indian's borrowed plume," etc.,

where in performance *Ah ! how, Sophia*, sounds like *Our house on fire*, and *Go fetch the Indian's* like *Go fetch the engines*. It may seem a feeble joke, but the contrivance called forth much musical ability and humour, seldom, it is to be regretted, of so innocent a nature as the one we have quoted. The popularity of such compositions was unbounded in an age which was characterized by no great delicacy of feeling. Many clubs were founded for their performance, and many collections of them were published. Out of evil, however, came good, and this was the invention of the "glee," a kind of composition which has been confined exclusively to this country, and which has called forth a large amount of musical genius. A glee may be defined as a composition for three or more voices in harmony, each voice, however, having a separate melody of its own, the lower parts not simply forming an accompaniment, as in a part-song. It comprises two movements at least, which are contrasted in character, and is performed with one voice only to a part, whereas the madrigal required several. In some of Playford's publications the term "glee" is attached to certain compositions, but the form was not settled till later. The merit of doing this is mainly to be attributed to Samuel Webbe, a man of very remarkable talents, which were shown in many ways. He was born of English parents in a fair position of life in the island of Minorca in the year 1740. While an infant his father died, leaving his mother in straitened circumstances. She returned to London with her child, and at an early age he was apprenticed to a cabinet-maker. He found opportunities, however, of improving his education, and became eventually an excellent linguist. Chafing at the restraints of a mechanical pursuit, he soon abandoned business, and managed

17

to earn a precarious livelihood by copying music, gradually acquiring at the same time an excellent knowledge of the art.

Among the clubs founded for the performance of vocal music was the " Noblemen and Gentlemen's Catch Club." It first met in 1761, having the support of several members of the nobility, and soon grew into a very fashionable and flourishing institution, most of the royal family becoming members of it. The members consisted of amateur and professional, and the latter comprised all the leading singers of the time.

From the performance of vocal compositions it was a natural step to the offering of prizes for new works. As early as 1763 the Club offered prizes for the two best catches, the two best canons, and the two best glees. The name of Webbe soon appears among those carrying off prizes, for catches as well as for glees, those for the latter with such compositions as *Discord, dire sister*, and *The Mighty Conqueror*. His masterpiece, *When winds breathe soft*, was sent in for competition in 1784, and it is incomprehensible that so noble a composition should not have received a prize. The work is a masterpiece; in the space of a few pages is depicted the gradual rising of the calm sea to a gale which "splits the sturdy mast," "when in an instant He Who rules the floods bids the waters and the winds be still." Nothing can exceed its dramatic power, and the musician who produced it deserves a prominent niche in the temple of fame.

If no other writer of glees was the equal of Samuel

Webbe in genius, many excellent compositions of this character were produced, and there was no lack of competitors for the prizes which the Club continued to offer. Among these must be mentioned Atterbury, Dr. Alcock, Bellamy, Danby, Lord Mornington, father of the Duke of Wellington, Dr. Cooke, the Paxtons, and John Stafford Smith, whose *Blest pair of sirens, While fools their time,* and *Return, blest days,* deserve their popularity. Stafford Smith has also claims on our gratitude as a musical antiquarian, in which capacity, in addition to affording Sir John Hawkins much assistance in his *History of Music,* he also published a well-known collection of ancient music under the title of *Musica Antiqua.* To these succeeded Reginald Spofforth, R. J. S. Stevens, and Dr. Callcott, the last of whom was the cause of an alteration in the rules of the Club, for in 1787 he sent in one hundred compositions in competition! The members decided that in future three compositions of each kind only should be accepted.

The first secretary of the Catch Club was E. T. Warren, who subsequently added the name of Horne to his patronymic. He was a man of indefatigable industry, for he copied out with his own hands the whole of the compositions sent in for competition, forming a vast collection, filling thirty-two volumes in oblong folio, which, after having formed part of several libraries, among others that of the late Mr. Greatorex, have now found a resting-place in that of the writer's brother. This vast series is of great interest as a means of tracing the history of the subject. But little more than a quarter of the works,

which amount to 2,269, have been printed. Many of those
which have been printed first saw the light in Warren's well-
known published collection—a work which at one time commanded a large price, copies having fetched at auction as much
as forty pounds. But the interest in this kind of composition
is now restricted to a few amateurs only, and a greater refine-
ment in taste renders the work not altogether a desirable
possession; it has thus happened that within the last few
years a copy in the choicest condition has been sold for fewer
shillings than it formerly fetched pounds.

To this country belongs the honour of producing the first
History of Music on a scale and completeness at all adequate
to the importance of the subject. A work of the same
nature had been projected by the eminent Padre Martini, but
it was planned on such large dimensions that time was not
vouchsafed to the author to complete more than the third
volume, which brought his history down to the destruction of
the Temple at Jerusalem. Strange to say, two Englishmen
attempted the task simultaneously, both of them being members
of THE club so well known to readers of Boswell. Of these
writers, one was a professor of position, Dr. Burney; the
other was an amateur, Sir John Hawkins, whose work has
achieved the greater success of being reprinted in our own
time. Both works will be found deficient viewed in the light
of the more critical knowledge of our own day, but to both,
subsequent writers on musical history have been greatly
indebted.

In the spring of the year 1764 the elder Mozart arrived in England, bringing with him his marvellous girl and boy.

Fig. 119.—Leopold Mozart, his daughter Marianne, aged eleven years, and his son J. G. Wolfgang Amadeus, aged seven years (engraved by Lafosse after Carmontelle, 1764).

The effect they produced was prodigious. So much interest was shown in their performance that the Hon. Daines

Barrington drew up a paper, which was read at the Royal Society, on the marvellous powers of the boy, who was then eight years of age, a fact which Barrington took the trouble to have verified by a certificate of his birth. The child's charm of manner, in addition to his precocious ability, won all hearts, and the visit to England was most successful. It is pleasant to read of his sitting at the harpsichord between the knees of J. C. Bach, who was then the Queen's music-master, each in turn playing a few bars of a sonata, as if by one pair of hands, and also to know that most of the English musicians who formed the orchestra at his concert would take no remuneration. Unfortunately the visit of the youthful master was never repeated at the time when his powers had arrived at maturity.

CHAPTER XII.

MUSIC IN FRANCE DURING THE EIGHTEENTH CENTURY.

Rameau as a Theorist and Composer—The "Théâtre de la Foire"—*La Serva Padrona* of Pergolesi in Paris and the "Guerre des Bouffons"—J. J. Rousseau—His Dictionary —Gossec—Monsigny—Gluck in Paris—Piccinni—Grétry—The Philidors—Foundation of the "Concerts Spirituels"—Instrumental Composers—Leclair—Couperin— The Ballet.

So far as we have as yet traced the history of music in France, that nation had produced no musician of the first rank. To Lully must be conceded the possession of genius, but he was French by naturalization only : his talent was essentially Italian, and the lustre which he without doubt shed on the French lyric stage redounded to the credit of that nation only to the extent of showing its power of appreciating excellence when brought under its notice. The successors of Lully, of whom we have spoken, made no advance on the model which he had set before them, and they have long been forgotten.

This reproach, however, was to be removed. On the 25th of September, 1683, there was born at Dijon, of a family of musicians, Jean Philippe Rameau, who was to make two separate and distinct musical reputations, the first in the capacity of a theorist of originality, the second—and that, strange to say, after middle life—as a composer. As his father

was a musician, the child picked up the rudiments of the art
as a matter of course, and showed much of the precociousness
which so often goes with a musical nature. His parents,
knowing how precarious a living music offered, had other
wishes for the boy, in furtherance of which they placed him
at the Jesuits' College in Dijon, with a view of educating him
for the law. Such pursuits, however, had no interest for the
boy. Music had taken so firm a hold upon him that he
paid no attention to his other studies, and finally the fathers
requested the elder Rameau to remove his son. Henceforth
all his energies were devoted to music ; in the pursuit of that
study there was no lack of industry ; but it is to be regretted
that the provincial town in which he lived offered so few
advantages for a thorough training in the theory of music.

A circumstance soon arose which taught him to regret the
neglect he had shown for the ordinary branches of education.
When only seventeen, he fell madly in love with a young
widow who lived near. She made him ashamed of the bad
spelling of the numerous letters which he addressed to her,
and he at once set to work to improve himself. To sever
this attachment, his father sent him to make a journey to
Italy, in which country, however, he got no further than
Milan, and, strange to say, seems to have shown no appreciation of the beauties of Italian music. In that city he made
the acquaintance of a theatrical manager, who was projecting
a tour through the southern towns of France, and with him
young Rameau engaged to travel in the capacity of first

violin in his orchestra. The company visited Marseilles, Lyons, Nismes, and other places, and the tour seems to have been of some duration. Occasionally he had the opportunity of giving an organ performance in the towns through which they passed, but from the account which he himself gives it is evident that his theoretical knowledge was as yet only rudimentary. For some time after this the circumstances of his life are involved in doubt, but in 1706 he was unquestionably in Paris, acting as organist of the Jesuits' church in the Rue St. Jacques, for he then published his first book of pieces for the harpsichord. It is not certain whether it was on this or on a subsequent visit to Paris that he was humiliated by the election of an inferior musician to a vacant organist's place, which injustice determined him to leave that city. He went to Lille first, and soon afterwards to Clermont, as organist, where he remained three or four years, devoting himself to an exhaustive study of the scientific principles of music by means of the treatises of Zarlino, Mersenne, and Descartes. He composed several motets, cantatas, and harpsichord pieces, showing great originality, but the most important result of his studies was the elaboration of a system of harmony, which he embodied in a work entitled *Traité de l'Harmonie réduite à ses Principes Naturels*. The comparative obscurity of a place like Clermont afforded no adequate opportunity for the production of the genius which was striving within him, and he was, moreover, anxious to publish his treatise. He determined therefore to visit Paris once more. This was not so easy as it would appear, for he had made an engagement of long duration with the chapter of the cathedral at Clermont. The latter had not been slow to discover what a fine musician they possessed in their organist, and were by no means disposed to release him from his engagement, and this difficulty was not readily surmounted. At last, however, he found himself in Paris, and in a short time succeeded in persuading Ballard, the famous printer of music, to purchase his treatise, which was published in 1722. It was the first attempt at a rational and scientific explanation of the laws of harmony. The author had already arrived at his thirty-eighth year without achieving the reputation he was so anxious to gain. The success of his book was not immediate, but the novelty of his theories soon began to attract the attention of those who were able to understand the difficulties of the subject, which were not lessened by the obscurity of his style. He lost no time in following up his advantage by the publication of other works, the chief of which was his *Nouveau Système de Musique Théorique*, in which he further develops his discovery of the "fundamental bass." His friend D'Alembert, the eminent mathematician, undertook the composition of a short work giving a popular account of his theories, which, if at that time they were more talked about than understood, had at least placed him in the foremost rank of musical theorists. The result of his great reputation was to make him the most famous teacher of the day. Many ladies of the highest birth became his pupils for the harpsichord, on which instrument he was an excellent performer. He also became organist of the Church of Sainte Croix de la Bretonnerie, where his playing became celebrated. But all these successes did not satisfy his ambition. He thirsted to make a name as an operatic composer, a wish which was not fulfilled without some difficulty. His friend Piron was enabled to obtain for him a commission to write the music for one or two of his own pieces, to be performed at the Opéra Comique of the Foire St. Germain. It was not a very dignified position for a man of his attainments, but it served to try his hand. It has been supposed that his reputation as a theorist stood in his way, the notion being common that learning and imagination do not go together. Fortunately he had among his pupils the wife of Leriche de la Popelinière, one of the richest and most influential of the farmers-general, who was an enthusiastic supporter of art. Every one celebrated in the world of music was received in his *salon*. To Rameau he showed the greatest kindness. The composer, no longer a young man, had lately married a lady many years his junior, and the pair passed much of their time in the houses of La Popelinière either in Paris or at Passy. La Popelinière undertook to obtain a suitable poem for the composer, and he was so far successful that he induced no less a man than Voltaire to write the words of an opera to be set to music by Rameau. The work was complete, and on the point of production, when a cabal succeeded in preventing the performance

of it on the score of the sacred nature of the subject.
Rameau's ambition was for the moment frustrated. The
kindness of his protector did not, however, stop. With some
difficulty he persuaded the Abbé Pellegrin, at that time a
notable character in the world of literature and art, to write
a poem for him. Strange to say, an opera on the subject of
Jephthah, set to music by Montéclair, the words of which were
by the Abbé, had just achieved a great success, although the
performance of *Samson* had not been considered decorous.
The consent of Pellegrin was not given with great readiness;
he stipulated that the composer should give him a bill for
five hundred livres as a security against the possible failure
of the work. After a short time the libretto was completed;
the title of it was *Hippolyte et Aricie*, and it was of course
founded on the *Phèdre* of Racine. But little time was lost
by Rameau in setting it to music. As soon as it was ready
La Popelinière invited his friends, and a trial performance took
place. It is only just to the Abbé Pellegrin to say that at
the end of the first act he addressed the composer as follows :
" Sir, when such music as yours is produced, there is no need
for any security," and destroyed the bill before the assembled
company. The true test of popularity, a public performance,
had still to be gone through. The work was at last produced
at the Opera on the 1st of October, 1733. The first impres-
sion produced on the public was that of surprise rather than
of complete satisfaction. The composer was disappointed, and
almost disposed to renounce the idea of writing for the stage.

But in truth the public had been so long habituated to the weary platitudes of the imitators of Lully that they were not prepared for so much vigour.   For the previous fifty years Lully and his disciples had held possession of the stage. During that period the character of the audience had altered. The popularity of Lully was ensured by the personal taste which Louis XIV. had for his music, and the frequenters of the Opera were largely made up of the courtiers who bowed to their sovereign's judgment.   On the death of Lully the King's interest in the opera waned, for he could with difficulty be induced to listen to the works of any new composer.   The main supporters of the opera were, at the time of which we are writing, the rich financiers and farmers-general, with a large admixture of the *philosophes*, who had become a power, thinking themselves equal to the task of deciding on the merits of any new work either in literature, the drama, or music, and, in fact, almost called on to put their opinion on record, even in spite of an absolute ignorance of the art which they presumed to judge.   The immediate result of the production of *Hippolyte* was the bursting forth of one of those curious wars of pamphlets which form so remarkable a feature of the period.   Fortunately the arguments of Rameau's supporters prevailed, and he was induced to continue the career of an operatic composer, which he had not entered upon until he had passed his fiftieth year.   Other operas followed: *Les Indes Galantes, Castor et Pollux*, which is generally looked on as his masterpiece, *Dardanus*, and many more, to the

number of thirty. He gradually conquered, and achieved a
position of such respect, that the whole audience was in the
habit of rising when he entered his box. In person he was

Fig. 120. –Rameau (from the portrait of Restout, engraved by Benoist).

tall and gaunt, and in face was considered to resemble Voltaire
in a remarkable manner (Fig. 120). His disposition was
reserved, and his manner abstracted, for he was in the habit

of walking through the streets taking no notice whatever of the acquaintances he chanced to meet.   He lived to the advanced age of eighty-one years, having succeeded by force of character in achieving a great reputation in all the branches of music which he attempted.   The principal characteristics of his style were the increased energy, the greater richness of his harmony, and the importance which he gave to the chorus. His instrumentation also showed a wonderful step in advance. The flutes, oboes, and bassoons, no longer double the string parts, but are treated independently, as indeed are frequently the brass and drums.   We have already drawn attention to the fact that the music of Rameau exercised an important influence on the career of Gluck.

As we have seen, Rameau's first dramatic efforts were made at the Théâtre de la Foire.   This was an institution about which a word must be said.   During the seventeenth and eighteenth centuries the difficulties of communication gave an importance to fairs, both for business and pleasure, which they have now generally lost.   In Paris there were at least two such fairs, one called the " Foire St. Laurent," held in the districts now known as the Faubourg St. Dénis and the Faubourg St. Martin ; the other, which was more aristocratic in its aims, was called the " Foire de St. Germain," and was held in the faubourg of that name.   Among the attractions of these fairs was a theatre, at which the artistic merit of the performances was much greater than might have been anticipated, and the short pieces represented were frequently the work of esteemed authors, Le Sage, for example, the author of *Gil Blas,* enjoying great popularity, as did Piron, to one or two of whose works Rameau had been content to set music. These entertainments had not been carried on without a struggle. In 1678 Lully, whose jealousy was soon aroused, had succeeded in obtaining a royal order forbidding singing on the stage, and confining the orchestra to four violins and a hautboy, while the Comédie Française also insisted on stopping the performance of comedies and farces. The theatre of the fair was in a bad way, but the ingenuity of the managers and the ready wit of the French audiences triumphed. Each performer went through his part in dumb show, but he came on the stage provided with a great placard, on which were written in large letters the words of the songs ; and when this was found inconvenient, the placard was lowered from the "flies." The four violins and the hautboy played the tunes, which were generally familiar, so that the audience was able to supply the vocal parts themselves, which they did with great merriment and satisfaction. The keen sense of the ludicrous which is so strong a characteristic of the French, as may be anticipated, soon triumphed, and a treaty of peace was made between the Academy of Music and Catherine Vanderberg, who at that time was proprietor of the theatre of the Foire St. Laurent. She acquired the privilege of representing dramatic pieces interspersed with songs, dancing, and instrumental interludes, in fact what are now known as *vaudevilles.* In a short time these pieces gained for the theatre of the fair the name of

" Opéra Comique," a title it also partly earned from the circumstance that many of the pieces were avowed parodies of
the more dignified works performed at the Académie. The
most successful of the directors of this enterprise was Jean
Monnet, a man who was at different times at the head of
several theatrical undertakings ; among others, he brought a
French company to this country. He was something of a
charlatan, and wrote an account of his life, which is far from
dull, under the title of *Supplément au Roman Comique.*

In the earliest years of the eighteenth century the discussion
of the relative merits of Italian and French music was initiated.
It was opened by the Abbé Raguenet, who, having accompanied
the Cardinal de Bouillon to Rome, became an enthusiastic
admirer of Italian music. He published his views in a work
entitled *Parallèle des Italiens et des Français en ce qui
regarde la Musique et les Opéras* in the year 1702, which
was soon afterwards translated into English. The admirers
of Lully and the French opera found an advocate in
Lecerf de la Vieville. Raguenet replied with a defence
of his *Parallèle,* and the strife was continued, but the
honours of the fight seem to have been carried off by
Raguenet. This discussion, however, had been long forgotten
when in the year 1752 an Italian company, under a director
named Bambini, were permitted to appear at the Académie.
On the 1st August, 1752, *La Serva Padrona* of Pergolesi
was produced. It had previously been played at the Comédie
Italienne, but the appearance of an Italian work on a stage

18

hitherto devoted exclusively to French opera provoked, as was
only natural, a comparison between the two schools of music.
The controversy broke out with extraordinary violence, and has

Fig. 121.—Leaving the Opera (after Moreau, eighteenth century).

become celebrated under the title of the "Guerre" or "Querelle
des Bouffons," the name by which the Italian company was
designated in France. The theatre at once became a field

of battle.   The national music received the support of the King and of Madame de Pompadour, and its defenders, ranging themselves under the King's box, were therefore called the " Coin du Roi ; " the advocates of Italian music took their places under that of the Que en, and were for that reason designated the " Coin de la Reine." Pamphlet after pamphlet, some witty, all straining after wit, appeared in quick succession, hardly a day passing without an addition to the paper war.   Every man who aspired to the character of a wit made his contribution to the literature of the controversy, which counted among its authors many of the leading writers of the day.   Among the most prominent were Grimm, D'Holbach, J. J. Rousseau, Cazotte, Travenol, Rameau, and even Frederick the Great of Prussia.   The veteran Rameau defended the French school against some of the charges which were so freely brought against it, but it is interesting to know that he appreciated the great beauties of the Italian school also.   He said with great sincerity on one occasion to the Abbé Arnaud, " If I were thirty years younger, I would go to Italy.   Pergolesi would become my model, and I would make my harmony subordinate to that truth of declamation which should be the only guide of the musician.   But when a man has passed sixty years of age, he feels that he must remain where he is ; experience points out what would be the right course to adopt : the will refuses to obey."

When there was a lull in the controversy, Jean Jacques Rousseau, who had taken but a small part in it, by way of

a judicial winding up of the discussion, brought out his *Lettre
sur la Musique Française.* The result was very different
from his intention : it stirred up the expiring embers, and
the flames burst forth with renewed fury. It is not remarkable that this was the case, for Rousseau declares that " the
French have no music, and cannot have any, and that if
they should succeed in having any, it will be so much the
worse for them." The advocates of the national cause were
beside themselves with rage, and the band of the Opera hanged
and burnt the author in effigy in the courtyard of the theatre.
Another storm of pamphlets burst forth, and it was long
before the atmosphere again became clear. M. Thoinan has
been at the pains of compiling a bibliography of this remarkable controversy, which may be found under the word
" Rousseau " in the supplement of Fétis's *Biographie des
Musiciens;* and he brings the number of publications up to
sixty-three !

The very remarkable man of whom we have just been
speaking came to Paris in the year 1742 with a scheme for
a new system of writing music in his pocket, which he succeeded in getting published, under the title of *Projet
concernant de Nouveaux Signes pour la Musique.* His plan
was mainly based on the use of numerals to distinguish the
notes of the scale, thus, like many others who have endeavoured to simplify the received notation, overlooking the
advantage offered by the *pictorial* representation of a musical
phrase which the received notation gives. Rousseau made

a precarious livelihood in Paris by copying music ; and although some of his friends endeavoured to force on him more than the ordinary remuneration for such work, he could never be induced to accept anything beyond the usual terms of payment. His scheme for the improvement of musical notation meeting with but little acceptance, he was next induced to try his skill as a composer, for which his deficient training but ill adapted him. He wrote an opera entitled *Les Muses Galantes*, which was tried at the house of the farmer-general La Popelinière. Rameau, who was present, declared that part appeared to be the work of a skilled artist, while the rest was written by a man ignorant of the first principles of music. Some went so far as to assert that the opera was not the work of Rousseau at all. It was publicly performed in 1747, without success.

Rousseau lived on terms of intimacy with Diderot and D'Alembert, and they therefore chose him as the writer of the articles on music in the *Encyclopédie*. His superficial knowledge of the subject made the attempt a very unwise one ; and although he devoted himself to some serious study, the time at his disposal was short, and the result was unsatisfactory. Rameau had been induced to suppose that the work would have been entrusted to him, and unquestionably that great musician and theorist was the fittest person to have undertaken it ; but differences had arisen between him and D'Alembert, and his claims were in consequence passed by. It would have been more than human for one so fond of controversy to allow the occasion to pass by unnoticed, and he was soon in the field with a pamphlet exposing the errors in a work which had laid claim to be a model of accuracy. Rousseau himself recognised his deficiencies, and determined to correct and amend them. This was the origin of his famous *Dictionnaire de Musique*, which was published at Geneva in the year 1767, and has since appeared in numerous editions and in many languages. Its success was enormous, although the work was very far from perfect. Its great deficiencies are in the theoretical portions ; the author was by temperament and education unfitted to cope with such subjects, which require the training of a mathematician. The critical portions show the taste which he undoubtedly possessed, and the charm of his style makes the book of great interest.

A few months after the production of *La Serva Padrona* at the Académie, and shortly after the appearance of his articles in the *Encyclopédie*, Rousseau succeeded in obtaining a hearing for his little opera *Le Devin du Village* before the court at Fontainebleau. The music was so simple and natural, that it was received with enthusiasm, and early in the following year —in March, 1783—it was transferred to the stage of the Opera, where it gave equal pleasure. Its popularity was unbounded. The deficiency of ordinary musicianship was still apparent, but the work was full of charm—a quality in which many compositions of much greater learning have been wanting—and the result was that it kept the stage for more than sixty years, and went the round of nearly all the theatres in France.

Even in this instance his enemies grudged him his success, and he was accused of passing off the work of another as his own. An obscure musician of Lyons, named Granet, was brought forward as the real composer, but there seems no ground for doubting that the work was actually by Rousseau.

De Fofe Delin.   C.Grignion Sculp!
M.^E LARUETTE et MR CLAIRVAL.
CATAU et LUCAS dans Julie Acte 2.^d
Comedie Italienne.
From the Collection of the R.^t Honble Lord Visc.^t Rusborough.
Published by Jefferys & Faden Corner of St Martins Lane Charing Cross, as the Act directs 1 May 1773.

Fig 122.—Madame la Ruette and Clairval in *Julie*, comic opera by Dezède, performed at the Comédie Italienne in 1772.

The last performance in Paris took place in 1829. On that occasion a large peruke descended on the stage ; there was some suspicion that it was launched by Berlioz, but it is only fair to say that he denies it in his autobiography. This proved its deathblow in the capital, although it was still to be heard occasionally in the provinces. After the death of Rousseau, a collection of a hundred songs was published under the title of *Les Consolations des Misères de ma Vie*, which show much the same touching simplicity as the melodies of *Le Devin du Village*.

Among the lesser lights of the musical world in France we must mention Gossec, who, having been brought up in the choir of the cathedral at Antwerp, found his way to Paris, and became conductor of the music at the house of La Popelinière, where he had the advantage of profiting greatly by the advice of Rameau. His early inclinations led him to cultivate instrumental music, and he was the first who attempted the composition of a symphony in France. He afterwards passed into the service of the Prince de Conti, employing the greater leisure which this position offered him in compositions of very varied character, among which some string quartets met with great success. In 1764 his career as a dramatic composer began with the opera *Le faux Lord*. He followed up his success with *Les Pêcheurs*, achieving even greater popularity, which was shared by several other operas of his composition. Many of the operas of Dezède enjoyed great appreciation (fig. 122), and Monsigny also is deserving of notice. Born of a good family, but thrown by the death of his father on his own resources, after some other employments he entered the service of the Duc d'Orléans. He had only followed music as an amateur, but a hearing of *La Serva Padrona*, then first produced in Paris, filled him with so strong an impulse to attempt composition that he began to study the art with greater

seriousness, and after a short time succeeded in bringing out
an opera: *Les Aveux Indiscrets.* Its reception encouraged him

Fig. 123.--Gluck (after Auguste de St. Aubin, 1781).

to continue, and in 1760 he produced *Le Cadi dupé*, the comic
force of which ensured it a great success. Several other works

followed, the best-known of which was *Le Déserteur*, his
masterpiece, and long a favourite on the French stage. His
last opera was written in 1777; and although he lived for forty
years afterwards, he made no further attempt at composition,
declaring that music was as though dead to him.

In 1774 a musician of a very different calibre arrived in
Paris. This was the renowned Gluck (fig. 123). In a former
chapter we have recounted the action of Du Rollet which led
to this visit. The personal influence of the Dauphiness, Marie
Antoinette, who had been the pupil of the great musician, was
necessary to surmount the difficulties which stood in the way
of Gluck's engagement; but these were at last overcome, and
the *Iphigenie en Aulide* was produced for the first time on the
19th of April, 1774, the composer having arrived at the ripe age
of sixty. This performance was an epoch in the history of
opera in France; no work of such breadth and loftiness of style
had as yet been heard in that country, and it was at first but
little understood. The rehearsals had given the composer
infinite trouble, for all the performers had to be educated in
their parts, and there was no great show of good feeling on
the part of many of them, as it was looked on almost as a
reproach that a foreigner should presume to set to music the
work of one of their greatest poets. The composer, however,
was the last man to be turned aside by any manifestations of
unwillingness. The public at once recognised that they were
face to face with a new departure; the dramatic truth and the
consistent earnestness of the new opera was a revelation. In

August of the same year *Orphée* was arranged for the French stage. Owing to the want of a contralto (a voice which is rare in France), the principal part had to be transposed, which somewhat detracted from its effect; but it was nevertheless

Fig. 124.—Music (a decorative picture, engraved after Lajoue by N. Cochin, eighteenth century).

hailed with enthusiasm, as was also *Alceste*, brought out in 1776. During the rehearsals of these works, the custom was introduced of allowing the public to be present, who found much amusement in the freedom with which the great musician

enforced his views on the performers. It was his practice to
remove his wig and to replace it by a nightcap on these
occasions ; and so great was his popularity that, at the end of
the rehearsal, great lords and even princes thought themselves
honoured by being allowed to hand him his wig or to help
him into his overcoat.

There were some, however, who were unable to appreciate
the superior merits of the great master. At their instance an
Italian composer of merit and celebrity, Piccinni, who had made
a reputation in Naples, Rome, and other parts of Italy, was
invited. He arrived in Paris at the end of 1776, and at once
set to work to compose an opera for the French stage. But
his ignorance of the language was complete, so that Marmontel,
who was entrusted with the task of compiling the libretto from
Quinault, was compelled to go through it word by word with
the composer to explain not only the meaning, but also the
prosody. In this laborious manner *Roland* was at last written,
but a whole year was occupied in the process, and the work
was not produced till January, 1778. The votaries of the rival
composer had not been idle, and all sorts of difficulties had
been created during the progress of the rehearsals, to such a
point that the composer had come to the opinion that its
failure was inevitable, and his family was in despair. Contrary
to his expectation, its success was complete. This was the
signal for the breaking out of another of those paper wars
which seemed inevitable at that time on the arrival of each new
candidate for fame on the stage of the French opera. Many

of those who had taken part in the war of the *bouffons* still
survived, and rushed into the fray like ancient war-horses.   Suard
and the Abbé Arnaud were at the head of the *Gluckistes ;*
Marmontel, the well-known critic La Harpe, Ginguené, and

Fig. 125.—Grétry at his pianoforte (after the picture by Isabey).

D'Alembert took the side of Piccinni.   The discussion was
continued till 1780, when Gluck returned to Vienna.   These
wars on matters of taste are a curious feature of artistic life
in Paris during the eighteenth century.   It must often have
been noticed how childish is the outburst of popular enthusiasm

in favour of a particular performer on the stage among those nations which enjoy no political freedom, or who still remain unaccustomed to the possession of it ; and one is almost tempted to believe that these fierce discussions in France were but a manifestation of the general upheaval of society which was so shortly to take place. It may be interesting to mention that the correspondence of the rival factions was collected and published in a volume by the Abbé Leblond, under the title of *Memoires pour servir à l'Histoire de la Revolution operée dans la Musique par M. le Chevalier Gluck*, in the year 1781, from the frontispiece of which work our portrait of the great composer is taken.

While Piccinni was engaged in the composition of *Roland*, Gluck had brought out his opera *Armide*. Its composer was not wanting in self-appreciation ; he addressed a letter to Du Rollet in which he declared that it nearly approached perfection, and when the Queen inquired one day if the opera was nearly complete, he replied, "Madam, that opera will soon be finished, and in truth it will be superb!" Authors, however, are frequently mistaken in their estimates of their own works, or at least the public judgment is not always in accord. The opera was received with coldness, although after a time it made its way.

It had been the original intention that *Roland* should be set to music simultaneously by Gluck and Piccinni; but when the former found that his rival was also to be entrusted with the libretto, he tore up what he had written, and declined to proceed with the work. This disinclination to enter into a trial of skill was afterwards got over, and both composers were induced to write an opera, *Iphigenie en Tauride*, although the words were written by different authors. That of Gluck, it will be readily believed, was the first completed. It was produced at the Académie in May, 1779, and was a crowning victory for the composer and his supporters. The work was a masterpiece. Some one remarking that there were five pieces in the opera, Arnaud, his great admirer, declared, "There is but one." "Which is that?" "The entire work," replied Arnaud. Piccinni's opera was not brought out until January, 1781; and although very melodious, it was completely overshadowed by the recollection of the work of his rival. Gluck's *Echo et Narcisse*, produced at the end of the same year, met with only moderate success. The great composer was now sixty-five years of age. He had undertaken to set to music the *Danaides*, the poem of which was in part by his friend Du Rollet; but an attack of apoplexy warned him of the necessity for rest. He returned to Vienna, handed over the libretto to Salieri, his friend and pupil, and, it is supposed, indicated to the latter his general ideas of the treatment of the subject. The opera, which had great success, was for the first few representations given under the name of the better-known composer, although it is not certain that he was privy to the deception. After a few years of retirement, a second attack of apoplexy carried him off on the 25th of November, 1787.

Piccinni, who was an amiable and worthy man, remained for a time in Paris, having some success at the Théâtre

Fig. 126.—The magic picture (from the opera *Zemire et Azor*, by Grétry.   From a
drawing by Touzé).

Italien; but his life seemed destined to be one of strife and
trouble, for no sooner had his great rival returned to Vienna

than Sacchini arrived in Paris to dispute his position. In 1791 the latter returned to Italy, the close of his life being clouded by pecuniary troubles, caused by the outbreak of the French Revolution. He was a most voluminous composer; the names of eighty of his operas are given by Fétis, and it is believed that this large number does not include the whole.

By that geographical comprehensiveness which is so marked a feature of the French nation, Grétry (fig. 125) is always claimed as a native of that country, although he was born in the year 1741 at Liége, which at the time formed no part of that kingdom. Grétry at a very early age showed a disposition for music, and was educated in the choir of one of the churches in his native city, his beautiful voice attracting great notice. The arrival of a company of Italian singers in Liége, who performed Pergolesi's *Serva Padrona*, at once confirmed him in his wish to become a composer. His ambition was so great that he could hardly be persuaded of the importance of theoretical study. Some of his symphonies having been performed with success, one of the canons of the cathedral suggested to him the idea of a journey to Rome. His parents were poor, but the Chapter came to his aid, and he actually performed the whole of the journey on foot. On his arrival he studied counterpoint with an esteemed master for some months, but he never arrived at the possession of great ease in the use of harmony, his heart being in the direction of expressive melody. His stay in Italy was extended to nine years; in that country his music was well received, but his

19

Fig. 127.—Card of a Parisian instrument-dealer in the eighteenth century.

desire was to write for the French stage. On his return he
visited Voltaire at Geneva, hoping to obtain from him the
poem of a comic opera. He received vague promises only,
but the presence of a French operatic company in that city
enabled him to try his hand at that style of composition. His
Isabelle et Gertrude had some success, and obtained for him
a number of pupils, who provided him with the means of life.
But he was now twenty-eight years of age, and had made no
reputation. Voltaire counselled him to go at once to Paris.
It is no easy thing for an unknown man to get a hearing, or
even a libretto to set to music. The last, after two years of
fruitless efforts, he succeeded in obtaining from an obscure
poet named Du Rozoy. The title of the work was *Les
Mariages Samnites.* The opera was written and rehearsed,
but the judgment of those who were invited to hear it was
unfavourable, and the work was withdrawn, to be produced
some years later, when the reputation of the composer was
established. One of the hearers did not agree with the general
verdict ; this was the Comte de Creutz, the Swedish envoy
and at his suggestion Marmontel was induced to entrust to
the composer his comedy *Le Huron.* It was produced in
August, 1768, at the Théâtre Italien, and formed the beginning
of a long series of triumphs. Space fails to give a complete
list of the whole of these ; we must be content to mention
Le Tableau Parlant, Zémire et Azor (fig. 126), *La Fausse
Magie,* and *Richard Cœur de Lion,* containing the airs *O
Richard ! ô mon roi !* and *Une fièvre brûlante.* Grétry also

claimed the suffrages of the public as an author, having written
a series of *Essais*, the main interest of which consists in the

Fig. 128.—Gentleman of quality playing the bass-viol (after J. de St. Jean, eighteenth century).

autobiographical account of his life, which is not diminished
by a pleasant vein of self-satisfaction which pervades the work.

During the reign of Louis XIII., there arrived in Paris

a hautboy-player of the name of Danican. He had the good
fortune to please the King, who asserted that his performance
recalled that of. an Italian named Filidori. On the strength of
the King's remark, Danican added the name of Philidor to his

Fig. 129.— Section of the new orchestra of the King's chapel at the château of Fontainebleau
(from a manuscript in the library at Versailles, 1773).

own, and he became the ancestor of a numerous family of
musicians—so numerous that to distinguish them it has become
customary to *number* the different members, as in the case of a
line of kings. Several of them achieved eminence as composers
and performers, but one rendered great service to the history

of music, for, having been appointed to the charge of the court
musical library, he succeeded in getting together an excellent
collection—which still bears his name—of the greatest interest
to those engaged in the investigation of the history of music
in France.   Another member of the family, François André
Danican Philidor, in addition to a reputation based on a series
of operas, which achieved a brilliant success, was still more
celebrated as the greatest chess-player of the day, and in the
latter capacity made several visits to this country, where his
society was much sought.   To still another member—Anne
Danican Philidor—Paris is indebted for the foundation of the
famous "Concerts Spirituels," which were the first public concerts
given in France.   As the Opera was closed on the festivals of
the Church, including Holy Week and a fortnight at Easter,
Philidor proposed to make use of the enforced holiday, and to
find employment for the musicians by a series of concerts during
that period, at which the music performed should be suitable for
the holy season; hence the name of "Concerts Spirituels."   He
acquired the privilege on the condition of paying to the Opera
a yearly contribution of six thousand livres.   The first of these
performances took place on the 18th of March, 1725, in one
of the halls of the Tuileries, and they were continued almost
without interruption till 1791.   It is hardly necessary to add
that the company was a fashionable one; in fact, the concerts
were as exclusive as our own "Antient Concerts."   To make an
appearance at them was the honourable ambition of every artist;
Mozart's heart-burnings over his negotiations with the director

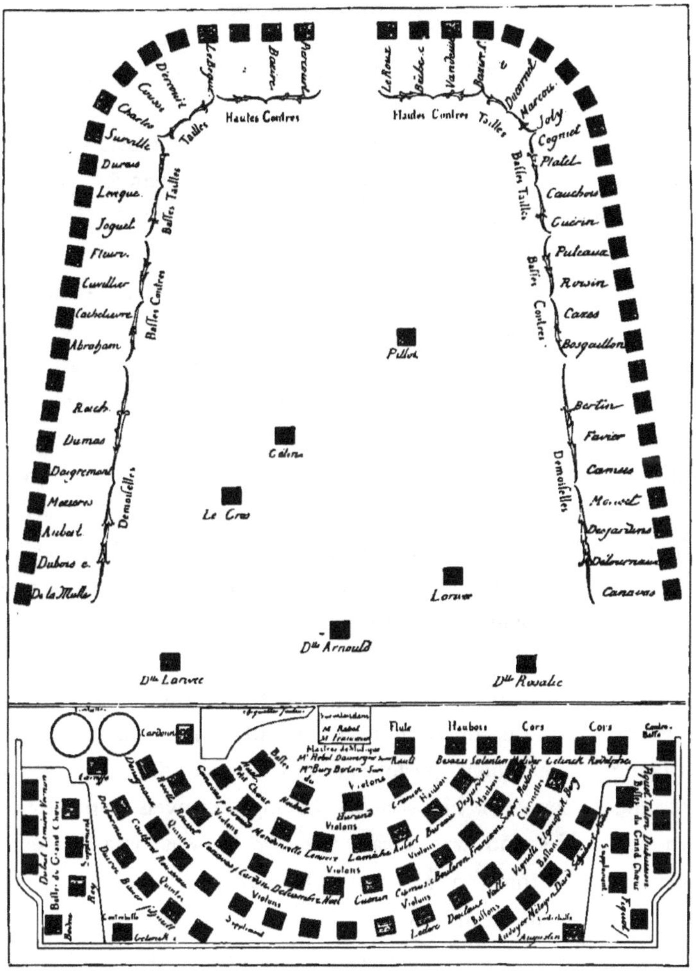

Fig. 130.--Plan of the arrangement of the orchestra and singers in the King's Theatre at Versailles in 1773 (from a manuscript in the library at Versailles).

of these concerts will be remembered by those who have read his life.

During the eighteenth century instrumental music was much cultivated in France. Among the greatest changes was the gradual but definite abandonment of the viol family, in which the finger-board was *fretted*, in favour of that of the violins (fig. 128). The change was not brought about without a protest. A certain M. Hubert le Blanc, *docteur en droit*, wrote a little work under the title of *Défense de la Basse de Viole contre les Entreprises du Violon et les Prétentions du Violoncel* (Amsterdam, 1740). The title promises something amusing, but in truth it is a dull work, and it was with difficulty that the author succeeded in finding a publisher. When he heard of one in Amsterdam who was disposed to undertake it, he was so transported with the news that he started at once to Amsterdam just as he was—in dressing-gown, slippers, and nightcap.

The most famous player on the violin during this period in France was Leclair, born in Lyons in 1697, who, in addition to being an excellent performer, also wrote admirably for his instrument, some of his sonatas having survived even to our own day. His end was a sad one, for he was assassinated at his own door on the night of October 22nd, 1764, and his murderer was never discovered. Jean Pierre Guignon was also a fine violinist; and Gaviniés, an excellent performer and also a successful teacher, may be considered the founder of the French school of violin-playing.

Fig. 131.—Annette and Lubin—last scene of the comic opera of that name, words by Favart, music by Blaise (from a coloured engraving by Debucourt). The character of Annette was played by Madame Favart, and that of Lubin by Caillot.

We have seen that in the case of the family of the Philidors nearly every member was distinguished as a musician. In another family of French musicians this also happened. Their name was Couperin, and they nearly all acquired some celebrity as organists or players on the harpsichord. One member of

Fig. 132.—A zephyr (from a ballet after Martin, eighteenth century).

the family, however, François, excelled the rest so completely that he acquired the title of "Couperin le Grand." He became organist of St. Gervais, and was the only French organist whose treatment of the instrument was at all worthy of its capabilities.   He is perhaps better known as a writer for the harpsichord, for which he wrote several collections of pieces, a testimony to the merit of which is that they have been

Fig. 133.—A demon (from a ballet, after Martin, eighteenth century).

thought worthy of republication in Germany within the last few years.

We have mentioned that Lully introduced instrumental accompaniments into the services of the private chapel of

Fig. 134.—Court ballet of the *Prince de Salerne*, performed at Fontainebleau (1746).

Louis XIV. The custom at once took root, and the band
was maintained with a high degree of efficiency (fig. 129).
At Versailles a theatre formed part of that enormous pile of

Fig. 135.—Mademoiselle Sallé, a celebrated-dancer (after Lancret)

building, which also demanded the services of a large body of
instrumentalists in the orchestra (fig. 130).

It cannot be claimed for the French school of music

that it was very fruitful in the production of singers of
eminence. Among the most eminent was Mademoiselle
Chantilly, who afterwards became Madame Favart (fig. 131).
She appeared at the Opéra Comique, where she delighted
the public both by the charm of her singing, as well as by
the grace of her dancing. Sophie Arnould is remembered for
her wit and her waywardness better perhaps than for her
powers as a singer. At the time of which we are writing
prima donnas were not allowed in France to indulge their
caprices with impunity, and any serious breach of engagement received the punishment of a few days' seclusion. Madame
Saint-Huberty was a singer of great dramatic power, which
Gluck did not fail to discover. For a long time she filled the
leading parts, and ultimately married the Comte d'Entraignes,
with whom she settled in England, where both she and her
husband were assassinated by a servant, for reasons which
have never been explained, although it is believed that they
were political. Of men-singers the only one who need be
mentioned here is Jélyotte.

The ballet continued to be a favourite form of entertainment at the French court, although the royal family ceased
to take part in the performances, content to remain as
spectators. They were also produced with great splendour
at the Opera. Among the most celebrated dancers were
Mademoiselle Sallé (fig. 135) and Mademoiselle Camargo.
These were the days of Noverre and the elder Vestris, who
brought great skill to bear on the arrangement of such spectacles

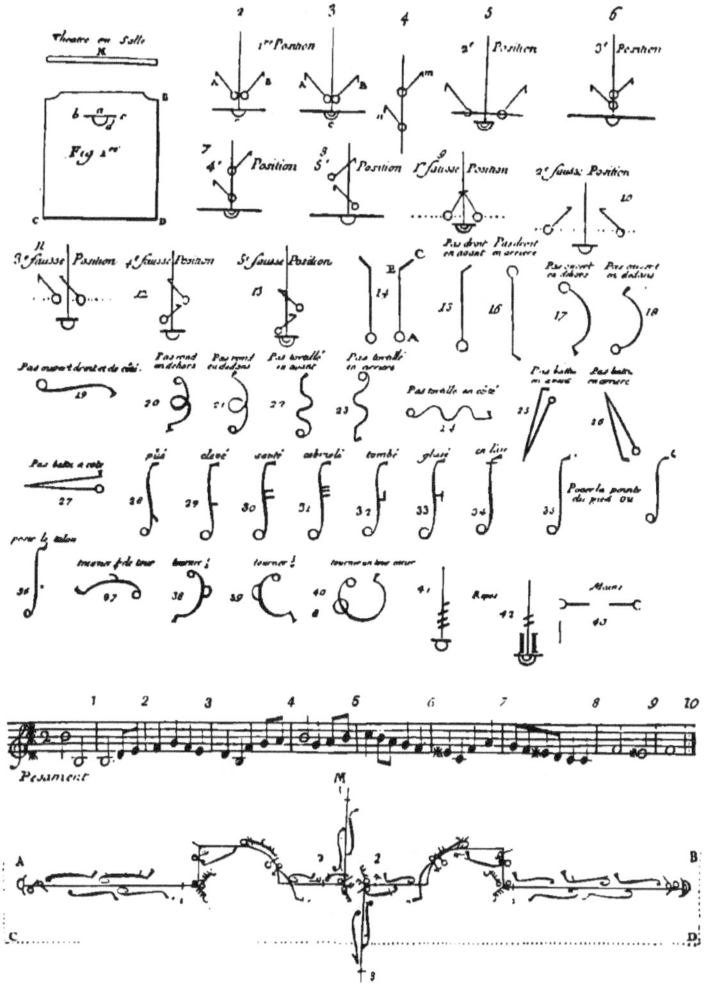

Fig. 136.—Examples of choregraphic notation (from the *Encyclopédie*). The first example represents the signs used for indicating the different steps, the second these signs grouped for the performance of a portion of a ballet (*Les Fêtes Grecques et Romaines*) to the given melody.

It may not be generally known to our readers that the mazy intricacies of a ballet are capable of being set down on paper in a species of notation quite understood by the initiated. We give a specimen which cannot fail to prove interesting, if not perhaps very intelligible.

Here we must bring this work to a close. We have traced the development of musical notation, without which that marvellous impulse which, taking its rise in the Netherlands, made itself felt throughout the whole of civilized Europe, would have been impossible; we have seen religious music receive its most worthy expression under Palestrina; the infancy of the oratorio has achieved vigorous manhood under Handel; John Sebastian Bach has exhausted the resources of fugal art; the opera, taking its rise from a pedantic admiration of antiquity, has become a fashionable amusement of society; and we leave our subject at the moment when Haydn and Mozart are about to reveal the power of instrumental music and the beauties of orchestral colouring, which culminate during the present century in the works of Beethoven, and in the elaborate scores of Berlioz and Wagner.

INDEX.

Abhandlung von der Fuge, by Marpurg, 184.
Academy of Antient Musick, 254.
Acis and Galatea, cantata by Handel, 229, 236, 237.
Adam and Eve, opera by Theile, 169.
Adam de la Halle. See "Halle, Adam de la."
Addison, remarks in the *Spectator* on Italian opera, 223, 226 ; his opera *Rosamund*, 223.
Admeto, opera by Handel, 234.
Agricola, Alexander (14—[?]—1526[?]), 67.
Agricola, J. F. (1720—1774), 165.
Agrippina, opera by Handel, 176.
Ah! how, Sophia, Callcott's catch, 256.
Aichinger, Gregoir (1565—   ), 80.
Albert V. of Bavaria, Duke, his friendship for Orlando di Lassus, 71.
Albinoni, T. (1674—1745), 116.
Albion and Albanius, opera by Grabu, 200.
Alceste ; ou, Le Triomphe d'Alcide, opera by Lully, 138.
Alcestis, opera by Gluck, 189, 283.
Alcina, opera by Handel, 240.
Alcock, Dr. John (1715—1805), 259.
Alessandro, opera by Handel, 233.
Alexander Balus, Handel's oratorio, 247.
Alexander's Feast, cantata by Handel, 241, 243.
Allegri, Gregorio (1560—1652), 77.
Allison, Richard (1565[?]—   ), 100.
Almira, opera by Handel, 174, 175.
Altnikol, J. C.,(   ), 165.
Amadigi, opera by Handel, 227, 228.
Amati, Andreas (—1577[?]), 59.
Ambrose, St. (340—397), collects the ancient Church melodies, 2 ; his reforms in Church music, *ib.*

Amour Médecin, incidental music to, by Lully, 136.
Amphion Anglicus, collection of songs by Dr. Blow, 202.
Amphitryon, Dryden's, incidental music by Purcell, 208.
Ancient Christian melodies, corruption of, 2.
Ancient music, exaggerated appreciation of, at the Renaissance, 102.
Andromeda, words by Corneille, music by D'Assoucy, 129.
Anerio, Felice (1560—   ), 77.
Anerio, Francesco (1567—   ), 77.
Angels ever bright and fair, song from Handel's *Theodora*, 247.
Angilbert, his song on the battle of Fonte-nailles, 8.
"Anglican" chant, introduction of, 202.
Animuccia, Giovanni (1505—1571), 77, 108.
Anjou, Count of, 17.
"Antient Concerts," 209, 254.
Antigone, opera by Hasse, 180.
Antiphonarium of St. Gregory, 3, 5.
Arcadelt, Jacques (1490[?]—1575[?]), 67.
Archlute, 55.
Ariana, opera by Monteverde, 105.
Ariane ; ou, Le Mariage de Bacchus, opera by Cambert, 131, 221.
Arianna, opera by Handel, 240.
Ariodante, opera by Handel, 240.
Ariosti, Attilio (1660—   ), 172, 231.
Armide, opera by Gluck, 286.
Armide, opera by Lully, 139, 141.
Arminio, opera by Handel, 241.
Arnaud, Abbé (1721—1784), 275, 285, 287.
Arne, Thomas Augustine, Mus. Doc. (1710—1778), 223, 249 ; his *Artaxerxes*, 250, 253.

Arne, Miss (Mrs. Cibber), singer (1714—1766), 237.
Arne, Mrs. (Cecilia Young) (—1795), singer, 250.
Arnould, Sophie (1744—1802), singer, 302.
Aron, Pietro (1490[?]—), 80.
Ars Canendi of Sebaldus Heyden, 85.
Arsinoe, Queen of Cyprus, opera by Clayton, 222.
Artaserse, opera by Hasse, 240.
Artaxerxes, opera by Dr. Arne, 250, 253.
Artusi, G. M. (1554—), 107.
As from the power, chorus from Handel's Ode for St. Cecilia's Day, 243.
Astarto, opera by G. B. Buononcini, 231.
Astorga, Baron É. (1681—1736), 254.
As when the dove, air in Handel's *Acis and Galatea*, 229.
Atalanta, opera by Handel, 241.
Atterbury, L. (c. 1740—1796), 259.
Atys, opera by Lully, 139.
Augelletti che cantate, air from Handel's *Rinaldo*, 226.
Aureng-Zebe, Dryden's, music for, composed by Purcell, 206.
Aveux Indiscrets, Les, opera by Monsigny, 281.
Avison, Charles (1710—1770), 113.

Bach, Carl Philipp Emmanuel (1714—1788), 159, 164.
Bach family, the, 154.
Bach, Johann Christian (1735—1782), 165, 262.
Bach, Johann Sebastian (1685—1750), 154; appointed organist at Arnstadt, 156, at Mühlhausen, *ib.*, and at Weimar, *ib.*; enters service of the Prince of Anhalt-Coethen, 157; appointed "Cantor" of the Thomas-schule, Leipzig, 158; visit to Potsdam, 160; his death, *ib.*; his works, *ib.*; the B minor mass, 161; his writings for the harpsichord, 162; his pupils, 165;—177, 304.
Bach, Wilhelm Friedemann (1710—1784), 164, 178.
Bagpipes, 36; Calabrian, 37; Scotch, *ib.*; Irish and Lowland Scotch, *ib.*
Baïf, Antoine de (1532—1589), 121.
Ballad operas, English, 253.
Ballet at the Paris Opera, 302.
Ballet Comique de la Royne, 123.
Ballet, notation of, 303.

Ballets, popularity of, 126.
Banister, John (1630—1679), his concerts, 254.
Bannieri, Antonio (1638—1740), 130.
Barnard, Rev. John, his collection of *Church Musick*, 98, 211.
Barrington, Hon. Daines, his account of Mozart, 261.
Basilius, opera by Keiser, 170.
Bassani, G. B. (1657[?]—1716), 114.
Bassoon, 45.
Bates, Joah (1740—1799), 255.
Bateson, Thomas (1575[?]—), 93.
Battishill, Jonathan (1738—1801), 212.
Bauderon, Antoine, his *Lettre de Clément Marot*, 140.
Beaujoyeulx, Baltasar de, 123.
Beaulieu (living 1582), 125.
Bedford, Rev. Arthur, his *Great Abuse of Musick*, 219; *Temple Musick*, 220.
Beethoven, L. van (1770—1827), 193, 304.
Beggar's Opera, The, 235, 236.
Bellamy, Richard (1745[?]—1813), 259.
Bellay, du, Cardinal, 67, 68.
Belleville, 126.
Bells, 31.
Belshazzar, Handel's oratorio, 246.
Belshazzar, oratorio by Carissimi, 109.
Bercan (Berchem), Jacques (—1565[?]), 68.
Berenice, opera by Handel, 241.
Berg, Adam, *Patrocinium Musices* of, 73.
Berlioz, Hector (1803—1869), 279, 304.
Bertolazzi, Margarita, singer, 128.
Beza, Theodore, completes Marot's translation of the Psalms, 121.
Binchois, Egidius (1400—1465), 61, 64.
Biographie des Musiciens of Fétis, 276.
Blanc, Hubert le, his *Défense de la Basse de Viole*, 296.
Blest pair of sirens, glee by J. Stafford Smith, 259.
Blondeau de Nesle, 17.
Blow, Dr. John (1648—1708), 196, 202, 206, 207, 210, 211, 214, 217.
Blow, thou wintry wind, air by Dr. Arne, 250.
Boethius (455—526), author of first Latin treatise on music, 1; popularity of his treatise, 13, 80.
Bonanni, his *Gabinetto Armonico*, 26.
Booke, The, of Common Praier Noted, 88.
Borjon, C. E., his *Traité de la Musette*, 146.

Borromeo, Cardinal, 75.
Boscherville, bas-relief of concert at, 56, 57.
- Bouffons," "Guerre des, 274.
Bourgeois Gentilhomme, Le, incidental music to, by Lully, 136.
Boyce, Dr. William (1710—1779), 211 ; his *Cathedral Music, ib.*
Brabant, Duke of, 17.
Bracegirdle, Mrs., singer (1663—1748), 222.
Brady and Tate, their "New Version" of the Psalms, 101.
Breitkopf and Härtel, their edition of Palestrina's works, 77.
Britton, Thomas, "the musical small-coal man " (1651—1714), 251, 254.
Broschi, R., 231.
Brouncker, Lord, his translation of Descartes' *Compendium Musicæ,* 148.
Brumel, Antonio (1460[?]—15—), 67.
Bruyer, 67.
Bull, Dr. John (1563[?]—1628), 96, 97.
Buononcini, G. B. (1665[?]—1750), 172, 185, 231, 238.
Buononcini, M. A. (1655—1726), 222.
Burci or Burtius, Nicolas (1450[?]—15—), 79.
Burney, Dr. (1726—1814), his edition of music for Holy Week sung in the Sistine Chapel, 78; his *History of Music,* 260.
Buxtehude, Dietrich (1637—1707), 151, 156, 173.
Byrd, Thomas, 97.
Byrd, William (1537[?]—1623), 90; his patent for printing music with Tallis, *ib.,* 96.

Caccini, Giulio (1558[?]—1640), 104.
Cadi Dupé, Le, opera by Monsigny, 281.
Cadmus, opera by Lully, 137.
Caduta de' Giganti, opera by Gluck, 252.
Caffarelli, G. M. (1703—1783), 114.
Caldara, Antonio (1678—1763), 186, 188.
Callcott, Dr. J. W. (1766—1821), 256, 259.
Calvin on sacred music, 122.
Calzabigi, poet, writes Gluck's libretti, 189.
Camargo, Mademoiselle, dancer, 302.
Cambert, Robert (1628—1677), 130; his opera *La Pastorale,* 131; his *Ariane; ou, Le Mariage de Bacchus, ib.*; his *Pomona,* 132; supplanted by Lully, 136; 141, 221.
Camelin, 67.

Camilla, opera by M. A. Buononcini, 222.
Campanile, 31.
Campra, André (1660—1744), 144, 146.
Cantiones Sacræ, by Tallis and Byrd, 90.
Capistrum, or mouth bandage, 35.
Cara sposa, air from Handel's *Rinaldo,* 226.
Carestini, Giovanni, singer (1705—1763), 240, 241.
Carey, Henry (1685[?]—1743), 250.
Carillon, 32.
Carissimi, Giacomo (1604[?]—1674), 109.
Castor et Pollux, opera by Rameau, 269.
Catch Club, Noblemen and Gentlemen's, 258.
Catch, the, 256.
Cathedral music, Boyce's collection of, 211.
Cathedral Service, Short Direction for the Performance of, by E. Lowe, 203.
Catone, opera by Leonardo Leo, 238.
Caurroy, Eustache de (1549—1609), 127.
Cavaliere, Emilio del (1550[?]—1598[?]), 104, 108.
Cavalli, P. Francesco (1599[?]—1676), 107.
Cazotte, Jacques (1720—1793), 275.
Cecilia, St., Cologne, bell at, 31.
Cecilia's, St., Day, 208, 209.
Cecilia's Day, ode for St., Handel's, 243.
Cesti, Marco Antonio (1620—1675), 108.
Chalumeau, 44.
Champeron finances the opera founded by Perrin and Cambert, 131, 132.
Chandos *Anthems* and *Te Deums,* Handel's, 229.
Chandos, Duke of, 228.
Change-ringing, 34.
Chanterelle, 55.
Chantilly, Mademoiselle, singer (Madame Favart), 275.
Chant sur le Livre, 16.
Chapel, the Royal, in France, 299.
Chapel Royal, London, at the Restoration, choir of, 195; introduction of instrumental music in, 198.
Chappell, Mr. W., his *Popular Music of the Olden Time,* facsimile of *Sumer is icumen in,* 86.
Charlemagne endeavours to introduce uniformity of ritual, 5; dirge on death of, 8; receives an organ from Haroun Alraschid, 39.
Charles II. of England, music at his court, 219.
Charles VI., Emperor of Austria, 186.

Charles VII. of France, 64.
Charles VIII. of France, 64.
Charles IX. of France, 120.
Charmante Gabrielle, the air, 127.
Che faro senza Euridice, from Gluck's *Orfeo*, 189.
Chelys. See " *The Division Violist,* Simpson's."
Cherubini, M. L. C. Z. S. (1760—1842), 252.
Chest of viols, 58.
Child, Dr. William (1606—1697), 196.
Chimes, 32.
Chittarrone, 55.
Choir-schools established by St. Gregory, 5.
Chorales, introduction of, 82.
"Chorus" (musical instrument), 36.
Christian religion, effect of, on music, 2.
Chrysander, Dr. F., his edition of Carissimi's oratorios, 109 ; Life of Handel, 228.
Cibber, Mrs., singer (1714—1766), 222.
Cithara, Hebrew, 28 ; described by Gerbert, 46.
Clarionet, 45.
Clark, Dr. Jeremiah (1668[?]—1707), 203.
Clavichord, 61.
Clavicytherium, 51.
Clayton, Thomas (1665[?]—), 222, 223.
Clemens non Papa (first half 16th century), 67.
Cleopatra, opera by Mattheson, 174.
Clovis, baptism of, 3 ; treaty with Theodoric, *ib.*
" Coin du Roi," " Coin de la Reine," 275.
Colasse, Pascal (1639[?]—1709), 140, 142, 143.
Cologne, bell at, 31.
Colomban, his dirge on Charlemagne, 8.
Come if you dare, from Purcell's *King Arthur*, 208.
Come unto these yellow sands, from Purcell's *Tempest*, 208.
Commandments, Matthew Lock's responses to, 196.
Compendium of Practical Musick, Simpson's, 217.
Compère, L. (15th century), 67.
" Concert of Antient Musick," 254.
Concerts, early, in England, 254.
Concerts spirituels founded by A. D. Philidor, 294.
Concertos, organ, by Handel, 241.
Consilion, J. (first half 16th century), 68.

Consolations des Misères de ma Vie, songs by J. J. Rousseau, 280.
Constantine, Christian worship under, 2.
Constantine Copronymus sends an organ to Pépin, 39.
Contrabasso introduced into French orchestra by Montéclair, 146.
Contralto voice, rarity of, in France, 283.
Contrapunto a mente, 16.
Cooke, "Captain" Henry (1610[?]—1672), 195, 196, 201, 206.
Cooke, Dr. Benjamin (1732[?]—1793), 212, 259.
Corelli, Arcangelo (1653—1713),114, 176, 209.
Corneille, P., writes words of the opera *Andromeda*, 129.
Cornemuse, or bagpipes, 36, 37.
Coronation anthems by Handel, 234.
Costanza e Fortezza, opera by Fux, 186.
Cotton, John (11th century), his explanation of *organum*, 15.
Coucy, Châtelain de (—1192), 17.
Couperin, family of the, 298.
Coussemaker, C. E. H. de (1805—1876), his facsimiles of ancient manuscripts, 8 ; on early harmony, 14; his collection of the works of Adam de la Halle, 21 ; and of liturgical dramas, 23 ; on manuscript of *Sumer is icumen in*, 87.
Cremona violins, 59.
Crétin, Deploration sur le Trépas de feu Okeghem, 64.
Cristofali, Bartolomeo (1651—1731), inventor of pianoforte, 53.
Critica Musica, Mattheson's, 178.
Croce, Giovanni della (1550[?]—1609), 78.
Croft, Dr. William (1677—1727), 203, 204, 211.
Cromwell, 194.
Crwth, 57.
Cuzzoni, Francesca, singer (1700—1770), 232, 233, 234, 238.
Cymbals, 30. See also "Crotala."

Dafne, by Jacopo Peri, 104.
D'Alembert, J. le R. (1717—1783), 266, 277, 285.
Damasus, Pope, introduces chanting the Psalms, 3.
Danaides, Les, opera by Salieri, 287.
Danby, John (1757—1798), 259.
Danican. See "Philidor."
Dardanus, opera by Rameau, 269.

D'Assoucy, C. Coypeau (1604—1679), 129.
Davis, Mrs. Mary, singer, 222.
Deborah, oratorio by Handel, 237.
Deeper and deeper still, recitative from Handel's *Jephtha*, 247.
Défense de la Basse de Viole, by H. le Blanc, 296.
Deidamia, opera by Handel, 242.
De la Fage, Pierre (second half 15th century), 67.
De la Rue, Pierre (second half 15th century), 67.
Délivrance de Renaud, ballet of, 127.
Descartes, Réné, his *Compendium Musicæ* (1596—1650), 147.
Déserteur, Le, opera by Monsigny, 282.
Desmarets, Henri (1662—1741), 142.
Destouches, A. C. (1672—1749), 145.
Dettingen *Te Deum*, Handel's, 246.
Deuteromelia, by T. Ravenscroft, 98.
Devin du Village, Le, opera by J. J. Rousseau, 278.
Dezède (1740—1793), 280.
Diaphony, or *organum*, 15.
Dibdin, Charles (1745—1814), 253.
Dictionary, Musical, of Tinctoris, 65.
Dictionnaire de Musique, by J. J. Rousseau, 278.
Diderot, D. (1712—1784), 277.
Dido and Æneas, opera by Purcell, 207.
Diocletian; or, The Prophetess, incidental music by Purcell, 208.
Discant, introduction of, 15.
Discord, dire sister, glee by S. Webbe, 258.
Division Violist, Simpson's, 218.
Dodecachordon of Glareanus, 62.
Doles, J. F. (1715—1797), 168.
Douland, John (1562—1626), 100.
Draghi, Antonio (1642—1707), 185.
Draghi, J. B. (17th century), 214.
Dragon of Wantley, burlesque opera by J. F. Lampe, 250.
Drums, 27, 30. See also "Kettledrums."
Dryden, John, poet, 200, 207, 208, 241.
Dublin, Handel's visit to, 244, 246; Harris's organ in Christ Church Cathedral, 215.
Duenna, The, opera by Linley, 253.
Dufay, Guillaume (1350—1432), 61.
Duiffoprugcar, Gaspar (first half 16th century), 58.
Dulcimer or psaltery, 51.
Dunstable, John of (c. 1400—1458), 61, 87.
Dupuis, Dr. T. S. (1733—1796), 212.

Durante, Francesco (1684—1755), 110.
Durastanti, Signora, singer (18th century), 231.
D'Urfey, Thomas (—1723), 203; his *Wit and Mirth; or, Pills to Purge Melancholy*, 219.
Durham, Smith's organ at, 216.

Early history of music, 1.
Early secular music, 16.
Echo et Narcisse, opera by Gluck, 287.
Edward VI., Reformed Prayer-book of, 88.
Edwards, Richard (1523—1566), 88.
Ehrenpforte, Grundlage einer, by Mattheson, 179, 187.
Ein' feste Burg, the chorale, 82.
Elizabeth, Queen, her fondness for the virginal, 52; celebrated in the *Triumphs of Oriana*, 94, 96.
Encyclopédie, L', J. J. Rousseau's articles in, 277.
Engel, Carl, catalogue of musical instruments in the South Kensington Museum, 27.
Envy, eldest-born of Hell, chorus from Handel's *Saul*, 243.
Epine, Margherita de l' (—1746), 222.
Equal temperament advocated by Bach, 162.
Erasmus, Desiderius, 62.
Ercole d'Este, Duke of Ferrara, 65.
Escobedo, Bartolomeo (1510—), 77.
Essais sur la Musique, by Grétry, 292.
Esther, Handel's oratorio, 229, 237.
Est's *Psalms*, 100.
Euridice, by Rinuccini, set to music both by Peri and Caccini, 104.
Ezio, opera by Handel, 236.

Fairfax, Dr. Robert (second half 15th century), 87.
Faramondo, opera by Handel, 242.
Farinelli (Carlo Broschi called) (1705—1782), 114, 240, 241.
Farmer, John (1565[?]—), 100.
Farnaby, Giles (1560—), 100.
Farrant, Richard (1530[?]—1581), 90.
Fausse Magic, La, opera by Grétry, 291.
Faustina Bordoni, wife of Hasse (1700—1783), 180, 233, 234.
Faux Lord, Le, opera by Gossec, 280.
Favart, Madame, singer and dancer (1727 —1772), 302.
Fenton, Lavinia (Duchess of Bolton) (18th century), 236.

Ferrari, Benedetto (—1681), 107.
Festa, Constanzo (1490[?]—1545), 68.
Festes de l'Eté, opera by Montéclair, 146.
Fêtes de l'Amour et de Bacchus, opera by Lully, 137.
Fétis, F. J. (1784—1871), remarks on Guido d'Arezzo, 13;—276.
Fevin, Antoine (1481—), 67.
Finta Pazza, La, performed in Paris, 1645, 127.
Five times by the taper's light, quartet by Storace, 253.
Fixed in His everlasting seat, chorus in Handel's *Samson*, 246.
Flageolet, 29, 35.
Flavio, opera by Handel, 232.
Flores Musicæ, by Hugo von Reutlingen, 82.
Floridante, opera by Handel, 232.
Florid Song, Treatise on the, by Tosi, 185.
Flute, the, 27, 35; double, 35; horizontal or "German," *ib*; à-bec, *ib*.
Foire, Théâtre de la, 271.
Fontenailles, Angilbert's song on the battle of, 8.
Foolish Virgins, song of the, 23.
Foundling Hospital, Handel's interest in the, 245.
Four-line staff introduced, 12.
Fournival, Richard de (13th century), 17.
Franc, Guillaume (16th century), his music to Marot's *Psalms*, 122.
Francis I. of France, 120.
Frederick the Great of Prussia, 159, 182, 275.
French and Italian music, comparison between, 273.
French singers, 302.
Frescobaldi, Girolamo (1587—1654), 118.
Froberger, J. J. (1615—1667), 151.
Froissart, figure of monochord from MS. copy of, 60.
From the censer, chorus in Handel's *Solomon*, 247.
Frost scene in Purcell's *King Arthur*, 208.
Full fathom five, from Purcell's *Tempest*, 208.
Funeral service by Dr. Croft, 204.
Fux, Johann Josef (1660—1741), 186, 188.

Gabinetto Armonico of Bonanni, 26.
Gabrieli, Andrea (1510—1586), 78, 117.
Gabrieli, Giovanni (1557—1613), 78, 117.

Gaforius (or Gaffurius) (1451—1522), writer on theory of music, 78.
Galatea, dry thy tears, chorus from *Acis and Galatea*, 229.
Galilei, Vincenzo (1533[?]—), his dialogue on the music of the ancients, 103.
Galuppi, Baldassare (1701 [1706?]—1785), 111.
Gardano, Antonio (16th century), music-printer, 68.
Gardiner, Bishop, 88.
Gascogne, M. (beginning of 16th century), 67.
Gaspar di Salo (end of 16th century), 59.
Gastoldi, Giangiacomo (1532—1598), 78.
Gates, Bernard (1686—1773), 237.
Gaviniés, Pierre (1728—1800), 296.
Gavotte of Louis XIII., 125.
Geminiani, F. (1680—1762), 116, 250.
Gerbert, Martin (1720—1793) (prince abbot of St. Blaise, in the Black Forest), 8, 46, 57.
Germany, early history of music in, 80.
Gewandhaus concerts, foundation of, 168.
Gheyn, Matthias van den (1721—1785), 33.
Gibbons, Christopher (1615—1676), 196.
Gibbons, Ellis (1580[?]—1650), 94.
Gibbons, Orlando (1583—1625), his madrigals, 93; his *Fantasies in three parts*, 96.
Gilbert, Gabriel, writes poem of *Les Peines et les Plaisirs d'Amour*, opera by Cambert, 133.
Ginguené, P. L. (1748—1816), 285.
Giulio Cesare, opera by Handel, 232.
Giustiniani's *Psalms* set to music by Marcello, 112.
Giustinio, opera by Handel, 241.
Gizziello (Gioacchino Conti called) (1714—1761), singer, 241.
Glareanus, Henricus Loritus (1488—1563), 62, 80, 85.
Glee, introduction of the, 257; definition of, *ib*.
Gluck, Christopher Willibald (1714—1787), 188; his *Orfeo*, 189; *Alcestis, ib.*; principles of dramatic composition, *ib.*; *Paride ed Elena*, 191; *Iphigénie en Aulide, ib.*; visits Paris, 192, 282; visits London, 252, 271; *Iphigénie en Aulide* in Paris, 282; *Orphée*, 283; *Alceste, ib.*; rivalry with Piccinni, 284; *Amide*, 286; *Iphigénie en Tauride*, 287; his death, 287;—302.

Gluckistes and Piccinnistes, controversy of the, 284.
God is gone up, anthem by Dr. Croft, 204.
Gombert, Nicolas (1495—1570[?]), 67.
Gosling, Rev. John (1652—1733), 207.
Gossec, F. J. (1733—1829), 280.
Goudimel, Claude (1510—1572), 67, 76.
Grabu, Louis (living 1685), 200.
Gradus ad Parnassum, by Fux, 187.
Graun, C. H. (1701—1759), 182.
Great Abuse of Musick, Rev. A. Bedford's, 219.
Greatorex, Thomas (1758—1831), 255.
Greece, musicians in Rome from that country, 1; musical instruments of, 27.
Greene, Dr. Maurice (1696[?]—1755), 211.
" Gregorian " music, 4.
Gregory, St., the great (542—604), his services to Church music, 3; his method of notation, 4; his claim to the invention of neums, 5.
Gregory of Tours, 3.
Gresham, Sir Thomas, his college, 97.
Grétry, A. E. M. (1741—1813), 289.
Grimm, F. M. Baron (1723—1807), 275.
Groppo, Antonio, his catalogue of *drammi in musica* played in Venice, 107.
Grove, Sir G., his *Dictionary of Music*, facsimile of *Sumer is icumen in*, 86.
Guarnerius, Joseph (1683—1745), 59.
Guerrero, Francesco (1518—1599), 77.
Guesdron, 126.
Guido d'Arezzo (c. 990—1070), his invention of *solfeggio*, 13; theories attacked by Ramis de Pareja, 79.
Guignon, J. P. (1702—1775), 296.
Guitar, 55.
Gumpelzhaimer, Adam (1560—   ), 151.

Halle, Adam de la (13th century), 17; his compositions, 21.
Hallelujah Chorus in Handel's *Messiah*, 245.
Hamburg, first public performance of opera in Germany given in, 168.
Handbuch bey dem Generalbasse, by Marpurg, 184.
Handel, George Frederic (1685—1759), his youth, 170; settles in Hamburg, 173; relations with Mattheson, *ib.*; his opera *Almira*, 174; and *Nero*, 175; visits Italy, *ib.*; appointed Capellmeister at Hanover, 177; his arrival in

England, 224; operatic career, *ib.*; Utrecht *Te Deum* and *Jubilate*, 227; "Water Music," *ib.*; enters service of the Duke of Chandos, 228; production of his first oratorio, *Esther*, 229; foundation of the Royal Academy of Music, 230; coronation anthem, 234; collapse of the Royal Academy, 235; partnership with Heidegger, 236; production of *Acis and Galatea* and *Deborah*, 237; partnership with Rich, 240; his bankruptcy and illness, 241; his oratorios, 242; *The Messiah*, 244; his visit to Dublin, 244; his second bankruptcy, 246; his blindness, 247; and death, 248.
Handel's fondness for the trumpet, 44.
Handel, Life of, by Mattheson, 179.
Händl, Jakob (1550—1591), 80.
Hannibal, opera by Keiser, 171.
Happy we, chorus from Handel's *Acis and Galatea*, 229.
Harmonia Sacra, Playford's, 217.
Harmonie Universelle, by Mersenne, 148.
Harmonious Blacksmith, Handel's, 230.
Harmony, early attempts at, 14.
Haroun Alraschid sends an organ to Charlemagne, 39.
Harp, the, 47; of O'Brien, 48; Welsh triple, *ib.*; pedal, 50; Erard's improvements, 51.
Harpsichord, 53.
Harris, Renatus, organ-builder (—1725), 213.
Hasse, John Adolph (1699—1783), 110, 180, 240.
Hassler, Hans Leo (1564—1612), 78.
Haste thee, nymph, air and chorus from Handel's *L'Allegro*, 243.
Haunted Tower, The, opera by Storace, 253.
Hawkins, Sir John, his *History of Music*, 259, 260.
Haydn, F. J. (1732—1809), 193.
Hayes, Dr. Philip (1738—1797), 212.
Hayes, Dr. William (1707—1777), 212.
Heidegger, James, 227, 230, 236, 237, 242.
Henri II. of France, 120.
Henry VIII. of England, 71.
Heyden, Sebaldus (1498—1561), his *Ars Canendi*, 85.
Hiller, Johann Adam (1728—1804), 168, 184.

Hilton, John (1575[?]—1657), 90 ; his *Catch that catch can*, 98.
Hippolyte et Aricie, opera by Rameau, 268.
Histoire de la Revolution Opérée dans la Musique par M. le Chevalier Gluck of Leblond, 286.
Historisch-kritische Beytrage zur Aufnahme der Musik, Marpurg's, 184.
Histrio-Mastix, Prynne's, 126.
Hobrecht (1430[?]—1507), 62, 63, 67.
Holbach, P. Thyry, Baron d' (1723—1789), 275.
Holborn, St. Andrew's, Harris's organ in, 215.
Holy Week, music for, in Sistine Chapel, 77.
Hucbald (840[?]—930), his treatise *Musica Enchiriadis*, 15.
Hugo von Reutlingen (14th century), his *Flores Musicæ*, 82.
Humfrey, Pelham (1647—1674), 196, 199, 206.
Huron, Le, opera by Grétry, 291.
Hush, ye pretty, warbling choir, air in Handel's *Acis and Galatea*, 229.

I attempt from love's sickness to fly, from Purcell's *Indian Queen*, 209.
I beheld, and lo! a great multitude, anthem by Dr. Blow, 202.
Il tricerbero umiliato, air from Handel's *Rinaldo*, 226.
Indes Galantes, opera by Rameau, 269.
Indian Queen, Purcell's, 209.
In going to my naked bed, madrigal by R. Edwards, 88.
Instrumental music, early, 96 ; in France, 146, 296.
Instruments, musical, history of, 24.
Introduction to the Skill of Musick, Playford's, 217.
In una siepe ombrosa, madrigal by Lotti, 111, 239.
Iphigénie en Aulide, opera by Gluck, 191, 282.
Iphigénie en Tauride, opera by Gluck, 287.
I rage, I melt, I burn, recitative in Handel's *Acis and Galatea*, 229.
Iron Chest, The, opera by Storace, 253.
Isaak, Heinrich (1445[?]—1518[?]), 80.
Isabelle et Gertrude, opera by Grétry, 291.
Isidore, St., Bishop of Seville (c. 570—636), on the use of neums, 10.

Israel in Egypt, Handel's oratorio, 243.
Issé, opera by Destouches, 146.
Italian and French music, comparison between, 273.
Italian singers introduced into France by Cardinal Mazarin, 127.
Italy, early history of music in, 74.
I was in the Spirit, anthem by Dr. Blow, 202.

"Jack" action in keyed stringed instruments, 52.
Jackson, William, of Exeter (1730—1803), 212.
Jannequin, Clément (c. 1480—   ), 67.
Jélyotte, Pierre, singer (1711—1782), 302.
Jennens, Charles, selects the words of Handel's *Messiah*, 244, 245.
Jephtha, Handel's oratorio, 247.
Jephtha, oratorio by Carissimi, 109.
Jerome, St. (331—420), his letter on musical instruments, 28.
Jewish influence on early Christian music, 2.
Jolly Young Waterman, song by Dibdin, 254.
Jomelli, Nicolo (1714—1774), 111.
Jonah, oratorio by Carissimi, 109.
Jongleurs, 17.
Joshua, Handel's oratorio, 247.
Josquin de Près (1450[?]—1521), 64, 65, 67, 68, 73, 80, 120.
Journet, Mademoiselle, as Mélisse in *Amadis de Grèce*, by Destouches, 145.
Jubilate, by Purcell, 208, 210.
Judas Maccabæus, Handel's oratorio, 246.
Judgment of Solomon, oratorio by Carissimi, 109.
Julien, St., des Menestriers, Church of, 19.
Julius III., Pope, appoints Palestrina a singer in the Sistine Chapel, 76.

Keiser, Reinhard (1673—1739), 170, 175, 180.
Kettledrums, orchestral, 30.
Kielmansegge, Baron, 177, 227.
King Arthur, Dryden's, incidental music by Purcell, 209.
King, Charles (1687—1748), 212.
Kirkman, maker of harpsichords, 53.
Kirnberger, J. P. (1721—1783), 165.
Krebs, J. Ludwig (1713—1780), 165.
Kritische Briefe über die Tonkunst, Marpurg's, 184.

Kritischer Musicus of Scheibe, 183.
Kritischer Musikus an der Spree, Marpurg's, 184.

La Harpe, J. F. de (1739—1803), 285.
L'Allegro, Il Penseroso, ed Il Moderato, Handel's cantata, 243.
Lalouette, J. F. (1651—1728), 140.
Lambillotte, Père (1797—1855), 7.
Lamentabatur Jacob, motet by Cristoforo Morales, 77.
Lampe, J. F. (1692[?]—1751), 250.
Lascia ch'io pianga, air from Handel's *Rinaldo*, 175, 226.
Lassus, Orlando di (1520[?]—1594), 70, 74; collection of his works at Munich, 71;—103.
Lateran, St. John, Church of, Palestrina made director of the music at, 76.
Lattre, Roland de. See "Lassus, Orlando di."
Laudi Spirituali, 108.
Lawes, Henry (1595—1662), 101, 194, 195, 217.
Leblond, Abbé (1738—1809), 286.
Lecerf de la Vieville, J. L. (1647—1710), 273.
Leclair, J. M. (1697—1764), 296.
Le Jeune, Claude (1528[?]—1606[?]), 67, 127.
Lenten oratorios given by Handel, 240.
Leo, Leonardo (1694—1746), 110, 238.
Leroy, Etienne (16th century), 121.
Let the bright seraphim, air from Handel's *Samson*, 246.
Let their celestial concerts all unite, chorus in Handel's *Samson*, 246.
Let thy hand be strengthened, coronation anthem by Handel, 234.
Lettre sur la Musique Française, by J. J. Rousseau, 276.
Let us take the road, song in the *Beggar's Opera*, 235.
L'Homme Armé, the air, 22, 74.
Li Gieus de Robin et de Marion, by Adam de la Halle, 22.
Linley, Thomas (1725—1795), 253.
Liturgical dramas, 22.
Locatelli, P. (1693—1764), 116.
Lock, Matthew (1628[?]—1677), 195, 196.
Lord, for Thy tender mercies' sake, anthem by R. Farrant, 90.
Lorenzo de Medici, 65.

Lotario, opera by Handel, 236.
Lotti, Antonio (1667[?]—1740), 111, 239.
Louis XI. of France, 64.
Louis XII. of France, 65.
Louis XIV., his musical acquirements, 130.
Love in her eyes, air in Handel's *Acis and Galatea*, 229.
Lowe, Edmund (1610[?]—1682), 196, 202.
Lully, Jean Baptiste (1633—1687), 134; protected by Louis XIV., 135; composes ballets, 136; obtains Perrin's privilege for performing opera, *ib.*; his career as a writer of opera, 137; his death, 140; his Church music, *ib.*, 198, 200, 221, 263, 272, 273, 299.
Lully, Jean Louis de, 142.
Lully, Louis, 142.
Luscinius (Nachtigall), Ottomar (1487—), 83.
Lute, the, 54.
Luther, Martin, his love for music, 80.
Lyre, the, 27, 45.

Macbeth, music to, 196, 206.
Mace, Thomas (1613—1709), his *Musick's Monument*, 218.
Madden, Sir F., on manuscript of *Sumer is icumen in*, 87.
Madrigalian Era in England, 90, 256; in Netherlands, 68.
Madrigals, rareness of complete printed sets of, 69, 94.
Magnum Opus Musicum of Orlando di Lassus, 73.
Mainwaring, Rev. John, his translation of Mattheson's *Life of Handel*, 179.
Marais, Marin (1656—1728), 142.
Marcello, Benedetto (1686—1739), 111.
March from Handel's *Rinaldo*, 226.
Marchand, Louis (1669—1732), 156.
Marenzio, Luca (1550[?]—1599), 77.
Marguerite de Valois, 121.
Mariages Samnites, Les, opera by Grétry, 291.
Marmontel, J. F. (1723—1799), 284, 285.
Marot, Clément (1495—1544), his translation of the Psalms, 121.
Marot, Clément, Lettre de (satire on Lully), 140.
Marpurg, F. W. (1718—1795), his critical and theoretical writings, 183.
Martini, G. B., Padre (1706—1784), 192 260.

Mattheson, Johann (1681—1764), 173; his
    opera *Cleopatra*, 174; his critical and
    theoretical writings, 178, 187.
Mauduit, Jacques (1557—1627), 126.
Maximilian I., Emperor, 65, 80.
Maximilian II., Emperor, ennobles Orlando
    di Lassus, 71.
May no rash intruder and succeeding
    choruses in Handel's *Solomon*, 247.
Mazarin, Cardinal, introduces Italian opera
    into France, 127; enormous sums
    spent on it by him, 129.
Meistersingers, the, 18; their election, *ib.*
Melothesia, Lock's, 198.
Menestriers, Confrérie des, 18; receive sanc-
    tion of the Provost of Paris and of
    Charles VI., 20; of Louis XIV., 21;
    abuse of their privileges, 20.
Merbecke, John (1512[?]—1585), 88.
Mersenne, Marin (1588—1648), 148.
Messiah, The, Handel's oratorio, 244, 246,
    256.
Military trumpet, 43.
Milton, John (father of the poet) (c. 1576—
    1647), 101.
Milton, John, the poet, 194.
Minnesingers, the, 18.
Minstrels, 17. See also " Menestriers."
Minstrels," " King of the, 20.
Missa Papæ Marcelli, by Palestrina, 76,
    104.
Mizler, Lorenz(1711—1778), his *Neueröffnete
    Musikalische Bibliothek,* 183, 187.
" *Modern Church Musick, Preaccused,*" etc.,
    by Matthew Lock, 197.
Molière, his intimacy with Lully, 136.
Monnet, John (—1785), 273.
Monochord, 59.
M. de Porceaugnac, incidental music to, by
    Lully, 138.
Monsigny, P. A. (1729—1817), 280.
Monte, Philippe de (1521—1603), 67.
Montéclair, M. P. de (1666—1737), 146, 268.
Monteverde, Claudio (1568—1643 [? 1651]),
    105; his instrumentation, 106, 129.
Morales, Cristoforo (16th century), 77.
Morley, Thomas (1563—1604), his madri-
    gals, ballets, and canzonets, 93; his
    *Plaine and Easie Introduction to
    Practicall Musicke*, 94.
Mornington, Lord (1735—1781), 259.
Moscow, great bell of, 34.
Motets, collection of, by O. di Lassus, 73.

Motteville, Madame de, her opinion of the
    Italian opera, 128.
Mouton, Jean (16th century), 67.
Mozart, W. A. (1756—1791), 78, 182, 193,
    253, 261, 304.
Mulliner, Thomas (15th century), 87.
Muses Galantes, Les, opera by J. J. Rous-
    seau, 277.
Musette, 37, 146.
Music, early treatises on, 80; in England,
    86; widespread knowledge of, during
    the 16th and 17th centuries, 94.
Musica Antiqua, J. Stafford Smith's, 259.
Musica Transalpina, published by N. Yonge,
    91.
Musical Antiquarian Society, 95.
Musical Century, Henry Carey's, 250.
Musicalische Patriot, Der, by Mattheson,
    179.
Musick's Monument, Mace's, 218.
Musikalische Bibliothek of Mizler, 183.
Muzio Scevola, opera by Ariosti, G. B.
    Buononcini, and Handel, 231.
My heart is inditing, coronation anthem by
    Handel, 234.

Nablum, 46.
Nacaire, 29.
Nachtigall. See " Luscinius."
Nanini, Bernardino (1545[?]—1620[?]), 77.
Nanini, Giovanni Maria (1530[?]—1607), 77.
Nardini, P. (1722—1793), 117.
Nares, Dr. James (1715—1783), 212.
Neri, St. Philip, his intimacy with Pales-
    trina, 76; founds order of Oratorians,
    108.
Nero, opera by Handel, 175.
Netherlands, musical influence of, 61.
Neums, invention of, attributed to St.
    Gregory, 5; suggested origin of, 7;
    nomenclature of, 8; used for both
    sacred and secular music, *ib.*
Noces de Thétis et de Pelée, opera by
    Colasse, 142, 143.
North, Hon. Roger (1650—1733), 216.
Nouveau Système de Musique Theorique,
    by Rameau, 216.
Noverre, ballet-master, 302.
Numitor, opera by Giovanni Porta, 230,
    231.
Nun danket alle Gott, the chorale, 82.

Occasional Oratorio, Handel's, 246

Ode for St. Cecilia's Day, Handel's, 243.
Oft on a plat, air from Handel's *L'Allegro*, 243.
Okenheim or Okeghem (1415[?]—1513[?]), 62, 64, 67, 68, 120.
Oliphant, 42.
Opera, origin of the, 102 ; first theatre for, in Venice, 107 ; foundation of, in France, 130 ; in Germany, 168 ; in England, 207, 221.
" Opera of the Nobility," 239.
Oratorio, origin of the, 108 ; Handel's oratorios, 242.
Orfeo performed in Paris in 1647-8, 129.
Orfeo, opera by Gluck, 189, 283.
Organ, 28, 38 ; hydraulic, 28, 38 ; in Italy, 117 ; in Germany, 165 ; in England, 212.
Organ concertos, Handel's, 241.
Organistrum, 57.
" Organizing " taught by the Roman singers to the French, 14.
Organum, or diaphony, 15.
Oriana, Triumphs of, 93.
O Richard ! ô mon roi ! air in Grétry's *Richard Cœur de Lion*, 291.
Orlando, opera by Handel, 236.
O ruddier than the cherry, air in Handel's *Acis and Galatea*, 229.
O the pleasures of the plains, chorus in Handel's *Acis and Galatea*, 229.
Ottone, opera by Handel, 232.
O where shall wisdom be found? anthem by Dr. Boyce, 211.

Pachelbel, Johann (1653—1706), 151, 155.
Pagan influence on early Christian music, 2.
Palestrina, Giovanni Pierluigi da (1524[?]—1594), 75 ; summary of his works, 76, 104, 304.
Pammelia, by T. Ravenscroft, 98.
Pan's pipes or syrinx, 34.
Parallèle des Italiens et des Français, Raguenet's, 273.
Partenope, opera by Handel, 236.
Parthenia, 96.
Pastorale, La, opera by Cambert, 131.
Pastor Fido, opera by Handel, 227.
Patrocinium Musices of Adam Berg, 73.
Paul IV., Pope, deprives Palestrina of his post in the Sistine Chapel, 76.
Paul's, St., Cathedral, Smith's organ in, 216.

Paxton, Stephen (1735—1787), 259 ; Paxton, William (—1781), *ib.*
Pêcheurs, Les, opera by Gossec, 280.
Pellegrin, Abbé (1661—1745), 268.
Pépin receives an organ from Constantine Copronymus, 39.
Pepusch, Dr. (1667—1752), 222, 228, 235.
Pepys, Samuel, extracts from his diary, 195, 199, 200, 212.
Percussion, instruments of, 29.
Pergolesi, G. B. (1710—1737), 110, 273, 275.
Peri, Jacopo (16th century, living 1610), 104, 109.
Perrin, Abbé (—1676), 130 ; joins Cambert in founding the first opera-house in Paris, 131 ; quarrels with his partners, 133 ; sells his patent to Lully, 136.
Peter's, St., at Rome, organs in, 117.
" Petits violons du Roi," 135.
Petrucci, Ottaviano dei (1466—1524), music-printer, 64, 66, 68.
Phalèse, Pierre (1510[?]—), music-printer, 68.
Philidor (Danican), the family of the, 293.
Phillips, John, his *Duellum Musicum*, 198.
Philosophes and the opera, 269.
Pianoforte, invention of, 53.
Piccinni, Nicolo (1728—1800), 284, 287.
Pills to purge Melancholy, D'Urfey's, 219.
Pius IV., Pope, 75.
Plain-chant or plain-song, treatises on, 4, 80.
Playford, John (1623—1693), 198, 203, 217, 257.
Plectrum, 47.
Poisson, Père, translates Descartes' *Compendium Musicæ* into French, 147.
Polly Peachum in the *Beggar's Opera*, 236.
Pompadour, Madame de, 275.
Pontifical Chapel, the, 62, 65.
Popelinière, Leriche de la, 267, 277, 280.
Poro, opera by Handel, 236.
Porpora, N. A. (1686—1767), 114, 238, 239.
Porta, Costanzo (1520[?]—1601), 67, 78.
Porta, Giovanni (1690[?]—1740), his opera *Numitor*, 230.
" Portative " (small organ), 41.
" Positive " (small organ), 41.
Prætorius, Michael (Schultz) (1571—1621), his *Syntagma Musicum*, 83, 152.
Préludes de l'Harmonie Universelle, by Mersenne, 148.
Près, Josquin de. See " Josquin de Près."

Printers, early music, 68.
Prioris (end 15th and beginning 16th
    centuries), 67.
*Projet concernant de Nouveaux Signes pour
    la Musique*, by J. J. Rousseau, 276.
Protestantism, influence of, in France, 121.
Prynne's *Histrio-Mastix*, 126.
Psalmody, metrical, in the English Church,
    100; the "old" version, 100; the
    "new" version, 101.
Psalms, Marcello's, 112.
*Psalms, Sonets, and Songs of Sadnes and
    Pietie*, by W. Byrd, 90.
Psalms, Songs, and Sonnets, by Byrd, 90.
Psalterium, 46.
Psaltery or dulcimer, 51.
Psyche, Matthew Lock's, 197.
Purcell, Henry (1658—1695), 203 ; his
    youth and education, 204; his early
    works, 206; his *Dido and Æneas*, 207 ;
    Te Deum and *Jubilate*, 208, 210; *The
    Tempest, Diocletian*, and *King Arthur,
    ib.*; *Indian Queen*, 209; his death, 210;
    his *Orpheus Britannicus*, 211, 214, 217.
Purcell, Thomas (—1682), 206.
Pur dicesti, song by Lotti, 111.

Quæstiones Celeberrimæ in Genesim, by
    Mersenne, 148.
Quantz, Johann Joachim (1697—1773), 159.
Quarter-notes introduced into Temple organ,
    216.
Quinault (1635—1688) writes most of the
    books of Lully's operas, 137, 284.

Rabelais, account of two concerts given by,
    67.
Racine, his *Iphigénie en Aulide* arranged as
    an opera and set to music by Gluck,
    191 ; *Hippolyte et Aricie (Phèdre)*, by
    Rameau, 268.
Radamisto, opera by Handel, 230, 231.
Raguenet, Abbé (1660[?]—1722[?]), 273.
Rameau, Jean Philippe (1683—1764), 189,
    191, 263 ; his theoretical publications,
    265; his career as a composer, 267 ;
    opinion of Italian music, 275, 277.
Ramis de Pareja (1440[?]—living 1521), 79.
Rappresentazione di Anima e di Corpo, ora-
    torio by E. del Cavaliere, 108.
Ravenscroft, Thomas (1582[?]—1635), 98 ;
    his *Psalms*, 101.

Recitative, accompanied, invented by
    Carissimi, 109.
Recorder, 45.
Redford, John (16th century), 88.
Reed, the, 34.
Reformation, effect of the, on music, 80.
Reform in Church music effected by Pales-
    trina, 75.
"Regal" (small organ), 41.
Restoration, music in England at the, 194.
Resurrezione, oratorio by Handel, 176.
Return, blest days, glee by J. Stafford Smith,
    259.
Return, O God of hosts, air in Handel's
    Samson, 246.
Reuchlin, Johann (1455—1522), his *Scenica
    Progymnasmata*, 168.
Rheims, House of Musicians at, 29.
Ricciardo Primo, opera by Handel, 234.
Richafford (second half of 15th century), 68.
Richard Cœur de Lion, opera by Grétry,
    291.
Rinaldo, opera by Handel, 175, 224 ; Rossi's
    excuse for the libretto, 225 ;—227, 228,
    235.
Rinuccini, Ottavio, poet, 104; his *Dafne* set
    to music by H. Schütz, 168.
Rodelinda, opera by Handel, 232.
Rodrigo, opera by Handel, 175.
Roland, opera by Piccinni, 284, 286.
Rollet, Bailli du, his relations with Gluck,
    191, 282, 287.
Romans, music among the, 1 ; musical in-
    struments of the, 27.
Rore, Cipriano di (1516—1565), 67, 78.
Rosamund, Addison's, set by Clayton and
    subsequently by Arne, 223.
Rota, or hurdy-gurdy, 57.
Rotta, or crwth, 57.
Rousseau, J. J. (1712—1778), 275, 276.
Rowbotham, Mr. J. F., his classification of
    instruments, 28.
"Royal Academy of Music," foundation of,
    230.
Royal Society of Musicians, 256.
Rule Britannia, air by Dr. Arne, 250.
Russian bells, 34.

Sacchini, A. M. G. (1734—1786), 289.
Sachs, Hans (1486—1567), 18.
Sackbut, 44.
Sacrati, Francesco Paolo (—1650),
    108.

Sacred Harmonic Society, 255; its library, 99.
Sacred music, corruptions of, 75.
St. Gall, its MS. of Gregory's *Antiphonarium*, 5; facsimile of a portion of, 6.
Saint-Huberty, Madame (1756 — 1812), singer, 302.
Salaries of singers in time of Handel, 233.
Salieri, Antonio (1750—1825), 287.
Sallé, Mademoiselle, dancer, 302.
Sally in our alley, song by Henry Carey, 250.
"Salmon and Lock" controversy, 197.
Salmon, Jacques (living 1582), 125.
Sambuca, 28.
Sammartini, G. B. (about 1700[?]—living in 1770), 188, 192.
Samson, Handel's oratorio, 246, 247.
Samson, opera by Rameau, 268.
Saul, oratorio by Handel, 243.
Scarlatti, Alessandro (1659—1725), 109, 180.
Scarlatti, Domenico (1683—1757), 119, 177.
Scenica Progymnasmata of Reuchlin, 168.
Scheibe, J. A. (1708—1776), his *Kritischer Musicus*, 183.
Schmidt, Bernard ("Father Smith") (1630 [?]—1709), 212.
Schools, choir-, established by St. Gregory, 5.
Schütz, Heinrich (Sagittarius) (1585—1672), 168.
Scipio, opera by Handel, 232, 236.
Scotto, Girolamo (—1573), music-printer, 68.
Senesino(Francesco Bernardi)(1680—1750), singer, 230, 231, 233, 236, 237, 238.
Senfl, Ludwig (1490[?]—1555), 80.
Serva Padrona, La, opera by Pergolesi, 110, 273, 278, 280, 289.
Sesostrate, opera by Hasse, 180.
Shawm, 44.
Shepherds' trumpets, 43.
Sheppard, John (16th century), 87.
Sheridan, R. B., 253.
Shield, William (1748—1829), 253.
Shophar, 42.
Siege of Belgrade, opera by Storace, 253.
Siena, ancient bell at, 32.
Silver Swan, madrigal by Orlando Gibbons, 93.
Simpson, Christopher (1640[?]—), *Chelys; or, The Division Violist*, 218; *Compendium of Practical Musick*, 217.

Siroe, opera by Handel, 234.
Sistine Chapel, performance of the *Missa Papæ Marcelli* in, 76; Palestrina appointed composer to, *ib.*; excellence of unaccompanied vocal music in, 77; music in Holy Week, *ib.*
Sistrum, the, 27, 30.
Sixtus IV., Pope, 65.
Slide-trumpet, 44.
Smith, J. Stafford (1746[?]—1836], 259.
Soissons, Count of, 17.
Solomon, Handel's oratorio, 247.
"Sonata," the word first used by G. Gabrieli, 118.
Sonatas, Purcell's, 209.
Songs of Sundrie Natures, some of Gravitie and others of Myrth, by W. Byrd, 90.
Sourdéac, Marquis de, joins Perrin, Cambert, and Champeron in founding the French Opera, 132.
South Kensington Museum, C. Engel's catalogue of musical instruments at, 27.
Spartaro, G. (1460[?]—1541), 80.
Spinet, 52.
Spofforth, Reginald (1768—1827), 259.
Stabat Mater by Astorga, 254; by Pergolesi, 110.
Stadt-pfeiffer, or town-musicians in Germany, 151.
Staff, musical, development of, 10.
Steffani, Abbate (1655—1730), 177.
Sternhold and Hopkins' *Psalms*, 100.
Stevens, R. J. S. (1753—1837), 98, 259.
Storace, Anna S., singer (1765[?]—1817), 253.
Storace, Stephen (1763—1796), 253.
Strada, Anna, singer, 236, 237, 241.
Straduarius, Antonius, 59.
Stringed instruments, 45.
Suard, J. B. A. (1734—1817), 285.
Suite de Pièces pour le Clavecin, by Handel, 230.
Sumer is icumen in, round, 86.
Supplément au Roman Comique of Jean Monnet, 273.
Susanna, Handel's oratorio, 247.
Sweelinck, J. P. (1540[?]—1621), 165.
Sweet bird, air from Handel's *L'Allegro*, 243.
Syntagma Musicum of Michael Prætorius, 85.
Syrinx or Pan's pipes, 34.

Tableau Parlant, Le, opera by Grétry, 291.
Tabour and pipe, 29.
Tallis, Thomas (1520—1585), 88, 89; his forty-part canon, *ib.*; his Evening Hymn, *ib.*; his patent for music printing with Byrd, *ib.*
Tambourin, 29.
Tambourine, 29.
Tamerlano, opera by Handel, 232.
Tartini, Giuseppe (1692—1770), 116.
Tate, Nahum, his *Dido and Æneas* set by Purcell, 208.
Taverner, John (first half 16th century), 87.
Teatro alla moda, Marcello's, 113.
Te Deum, by Graun, 182; by W. Jackson, of Exeter, 212; by Purcell, 208, 210.
Telemann, G. P. (1681—1767), 168.
Tempest, The, music to, by Purcell, 208.
Temple Church organ, 213; Smith's introduction of "quarter-notes" in, 216.
Temple Musick, Rev. A. Bedford's, 220.
Teseo, opera by Handel, 227.
The dead shall live, chorus from Handel's ode for St. Cecilia's Day, 243.
The king shall rejoice, coronation anthem by Handel, 234.
The mighty conqueror, glee by S. Webbe, 258.
The soldier tired, air by Dr. Arne, 250.
The trumpet's loud clangour, chorus from Handel's ode for St. Cecilia's Day, 243.
The ways of Zion do mourn, anthem by M. Wise, 199.
Theater of Musick, Playford's, 217.
Theile, Johann (1646—1724), 169.
Then round about the starry throne, chorus in Handel's *Samson*, 246.
Theodora, oratorio by Handel, 247.
Theorbo, 55.
Thésée, opera by Lully, 140.
They that go down to the sea in ships, anthem by Purcell, 207.
Thibaut, King of Navarre (1201—1254), 17.
" Third sound " of Tartini, 117.
Thirty Years' War, its effect on music in Germany, 151.
Thoinan, Ernest (A. E. Roquet), 276.
Thomyris, Queen of Scythia, opera, 222.
Tibia or flute, 35.
Tieffenbrücker. See "Duiffoprugcar."
Tinctoris, J. (1434[?]—1511), 65.
Tod, Der, Jesu, oratorio by Graun, 182.
Tofts, Mrs. (17th century), singer, 222.

Tolomeo, opera by Handel, 234.
Tom Bowling, song by Dibdin, 204.
Tosi, P. F. (1680[?]—1762[?]), 185.
Total eclipse, air from Handel's *Samson*, 246.
Town-musicians, or *Stadt-pfeiffer*, in Germany, 151.
Traité de l'Harmonie reduite à ses Principes Naturels, by Rameau, 265.
Travenol, Louis (1698[?]—1783), 275.
Travers, John (1706—1758), 212.
Treasury of Musick, Playford's, 217.
Treatises on music, ancient, all in Greek language, 1.
Tremolo invented by Monteverde, 107.
Trent, Council of, 75.
Triangle, 31.
Trionfo del Tempo, cantata by Handel, 176.
Triumph of Time and Truth, cantata by Handel, 176.
Triumphs of Oriana, 93.
Troubadours, their origin and constitution, 16.
Trumpet, 27, 42.
Trumpet-marine, 60.
Tschudi, maker of harpsichords, 53.
Tuba, St. Jerome's description of, 28.
Tye, Dr. Christopher (1508[?]—1570[?]), 88.

Under the greenwood tree, air by Dr. Arne, 250.
Une fièvre brûlante, air in Grétry's *Richard Cœur de Lion*, 291.
Utrecht *Te Deum* and *Jubilate*, Handel's, 227.

Vecchi, Orazio (1530[?]—1605), 78.
Venice, early school of music at, 78.
Veracini, F. M. (1685[?]—1750), 116.
Verdelot, Philippe (1490—1567), 67.
Versailles, theatre at, 300.
Verse anthem, introduction of, 202.
Vestris, ballet-master, 302.
Vielle (small hurdy-gurdy), 58.
Vienna, music in, 184.
Vincenti, music-printer, 68.
Viol, 58.
" Viola da Gamba," 58.
Violins, King of the, 20.
Viols, Mace's advice on their preservation, 219; abandoned in favour of violins in France, 296.

Virdung, Sebastian (16th century), his *Musica Getutscht*, 82.
Virginal, 52.
Vita Caduca, La, madrigal by A. Lotti, 111, 239.
Vittoria, T. L. (1540[?]—1608), 77.
Vivaldi, A. (1685—1743), 116.
Vive Henri IV., the air, 127, 128.
Vogler, J. C. (1698—1765), 165.
Vollkommene Kapellmeister, Der, Mattheson's, 179.
Voltaire, 267, 270, 291.

Waelrent, Hubert (1517—1595), 67.
Waft her, angels, song from Handel's *Jephtha*, 247.
Wagner, Richard (1813—1883), 304.
Wallis, Dr. John (1616—1703), 198.
Walsh, John, music-publisher (—1736), 226.
Ward, John (1580[?]—), 93.
Warren-Horne, E. T. (1730—1794), secretary of the Catch Club, 259; his MS. collection of glees, etc., *ib.*; his published collection, 260.
"Water Music," Handel's, 227.
Water parted from the sea, air from Arne's *Artaxerxes*, 250.
Watson, Thomas (1557[?]—1592), his *Italian Madrigalls Englished*, 93.
Webbe, Samuel (1740—1816), 257, 258.
Weelkes, Thomas (1578—1640[?]), 93.
Weldon, John (1676[?]—1736), 211.
Westminster Abbey, Smith's organ in, 213; St. Margaret's, Smith's do. at, *ib.*

We will rejoice, anthem by Dr. Croft, 204.
When winds breathe soft, glee by S. Webbe, 258.
Where the bee sucks, air by Dr. Arne, 250.
While fools their time, glee by J. Stafford Smith, 259.
Whitehall Chapel, organ in, 212.
Wilbye, John (1564[?]—1612[?]), 93.
Willaert, Adrian (1480[?]—1562), 67, 68, 78.
Winchester, early organ in cathedral, 40.
Wind instruments, 34.
Wise, Michael (1638—1687), 196, 199.
Wise and Foolish Virgins, liturgical drama of the, 23.
Wit and Mirth; or, Pills to purge Melancholy, D'Urfey's, 219.
Wolstan, description of organ in Winchester Cathedral, 40.
Wretched lovers, chorus from Handel's *Acis and Galatea*, 229.

Ye twice ten hundred deities, from Purcell's *Indian Queen*, 209.
Yonge, N. (1550[?]—), 91.

Zadok the Priest, coronation anthem by Handel, 234.
Zampogna, or Calabrian bagpipes, 37.
Zarlino, Gioseffo (1519 — 1590), 67, 80, 165.
Zémire et Azor, opera by Grétry, 291.
Zéphyre et Flore, opera by Louis and Jean Louis de Lully, 142.

Printed by Hazell, Watson, & Viney, Ld., London and Aylesbury.

www.ingramcontent.com/pod-product-compliance
Lightning Source LLC
Chambersburg PA
CBHW021211270326
41929CB00010B/1084